BUSINESS ETHICS

BUSINESS ETHICS

Perspectives on the Practice of Theory

Edited by

CHRISTOPHER COWTON
and
ROGER CRISP

OXFORD UNIVERSITY PRESS • OXFORD
1998

Oxford University Press, Great Clarendon Street, Oxford OX2 6DP
Oxford New York
Athens Auckland Bangkok Bogota Buenos Aires Calcutta
Cape Town Chennai Dar es Salaam Delhi Florence Hong Kong Istanbul
Karachi Kuala Lumpur Madrid Melbourne Mexico City Mumbai
Nairobi Paris São Paulo Singapore Taipei Tokyo Toronto Warsaw
and associated companies in Berlin Ibadan

Oxford is a registered trade mark of Oxford University Press

Published in the United States
by Oxford University Press Inc., New York

British Library Cataloguing in Publication Data
Data available

Library of Congress Cataloging in Publication Data

Business ethics: perspectives on the practice of theory / edited by
Christopher Cowton and Roger Crisp.
p.   cm.
Includes bibliographical references.
1. Business ethics.   I. Cowton, Christopher.   II. Crisp, Roger, 1961– .
HF5387.B8727   1998   98–23024
174'.4—dc21

ISBN 0-19-829031-4

1 3 5 7 9 10 8 6 4 2

Typeset in Great Britain
by J&L Composition Ltd, Filey, North Yorkshire
Printed in Great Britain on acid-free paper by
Biddles Limited, Guildford and King's Lynn

CONTENTS

CONTRIBUTORS

Christopher Cowton is Professor of Accounting at Huddersfield University Business School; he was previously University Lecturer in Management Studies and Fellow in Accounting, Templeton College, Oxford.

Roger Crisp is Fellow and Tutor in Philosophy, St Anne's College, Oxford.

Jane Garnett is Fellow and Tutor in Modern History, Wadham College, Oxford.

R. M. Hare FBA was, until recently, Professor of Philosophy, University of Florida, Gainesville; until his retirement from the post in 1981, he was White's Professor of Moral Philosophy, University of Oxford.

Brad Hooker is Lecturer in Philosophy, University of Reading.

J. R. Lucas FBA was formerly Reader in Philosophy and Fellow of Merton College, Oxford.

Richard Pring is Professor of Educational Studies, University of Oxford.

Tom Sorell is Professor of Philosophy, University of Essex.

J. Thomas Whetstone is an Assistant Professor of Management at Jacksonville University, Florida. He completed his doctoral studies while at Templeton College, Oxford.

S. N. Woodward was formerly Fellow in Organizational Behaviour, Templeton College, Oxford.

1

Introduction: Practising Theory

CHRISTOPHER COWTON AND ROGER CRISP

THE need to write an introduction to a collection of papers presents its editors with a choice. Should they restrict themselves to a brief indication of what is to come, presented as little more than a list; or should they be more ambitious, seeking to produce a coherent account of the contents and significance of the volume for which they are responsible? The answer for a volume which pretends to any kind of academic merit is obvious—at least until the time comes to get down to some serious writing. Conscious of the risks inherent in the more ambitious type of introduction—promising too much, forcing the chapters illegitimately into a mould, or even just boring the reader—we have nevertheless decided to map out some themes relating to the pursuit of business ethics and to show how the various chapters relate to those themes. But before embarking on that task, we thought it useful to provide some indication of how the book came about.

THE ORIGINS OF THE BOOK

Business ethics has developed greatly as a field of academic study in recent years. Reflecting that growth of interest and seeking to have it reflected in our own university (as it then was for both of us), we organized a series of seven seminars at Oxford in the Trinity (summer) Term of 1994.[1] The origins of this book lie in that seminar series, but it is by no means the 'book of the series'. Only two chapters (COWTON, SORELL[2]) are based on seminar presentations.

Within the general theme of business ethics, the topics addressed in the seminars were wide-ranging, in the hope of having 'something for

---

[1] We are grateful to St Anne's College for hospitality and to the School of Management Studies for the provision of financial support for external speakers.
[2] This style is used to indicate reference to chapters in this volume.

everyone'. The seminar series having been advertised widely within the University, the audience was diverse, including professors and other members of faculty, postgraduate and undergraduate students, and others with connections with the University. The disciplines or departments represented included philosophy, management, economics, education, and theology. Amidst all the diversity of topic and participant it seemed to us that the discussions, which were a major element of each seminar, threw up a number of general themes about the nature of business ethics and how it should be pursued. Several of the themes seemed important in taking stock of business ethics as it had developed, so we approached a number of the participants with an invitation to develop their ideas further. Thus, while only two of the chapters started life as formal presentations, virtually all the chapters are written by people who participated in some way in the seminar series.

This volume is not the first attempt to take stock of business ethics. In recent years, in books and scholarly journals, there have been several reviews of either the field as a whole or some particular theme or aspect related to its study. Some of those reviews are cited at various points in this book. Whatever their merits, it seemed to us that there was room for further reflection on the past and future progress of business ethics. This volume is the result. The tone of the volume sometimes resonates with the original discussions at the seminars, being in some cases rather less formal or more provocative than the writing ordinarily found in academic journals. Thus the opinions of the writers are frequently to the fore, and it is hoped that the collection is all the better for that. We hope that it provides readers—both those familiar with the field and those whose interest is less developed—with a stimulating and informative set of perspectives. How those perspectives relate to one another is the subject of the remainder of this introductory chapter.

DISSECTING THE TITLE

The true introduction to a book is not the opening essay but the title on the cover. There are plenty of books containing the term 'business ethics', so that in itself says little; or rather, the fact that it does say so little is a sign of the development of the field—a few years ago the publication of any book on business ethics was worthy of note. The appearance of so many books prompts the need for a subtitle to signal the particular aspects of business ethics that we are considering or the particular approach that we are taking. We have chosen 'Perspectives on the Practice of Theory'. Why?

First, the word 'perspectives' indicates that the contributors come from a number of different backgrounds or hold different points of view. While we will identify some of the common themes and points of agreement between them in this chapter, we make no attempt at a complete reconciliation. Indeed, the range of approaches and view-points, while not comprehensive, might be particularly useful for anyone new to the field.

What might we be trying to indicate by the phrase 'the practice of theory'? We are using it in a number of ways. Indeed, its ambiguity was one of its attractions. But the most obvious way is to indicate the development by academics of an abstract, general body of knowledge for understanding and coping with the world; or the process of discovery, analysis, and understanding using the tools that are the stock-in-trade of academics.

FINDING A SPACE

De George (1987) comments, quite rightly, that people have written about business ethics for many centuries. There is a long tradition of theological discussion of various issues which fall within the ambit of modern business ethics, such as the nature of work, just prices, fair wages, and the charging of interest; and there was considerable debate relating to commercial ethics in nineteenth-century Britain (GARNETT). More recently, with the appearance of business ethics as a recognizable field of academic specialization, there has been added a considerable body of work in the tradition of applied moral philosophy. That tradition, or set of traditions, is currently dominant in academic business ethics and is reflected in several chapters in this volume.

Perhaps the first question is to enquire what scope there is for a moral philosophical contribution. Are philosophers, in their ivory towers, equipped to offer insight into the messy world of everyday practice? CRISP argues that they are, and that the distinction between the worlds of theory and practice must anyway not be exaggerated. Philosophers, like nearly all human beings, engage at some level in business practice; and those in business will not act without thought—often philosophically implicated thought—beforehand.

In similar vein, in his consideration of the place of self-interest, HOOKER is asking whether there is practical space for business ethics; many people might think not, because of the profit motive in particular and the orientation of business management in general. This is an important question, not only because of its implications for business itself but also because of the way in which the methods and language of management and quasi-markets have entered many fields which traditionally have not been viewed as businesses, of which education is an important example (PRING). HOOKER concludes that there is another distinction which should not be exaggerated: that between self-interest and morality. Of course, there can be conflicts between the two, and he also shows why it is a mistake to think that self-interest should always, rationally, win.

Many business people and some academic commentators might be uncomfortable with this conclusion, preferring to pursue profitability as the sole goal, constrained only by law—a position often identified with Milton Friedman. But as LUCAS points out, law not only rests on the recognition of moral principles, but requires supplementation by them. As GARNETT's chapter on Victorian commerce shows, people in the past have seen it as legitimate to discuss the ethics of business, even (or especially) at a time when laissez-faire was probably at its height. And the content of the arguments remains relevant today.

APPROACHING THE TASK

However, while it might be accepted that there is room for a contribution by moral philosophers, that still leaves the question of how the tools of philosophical analysis are to be employed in business ethics. How philosophy should be conducted, in particular how it should be related to the world of affairs, is a concern in the chapters by HARE, LUCAS, and SORELL. Their views differ considerably. HARE's preferred procedure is to ensure that the general philosophical approach is right and then merely to have others, perhaps managers or others involved in business, add the detail. LUCAS, on the other hand, has a much more grounded approach. Proceeding not from abstract theory but from the nexus of relationships in which business decisions are made, he employs a stakeholder approach to generate a series of insights which can be used to think through practical business problems, providing a theoretical background for sensitivity required in actual ethical practice. Out of these relationships there emerge 'grounds of obligation' rather than a set of absolute moral duties. Critics of business ethics, such as Andrew Stark in his well-known *Harvard Business Review* article (Stark 1993), often view moral philosophy as impractically idealistic in its demands, even if pointing in the right direction. LUCAS's position might be received by them with some sympathy.

SORELL, in at least one sense, takes LUCAS a step further by suggesting how philosophers might ground their work in, and become more sympathetic towards, the world of business practice. One way is to talk to members of faculty in the business school or its equivalent. Another is to do some 'legwork' themselves, getting out into the field to meet business people. It is important for business ethicists to maintain a critical distance, but not at the cost of a gap of relevance—a gap largely created by ethicists, according to Stark.

Suggestions of 'legwork' raise the spectre of more systematic and directed acquisition of knowledge of the world of affairs, beyond the knowledge that might be entailed, in different ways, in the approaches of HARE and of LUCAS—or even of SORELL. How might systematic empirical knowledge be specially generated for use in business ethics? That theme is picked up in COWTON's chapter, which examines the possibility of drawing upon the methods of empirical social science. The challenges involved range from the abstract (how to relate *is* and *ought*), through the problems of researching sensitive issues, to the mundane but powerful influences on what is deemed to be prestigious, or even appropriate, research within leading business schools. Just like the philosophers (SORELL), social scientists interested in business ethics are often seen to be ploughing a barely legitimate furrow lacking in academic prestige.

THE WORLD OF PRACTICE

Although the original seminar series from which this book has developed was run by and for academics, the world of practical affairs was often mentioned during the discussions. The desire to learn about, and to respond to, practical detail, set against a background of an academic field of study which is strongly rooted in the West, particularly the USA, raises the question of whether business ethics can be applied throughout the world or whether it is culturally specific. Drawing on a wide range of literature, including anthropology, WOODWARD outlines the problems involved but, like CRISP, he does manage to identify grounds for the pursuit of ethics, including business ethics, in some universalist sense. However, he also identifies a universal problem in the way in which 'civilization' and organizations tend to function, serving to oppress or suppress the human spirit.

The notion of organizations as debilitating mechanisms appears to run counter to the purpose of educational institutions in particular, with their developmental orientation, but it seems that the model of business encouraged in, or imposed on, the education sector, at least in the UK, is a particularly crude one. As PRING argues, that imposition poses a significant challenge to many of the values that have long underpinned the education process at its best. Perhaps if that model included a well-developed ethical perspective, there would be a greater chance of its being consonant with the world of education. Ironically, this might require education itself to embrace more enthusiastically the teaching of business ethics, thereby influencing the next generation of managers and policy-makers.

Yet, as WHETSTONE notes in our final chapter, the teaching of business ethics is not without its difficulties. He reviews some of the criticisms that have been made and proposes a solution, to ensure that the approaches advanced by academics are used—a further method of encouraging 'the practice of theory'.

So, to conclude, the phrase 'practice of theory' concerns three broad questions discussed in this book:

(1) how we pursue the conventional academic endeavour, drawing on various traditions and approaches;
(2) how the academic enterprise comes to know the world of business and quasi-business practice;
(3) how theory might be practised in that world.

It is our hope that this volume makes a contribution, in some measure, to answering all of the above.

REFERENCES

De George, R. T. (1987), 'The Status of Business Ethics: Past and Future', *Journal of Business Ethics*, 6: 201–11.

Stark, A. (1993), 'What's the Matter with Business Ethics?', *Harvard Business Review,* May–June: 38–48.

REFERENCES

2

A Defence of Philosophical Business Ethics

ROGER CRISP

1. BUSINESS ETHICS

WHAT is meant by 'business ethics' (see De George 1990: ch. 1)? The phrase is sometimes used to refer to the ethical outlook, whether implied by behaviour or explicitly stated, of a company or individual engaged in business. Behaviour and statement can of course come apart, so that one might say of a certain corporation: 'Their ethic is allegedly one of service to the community, but their woeful environmental record shows what they really believe.'

In a second sense, business ethics is that set of principles or reasons which should govern the conduct of business, whether at the individual or collective level (cf. Lewis 1985: 381). If we assume that there are many ways in which people should not act in business, business ethics in this second sense refers to the way people *should* act.

In its final, and most commonly used, sense, business ethics is an area of philosophical enquiry, with its own topics of discussion, specialists, journals, centres, and of course a panoply of different ethical positions.[1] In this sense, I suggest, business ethics refers to the philosophical endeavours of human beings to grasp the principles constituting business ethics in its second sense, usually with the idea that these should become the 'ethic' of real businesses and business people (cf. Nash 1990: 5).

Philosophers have long thought about philosophy and its nature. The Platonic Socrates saw philosophy as preparation for death, while Aristotle viewed philosophy as the activity in engaging in which we are most like the gods. I shall not make a claim anywhere near as grand, but will suggest that philosophical business ethics is the best way we know to approach the truth about how our economic and

---

[1] For a slightly different definition, see Nash (1990: 5). An interesting history and discussion of the field until the mid-1980s is De George (1987). A useful discussion written from a European perspective is Van Luijk (1994: 12–31).

business life should be. (See Donaldson 1989: 106 for a similar commitment to truth in ethics and business ethics.) I shall proceed largely by fending off objections to philosophical business ethics, but the positive advantages of the practice should emerge as we go.

2. PHILOSOPHICAL SCEPTICISM

Philosophical scepticism is almost as old as philosophical reflection itself, and scepticism about the claims of morality or ethics as old as any form of scepticism. According to the sceptic, philosophical business ethics is misguided, and indeed pointless, because what it seeks is a chimera. There are no principles for philosophical business ethics to uncover.

There are several forms of this kind of scepticism. According to the first, egoism, we do indeed have reasons for action, but they are all egoistic or self-referring reasons. Ethics concerns my relations to others and the environment, but in fact rationality suggests that I should govern such relations only in accordance with my own self-interest. This kind of objection is particularly likely to emerge in business ethics, since business is often taken to be a paradigmatically self-interested enterprise (see HOOKER).

According to one moral theory common in business ethics, utilitarianism, egoism is utterly mistaken. For I should be concerned not with my own self-interest or happiness, but with that of everyone. I should be entirely impartial between my own interest and that of others, putting my own interests into the scale along with everyone else's, even at very great cost to myself. Utilitarianism is hard to believe. Whether a certain pleasure, or more strikingly perhaps, a pain, occurs within my life or someone else's is undoubtedly a matter that I should rationally be concerned about. Certainly no human being has ever behaved as if the difference between their own life and that of others was of no significance. (For discussion of the demand-ingness of some moral theories within business ethics, see Stark 1993.)

But egoism is equally hard to believe. Imagine that you work as an accountant for a large company which imports goods from the developing world. Under your contract, you are required to pay a very large amount to a certain medium-sized company in the Sudan by 1 August. It is now 2 July. You know that payment now will enable this company to survive, thus vastly improving the prospects of the well-being of its employees. The money is already in a payment account, where it is not gathering interest for your own company. Surely you have *some* reason, even if it is only a weak one, to send the cheque now rather than later? (For a general discussion of payment of debt, see Sorell and Hendry 1994: 139–44; also SORELL.) Once it is accepted that people can have some reason to offer great services to others at no cost to themselves, egoism is no longer an option, since it suggests that all reasons are self-interested. And once other-regarding reasons are accepted, it is hard to see why they should not trump self-interested reasons in certain cases. Imagine that sending the cheque now will require your walking across the road to a post-box, and it is a cold day. Is this enough to make your not sending the cheque rational or reasonable?

A complete denial of the force of moral principles, then, is implausible. It may be that moral principles in business have little force against the rationality of self-interest, of course, but that is a question to be decided within philosophical business ethics itself.[2]

Another sceptical line of argument involves pointing out how the moral principles accepted in various societies now and in the past to govern business have varied wildly (see WOODWARD). Compare, for example, attitudes in modern developed countries towards child labour with those of a century or so ago in those same countries, or with those which now exist in certain less developed countries. Does this huge variation in ethical view not suggest that there is no truth to be had in this area, and that moral principles are merely expressions of particular largely culturally determined attitudes? (For a version of this argument applied to ethics in general, see Mackie 1979: 36–8.)

One response here might be to claim that there is more homogeneity in moral belief than is often thought. But this response is less successful than one which accepts the possibility of huge variation in ethical belief but denies that this shows anything much about the status of moral principles themselves. Imagine two people looking at a light, one saying that it is red and the other that it is green. We have

---

[2] Some business ethicists, particularly those writing from a virtue ethical perspective, prefer to see ethical reasons and self-interested reasons not as in conflict but as subsumed under a more general heading of 'ethics', as opposed to 'morality'. See, e.g., Solomon (1992); cf. Olson (1995: 374).

a puzzle on our hands, but it is easy to solve, since one person is colour-blind. Similarly, we shall often be able to explain differences in moral view using sociological, anthropological, cultural, and other data. For example, views about child labour are often closely tied up with brute economic fact, or with views about the nature of children. Disagreement does not undermine the possibility of truth, in ethics as in science, though the defender of the possibility of truth should be prepared to say at least something about how errors arise.

A final form of scepticism about moral principle emerges from what is often called the 'Scientific World View' (SWV) (cf. McDonald and Donleavy 1995: 839–53). According to SWV, not only is it the case that everything is ultimately explicable in the terms of natural science (including psychology and sociology, perhaps), but this principle should govern our theorizing about the world. Postulating moral principles to govern people's behaviour in business or elsewhere is to introduce mysterious notions quite out of place in a modern rational outlook. (A well-known version of this objection applied to ethics in general is Mackie 1979: 38–42. It is discussed in the context of business ethics in McDonald and Donleavy 1995.)

SWV is closely related to what used to be called the 'Verification Principle', according to which the meaning of any statement consists in the conditions for its being verified. The species of verification given primacy by upholders of the Verification Principle was scientific. The problem with the principle was that it was self-undermining, since no one could come up with a plausible story about how it might itself be scientifically verified. The same sort of problem arises for SWV. The holder of SWV would like to believe that the world contains nothing mysterious—merely atoms, lumps of matter, and other objects governed by straightforward causal law (as if these were not mysterious!). But the claims of SWV are surely intended to have *meaning*, and to supply *reasons* for us to believe them. If not, then it is not at all clear what proponents of SWV take themselves to be doing. But if there are reasons for believing, and these must make sense within SWV, then there is no need to rule out reasons for action, including moral reasons for action. And these reasons could quite plausibly be captured at least partially in the principles of business ethics. (On the unreasonableness of scepticism in general, see Lucas.)

3. THE ABSTRACTNESS OF PHILOSOPHY

The arguments against business ethics I discussed in the previous section were general arguments against any kind of ethics, and have usually been developed by philosophers. Another strand of objection to business ethics is a particular case of a more general objection to philosophy, especially moral philosophy, as a whole, and it is often mounted, in the case of business ethics, by those engaged in business itself. According to this argument, philosophy's tools are ill-suited to deciding the everyday, practical, and contextually rich ethical questions which arise in business. Philosophers are trained in thinking about philosophy, and this is a discipline governed by universal and general modes of theoretical enquiry, which have little to offer the person seeking to deal with a real-life problem in business ethics, with all its messy particularities (see Solomon 1992: 99; Stark 1993: 38; Lucas). 'You have to be there', the philosopher is told.

There are at least two responses to this point about abstractness. The first is that the gap between philosophy and real life is not as great as the objector implies. One way to deal with a real moral problem is unthinkingly to do whatever you feel like doing at the time, and some people of course do exactly this. But most people stop to think, and when they do so they are doing moral philosophy, that is, seeking to provide the course of action they eventually choose with some kind of universal justification. A high-ranking employee of a multinational is asked to supply what appear to be bribes to an official in another country to secure a contract. 'What if everybody did that?' he or she thinks. This is one of the fundamental questions underlying Kantian ethics. Then, 'But everybody *is* doing this, so maybe it's not so bad after all. Still, wouldn't it do some good for a corporation as large and influential as ours openly to distance ourselves from such practices?' The idea that what we do should do some good is the thought animating consequentialist and utilitarian theories of ethics. And finally: 'But I just don't want to be the kind of person who gets messed up in dubious and possibly unjust practices like this, whatever the consequences.' These thoughts sit well with forms of virtue ethics influenced by Aristotle. And this list goes on. It is not as if our everyday moral thinking has arisen from nothing; it has emerged from those very traditions that lie behind contemporary moral theory.

The second response to the abstractness objection is to concede something to the objector. Philosophy, including moral philosophy, can be abstract, in that it consists in the articulation of rather general principles, with wide application, which require much interpretation if they are to serve as guides for everyday life. And if they are going to be applied to everyday problems of business ethics, whether in real life or in the pages of business ethics journals, this will require some understanding of those problems themselves (see HARE and SORELL). Consider, for example, the question of leveraged buyouts (LBOs). In the 1980s, some major US corporations contracted debts of unprecedented proportions. Almost no one will deny that there was (indeed is) *some* risk of this leading to serious economic problems in future, affecting the well-being of many thousands of people. Now there is an empirical question about the level of risk here, and of course that will require a proper grasp of the nature of LBOs. This question is independent of the ethical question of whether LBOs are morally acceptable, in that it can be answered independently of that ethical question. But the ethical question cannot be answered independently of the empirical question. A philosopher who is going to write about business ethics needs to know about business, at least that area of business about which he or she is making claims. This, I suggest, is one reason why case-studies are so important in the teaching of business ethics. Business ethics case-studies teach us about business as well as about ethics. (For a good discussion of the case-study method, see Beauchamp and Bowie 1988: 49–53.)

There is here a general point to be made about the nature of applied, practical, or normative ethics. Applied ethics, including business ethics, comes under criticism on two fronts. Those involved in the practice itself say that philosophy is too abstract to be of serious help, while some philosophers say that philosophy should deal only with the universal and leave the practical to those who understand it. But, as I have argued, this dichotomy between theory and practice is a mistake. Most of those engaged in business will think through some ethical issue at some stage in their career, and philosophy here can be of great help in suggesting lines of thought, opening up logical possibilities, or extending the imagination. But it must be philosophy grounded in an understanding of practice. Business ethics, as a philosophical discipline, has its own independent and important role in our society.

It is worth noting here the interesting fact that philosophical business ethics tends to meet with more raised eyebrows than philosophical medical ethics. This is, I suspect, because of the fact that our common-sense morality is deeply concerned with matters of life and death, and these are of course at the heart of medicine. Those involved in medicine realize this, and most are already thinking ethically and are ready to welcome any assistance philosophy can provide. Business, on the face of it, is not a matter of life and death, and its practitioners do not traditionally go in for much ethical thinking. But this attitude is mistaken, for two reasons. First, our common-sense morality may be mistaken. It may be, that is, that business is as challenging ethically as medicine. Secondly, business *is* a matter of life and death. Business interests maintain the world order: the distribution of goods, with all the pleasures and pains it brings along with it, is a matter of business; and the future of the world depends on the way business responds to the environmental crisis. And, of course, business affects people's lives in less dramatic ways all the time.

Before I close this section, I want to point out one of the consequences of allowing the abstractness objection more weight than it deserves. This can be seen by looking at any of the prominent business journals. Some writers on topics of business ethics who are themselves engaged in business appear almost deliberately to steer clear of even the most basic study of philosophy, as if either it will corrupt them or it is a waste of time. As I have pointed out, by writing on business ethics they are themselves doing philosophy, so they would be well advised to acquaint themselves with some of the more important writings of the last two and a half millennia: Plato's *Republic*, Aristotle's *Ethics*, Kant's *Groundwork*, Mill's *Utilitarianism*, and so on. In that way, business ethics will be further advanced by philosophical business people and not, as is mostly the case at present, by philosophers who have some knowledge of business.

4. PHILOSOPHY AS AN IDLE WHEEL

Another objection to philosophy, closely related to the abstractness objection, is based on claims not so much about the general nature of philosophy as about its place in our society. This objection suggests that philosophy has turned itself into a highly specialized discipline, and that its methods and style have led to its moving out of the public arena entirely and retreating to the universities. Business people, not necessarily because philosophy is too abstract (though this may of course be so) but because it is just too difficult to understand in its contemporary form, largely ignore philosophical business ethics. Meanwhile, though some philosophers clearly do have a deep understanding of business, they use this knowledge to develop arguments in journals and books for their colleagues, and do not trouble themselves to communicate with those really concerned with the ethics of business (Stark 1993: 44). Philosophers might as well concern themselves with the ethics of feeding Christians to the lions or the ethics of time-travel: all they use business for is as a source of interesting problems, and history and the imagination could supply them with what they want just as efficiently as does real life.[3]

There are several responses to make on behalf of philosophy here. First, let us for the sake of argument accept the main point of this objection. Let us assume, that is, that philosophical business ethics has made itself out of touch, through its excessive use of jargon and technicality. Even if this is true of contemporary business ethics, it is not true of Plato, Aristotle and most of the other great writers in the history of moral philosophy. Anyone could read their works and consider their implications for the way they live.

Secondly, however, we should note that this objection exaggerates in two ways. Not all contemporary business ethics is comprehensible only to practitioners of business ethics as a discipline (see Cavanagh et al. 1995; Monast 1995: 503). Indeed, I would argue that most of what is currently published in philosophical business ethics is accessible to most moderately intelligent business people (its quality, of course, is another matter). Nor is it correct that business people ignore philosophical business ethics; they themselves publish in the area, many business schools teach courses in philosophical business ethics, and conferences and meetings on business ethics—at least those I have attended—always include at least some business people. Though it might be unfair even to suggest this, it might be the case that any apparent stand-off that exists between contemporary business ethics and business itself is at least as much the fault of the majority of business people, who do not take the trouble to

---

[3] De George (1987) suggests that, because business ethics is an academic field, it does not matter whether business people have not been affected by it. Here I side with Aristotle: the point of the study of ethics is that people become better; without that, it is pretty pointless. See Aristotle *c*.330 BC / 1985: 1103b26–30.

discover even the basics of philosophical business ethics, as it is of over-technical philosophers.

It has to be admitted, however, that some of the most important writings on business ethics can become quite complex, and require some grounding in philosophy for them to be understood (cf. Derry and Green 1989). And if, as I have suggested, philosophical business ethics is seamlessly woven into philosophical ethics itself, we should admit that some contemporary ethical theory, with its talk of agent-relativity and agent-neutrality, for example, is quite complicated. But difficult questions are likely to require difficult answers, so a certain level of complexity is only to be expected. Sometimes, of course, philosophical technicality, formalization, and jargon are unnecessary, being added either because the author has forgotten the importance of communication to a wide audience in this area or because he or she is attempting to add a veneer of quality to an argument which may in fact be quite simplistic, vague, or implausible (see SORELL). But sometimes they are necessary. And here there is a task for the philosophical translators, those who are able to take the difficult concepts and arguments from contemporary discussion and translate them into ideas which can be grasped by and may be of use to business people who are seeking ethical understanding of their own lives.

Business people should be encouraged to think philosophically by any means at our disposal, whether it be through philosophical translation in generalist business journals and papers, or through education at business school (on moral education in business, see Whetstone 1995, and in this volume). Such education is itself part of moral education in general, and there is here a substantive point to be made about the relation between philosophical principle and everyday practice. Early in his *Ethics*, Aristotle tells us that you will become a better person not just by attending his lectures. That requires that you have been brought up or habituated in the right way by your parents, school, or whatever. You need some basic grip on ethics and its problems before philosophical reflection and principle can help. Education in philosophical business ethics is part of the moral education of business people in general. Again, we can see a role for case-studies, which sensitize those who study them to the salient features of cases of a kind which is likely to reoccur in real life.

5. ENDLESS DISAGREEMENT

In section 2 above we saw how the fact of disagreement between cultures is sometimes used by philosophers to suggest that there is no truth to be had in ethics. The fact of disagreement, however, can be turned against philosophy itself. We saw how disagreement is consistent with there being a truth, so the argument that disagreements among philosophers in business ethics suggest that there is no truth to be had will not succeed. But philosophers in business ethics do, of course, disagree greatly with one another, at every level, from that of general theory to its application to very specific cases. How, then, it might be asked, can they provide any guidance to business people (see Monast 1995: 504)? Of course, as a business person, I can go to philosopher *P* and ask for advice, and he will tell me to do *X*. But why should I listen to *P* when his or her colleague down the hall, *Q*, would give me philosophical arguments for doing *not-X*? Until philosophers can agree, they should not consider themselves entitled to offer advice they can be confident of.

It is important to recognize first that there is in fact a great deal of agreement in philosophical business ethics. Most philosophers in the area will agree that morality requires business people to respect the principle of client confidentiality, to pay debts, to ensure that any product is reasonably safe before releasing it onto the market, to pollute the environment as little as possible, and so on (this will be a very long list).

But, surely, it will be said, this is just to play into the hands of the objector. For if everyone agrees that something is right or wrong, why do we need philosophers? After all, it is not only philosophers who think that morality requires the things mentioned above. Here we can learn again from Aristotle's discussion of moral education (Aristotle *c.*330 BC / 1985: 1095b4–13). According to Aristotle, the person who starts thinking seriously about ethics should know 'the that', that is, should have the basic grasp of ethics I mentioned when discussing Aristotle in the previous section. The student at business school who quite sincerely thinks that it is an entirely open question whether to repay a debt, or whether to remove competitors by taking out contracts on them, is unlikely to learn much from Business Ethics 101. But knowing the that is not enough for the ethical life; one must also have some understanding of 'the because', of the reasons which lie behind one's ethical beliefs. Here, philosophy—including business ethics as it is taught in the business schools—can help.

Why should I repay a debt? Because it is unfair not to do so and violates the principle of respect for persons; because not doing so may have bad consequences; because it is dishonest. Or so proponents of Kantianism, utilitarianism, and virtue ethics, respectively, will tell us. But here again it may be said that I am playing into the hands of the objector. I have claimed that there is much agreement in business ethics, but in fact this agreement about the conclusions of certain arguments masks yet more fundamental disagreement about the premises of those arguments. Why should I listen to the utilitarian, when the Kantian has arguments just as good and which have persuaded many serious thinkers? But then why should I listen to the Kantian, when I see that the same can be said of virtue ethics?

Even at the theoretical level, however, disagreement is not as deep as the proponents of various ethical theories might suggest. Much contemporary moral philosophy, business ethics included, operates on a mistaken scientific model. If we are seeking to explain some phenomenon scientifically, only one of several competing theories can be accepted. But business ethics is not seeking to explain, but to justify. It is seeking those principles or reasons which should govern our actions. Here, most philosophers have been tempted to think that you have to nail your colours to a particular mast, picking one theory to justify a particular course of action. But reasons do not operate like this, since it is an obvious fact of everyday life that one can have more than one reason for doing something. If I say, 'I am going to the opera because I want to see my cousin sing', it would be absurd for you to conclude that therefore I am not going in order to enjoy the music. I might be going for both reasons. Why is it, then, that philosophers have not noticed that it is equally absurd to suggest that if you think it is wrong not to pay a debt because it violates a principle of respect for persons, you cannot think that it is wrong because of its consequences or because it is dishonest? In other words, you do not have to choose a single ethical theory and stick with it; you can take what seems most plausible from several theories and seek insights from all of them (Bowie 1982: 7; pluralism is implicit in, e.g., SORELL).

There are, of course, going to be instances—such as the question of the nature of the person, or of the weight of self-interest against morality—where genuine, deep, and fundamental disagreement persists. Here each reasonable person will want to make up his or her own mind in the light of the best evidence available. Part of that evidence, perhaps most of it, will be the various competing arguments available in the various philosophical traditions.

These disagreements at the theoretical level are a large part of what explains the fact that there is a great deal of practical disagreement in business ethics on certain issues. At one end of the spectrum is the non-payment of debt or the murder of competitors: these are pretty well universally condemned. But on many other topics in business ethics there is a great deal of serious disagreement. What, for example, is the nature of the corporation, and can it have responsibilities or obligations? Does company loyalty speak against whistle blowing? Is persuasive advertising immoral?

A strong objector to philosophical business ethics may here advocate that business people ignore philosophers until they can come to some consensus on, say, the nature of the person and its ethical implications. Until that time, listening to the arguments of any one philosopher will be largely a waste of time, since other philosophers will have quite different arguments which, the philosophical experts will agree, are to be taken equally seriously. If one insists on having a view here, one might as well just toss a coin, or rather several coins, and adopt one's views according to chance.

But this objection is highly misguided, and for several reasons. First, philosophy cannot be opted out of in this way. As I have already pointed out, everyday thought is on a continuum with the most abstract philosophy, and behind everyday decision-making will lie certain everyday assumptions about the nature of persons and the demands of morality. As David Wiggins has put it, harking back to a point of C. S. Peirce, 'If someone says he dispenses with all metaphysics and wants none, you will be wise to expect him to be bogged down in a metaphysic so poor that, if it were explicitly revealed, you would not know whether to laugh or cry.'

Secondly, even if there is disagreement at a high philosophical level about these fundamental ethical and metaphysical issues, there may be agreement among philosophers at a lower level about what sorts of view are untenable, or the undesirable implications that follow from certain views. Consider, for example, Ivan Boesky's tee-shirt aphorism, that 'He who owns the most when he dies, wins' (see Singer 1995: 56). Most philosophers could quickly point out at least two serious problems with this claim. First, it is hard to understand even in its own terms. If I live my life in such a way that I am very poor throughout, so that I can inherit a vast amount on my deathbed, it is not clear that I have made the right decision. Secondly, ownership itself, as Aristotle saw long ago, does not seem to be a good in itself. Owning property is merely a means to things which are goods in themselves. Of course, Boesky could modify his view to deal with these points. But then he would be doing philosophy.

Finally, the global benefits flowing from reflective attitudes must be considered. Imagine that an analogue of the strong objection had been accepted before the Scientific Revolution: clever scientists have been studying these problems for a long time, it might have been said, and they cannot agree, so we might as well give up. Science, through the working out of the fundamental disagreements of its practitioners, made the huge advances which lie behind the whole shape of the modern world. There is no good reason to think that philosophy is not capable of the same advances. This is to say that philosophical business ethics, if it is pursued vigorously and conscientiously by philosophers and business people, may make advances in ethical thinking on which there will be consensus in the future. We can hypothesize that business would be run on more moral lines if this were the case, and this is surely something to be welcomed. If it is not welcomed, then we must return to the arguments of section 2 against scepticism.

The scientific analogy opens up a serious issue concerning why it is that human beings do disagree about certain fundamental issues. In the case of science, the explanation was often belief in fundamentalist religion. Now, even most of those committed to the forms of religion which have emerged from this fundamentalism will admit that in previous centuries certain religious beliefs distorted people's vision when it came to scientific matters. Why is it that some philosophers now are committed utilitarians, while others are committed Kantians, virtue theorists, or holders of some yet other view? This is a question surprisingly little discussed in contemporary philosophy. But it is not just something that happens without explanation; there must be a reason. And if there is a truth in ethics, which one of these views has captured, or which none of them has, or which each of them has in part, then the probability is that some philosophers are being led astray by certain mistaken fundamental metaphysical or ethical assumptions.

This raises the further question of the ideal conditions for approaching truth in ethics, whether ethics in general or business ethics. These ideal conditions, I suggest, are somewhat similar to those in science: intelligence and impartiality on the part of the enquirer, and the necessary resources for enquiry. Some scientists make discoveries on their own. But many scientists in the past and present have made their discoveries only through discussing their views in free and open discussion with others. That is particularly important in philosophy, and indeed in business ethics. Shutting down channels of communication, from either end, between philosophers and business people can only impede the search for truth.

6. IMMORAL ETHICS?

The final objections to the practice of philosophical business ethics come from within philosophical ethics itself. According to these views, there are moral objections to philosophical business ethics.

The clearest form of this objection is utilitarian. The utilitarian will point to the vast amount of preventable suffering and the huge opportunities for increasing human happiness that exist in the world today, and criticize the business ethicist for doing nothing about it. What the business ethicist should do is to resign his or her position and, perhaps, take a job with a development charity, or even with a management consultancy, so that he or she can earn vast sums of money which can then be surrendered to development charities. This objection can also be mounted on Kantian or Aristotelian grounds, if a proponent of Kantianism or Aristotelianism lays a particularly great stress on a principle or a virtue of benevolence.

There are three responses to this objection, all of which deserve serious consideration. The head-on response is just to deny that more good would be produced by moving. Business is obviously of immense importance in the contemporary world, and the well-being of present and future generations depends centrally upon how it is conducted, and in particular on the ethical principles that will govern it. Philosophical business ethics can be seen not only as part of the search for and advance towards truth in ethics, but as part of the substructure which supports ethical activity itself. If philosophers pull out of business ethics, it is more than likely that business people themselves will treat the ethical aspects of their actions with less concern.

The second response is more concessive. According to this response, the utilitarian may be right to suggest that the world in which I resign my job and seek to maximize overall happiness in some other way will be better overall, from the impartial point of view, than the world in which I remain as a business ethicist. But the world places empirical constraints on what morality can demand. It would be absurd to claim that morality requires me, when I see someone falling from a cliff, to fly through the air to catch them. Similarly, it may be that human psychology places limits on the level of sacrifice that can be demanded from me in the name of the collective good. Maybe I really cannot, given my background, my nature, and my present circumstances, do what the objector is asking of me (see Griffin 1991: 112–13).

The final response is, if anything, more challenging than either of the first two. Most modern moral philosophers, in business ethics and elsewhere, are what we might call 'moralists.' That is, they believe that morality's reasons are either the only reasons or the overriding reasons. According to the utilitarian, my strongest reason at any time is to maximize overall happiness. But, as we saw in section 2, this view of the rationality of morality ignores the fact that my life is mine, and separate from that of others. Self-interest, in other words, provides a counter-balance to the claims of morality, morality being only one source of reasons among others.[4] To be sure, increasing human happiness is a worthwhile and reasonable aim. But the implications of more or less demanding moral lives for me, the person who lives the life, must be taken into account. If I am flourishing in business, self-interest may give me a strong self-interested reason to stay there.

The final objection to business ethics, though it comes from within philosophical ethics itself, is closely related to that discussed at the end of the previous section. Here, a proponent of a particular view in philosophical ethics will castigate the proponents of some other view for leading people away from the true path. Utilitarians have come in particularly for this sort of criticism in recent decades, the idea being that somehow they are likely not only to mislead people philosophically, but to corrupt them in some way.

---

[4] See Crisp (1996); on the conflict between the discourse of morality and other discourses, see GARNETT; on the need of business ethics to come to terms with self-interest, see SORELL.

But intellectual and practical toleration are essential if progress is to be made in ethics. Business ethicists, like all philosophers, indeed all reflective human beings, require a split mind. On the one hand, they may adhere to certain views about fundamental issues concerning the nature of the world, the nature of persons, and ethics, and views about the implications of these positions for issues of practical import in business. But, on the other hand, they must recognize that the disagreements that exist between equally serious, impartial, and reflective enquirers makes it rather unlikely that they themselves are in possession of the full truth. At this point, they should accept that the practice of reflective enquiry, in business ethics as elsewhere, must be encouraged through openness, and not stifled by those with closed minds.

REFERENCES

Aristotle (*c*.330 BC/1985), *Nicomachean Ethics*, trans. by T. Irwin (Indianapolis: Hackett).

Beauchamp, T. L. and Bowie, N. E. (1988), *Ethical Theory and Business*, 3rd edn (Englewood Cliffs, NJ: Prentice-Hall).

Bowie, N. (1982), *Business Ethics* (Englewood Cliffs, NJ: Prentice-Hall).

Cavanagh, G. F., Moberg, D. J., and Velasquez, M. (1995), 'Making Business Ethics Practical', *Business Ethics Quarterly*, 5: 399–418.

Crisp, R. (1996), 'The Dualism of Practical Reason', *Proceedings of the Aristotelian Society*, 96: 53–73.

De George, R. T. (1987), 'The Status of Business Ethics: Past and Future', *Journal of Business Ethics*, 6: 210–12.

De George, R. T. (1990), *Business Ethics*, 3rd edn (New York: Macmillan).

Derry, R. and Green, R. M. (1989), 'Ethical Theory in Business Ethics: A Critical Assessment', *Journal of Business Ethics*, 8: 521–33.

Donaldson, J. (1989), *Key Issues in Business Ethics* (London: Academic Press).

Griffin, J. (1991), 'Mixing Values', *Proceedings of the Aristotelian Society*, suppl. vol. 60: 101–18.

Harvey, B. (1994) (ed.), *Business Ethics: A European Approach* (Hemel Hempstead: Prentice-Hall).

Lewis, P. V. (1985), 'Defining "Business Ethics": Like Nailing Jello to the Wall', *Journal of Business Ethics*, 4: 377–83.

McDonald, G. M. and Donleavy, G. D. (1995), 'Objections to the Teaching of Business Ethics', *Journal of Business Ethics*, 14: 839–53.

Mackie, J. (1979), *Ethics: Inventing Right and Wrong* (Harmondsworth: Penguin).

Monast, J. H. (1995), 'What Is (and Isn't) Wrong with "What's the Matter . . . "', *Business Ethics Quarterly*, 4: 499–512.

Nash, L. (1990), *Good Intentions Aside: A Manager's Guide to Resolving Ethical Problems* (Boston, MA: Harvard Business School Press).

Olson, S. (1995), 'Old Guards, Young Turks, and the $64,000 Question: What is Business Ethics?', *Business Ethics Quarterly*, 5: 371–9.

Singer, P. (1995), *How Are We To Live?* (New York: Prometheus).

Solomon, R. (1992), *Ethics and Excellence: Co-operation and Integrity in Business* (New York: Oxford University Press).

Sorell, T. and Hendry, J. (1994), *Business Ethics* (Oxford: Butterworth-Heinemann).

Stark, A. (1993), 'What's the Matter with Business Ethics?', *Harvard Business Review*, May–June: 38–48.

Van Luijk, H. (1994), 'Business Ethics: The Field and its Importance', in Harvey (1994): 12–31.

Whetstone, J. T. (1995), 'The Manager as a Moral Person: Exploring Paths to Excellence', D.Phil. thesis, Oxford University.

3

Self-Interest, Ethics, and the Profit Motive

BRAD HOOKER

SOME people worry that business is powered by inherently non-moral—or even immoral—motivation. Obviously, most business decisions are driven by the profit motive. But what is the relation between self-interest, ethical considerations, and the profit motive? I shall try to answer this question. In order to do so, however, I need first to elucidate the concepts of self-interest, selfishness, and moral requirement. Once I have sketched a picture of the relation between ethical considerations and the profit motive, I shall consider some complications that arise when the correct moral rules for regulating business practice are not the rules that have in fact been laid down by professions or companies.

1. SELF-INTEREST AND PERSONAL WELFARE

The primary meaning of the term 'self-interest' is 'concern for one's own personal good'. Sometimes we use the term to refer, not really to someone's concern for his or her own personal good, but to that good itself. I shall take 'personal good' to be synonymous with 'welfare', 'well-being', 'flourishing', 'utility', 'advantage'. But what is this 'good' or 'welfare'?

There are three main theories about this (Parfit 1984: 493–502; Griffin 1986: Part One; Brink 1989: 221–36; Scanlon 1993; Crisp 1997: chs. 2–3). One is hedonism. Hedonism holds that welfare is merely *net pleasure*, i.e. pleasure minus pain, or perhaps, more broadly, *happiness*. A second kind of theory is the desire-fulfilment (or preference-satisfaction) theory. This theory holds that our welfare is maximized if and only if our desire-fulfilment is maximized. The desire-fulfilment theory holds that the fulfilment of my desire benefits me even if I get no pleasure, enjoyment, or happiness from it. The third kind of theory is perfectionism, sometimes called the 'objective list theory' (e.g. by Parfit 1984).

Perfectionism holds that certain things can add to our welfare even when they don't increase our pleasure or desire-fulfilment. Such things might include friendship, achievement, important knowledge, autonomy, etc. (Brink 1989; Hurka 1993; Crisp 1997: ch. 3).

There are interestingly different variants of each of these theories. What most matters here, however, is this point: we should not accept a theory of personal welfare such that *necessarily* people always do what is most advantageous to themselves. I discuss this theory in the next section.

2. PSYCHOLOGICAL EGOISM

The view that people always do what is most advantageous to themselves is called *psychological egoism*. In my experience, many people seem to believe psychological egoism, and there is one theory of welfare which, when conjoined with a popular philosophical theory about action, entails the truth of psychological egoism. Consider a variant of desire-fulfilment theory according to which one's own welfare is maximized by the fulfilment of one's strongest desires at the time of action. Call this *the present-desire-fulfilment theory* of welfare. Now suppose we add to this theory the popular philosophical theory of action that people always act to fulfil their strongest desires at the time of action. Putting the present-desire-fulfilment theory of welfare together with this theory of action, we get the conclusion that *necessarily* everyone always does what in fact maximizes his or her own welfare. In other words, psychological egoism is entailed by the conjunction of these theories.

The theory of action that is in play here can be challenged. Even more dubious, however, is the present-desire-fulfilment theory of welfare. It holds that fulfilling our strongest desires *at the time of action* is always what maximizes our own good. But this version of desire-fulfilment theory can completely ignore desires not present at the time of action, e.g. future desires. Fulfilling my current desires may benefit me now but then result in the frustration of much more intense and longer lasting desires that I will have later. Whether or not I now care about my future desires, or indeed my future welfare, what happens to me later is obviously part of my overall welfare. When I do what I now want and this will lead to greater losses later, I may be acting on my strongest current desires, but I am not really doing what is best for myself.

There is a second decisive objection to the present-desire-fulfilment theory of welfare. This theory ignores the possibility that desires can be incoherent, ill-informed, or otherwise misguided. Our current desires may be so wayward that their fulfilment constitutes no benefit at all to us. Suppose I want you to suffer and so try to bring this about. But suppose also that in the event I find that your suffering brings me no enjoyment or sense of accomplishment. Then my having fulfilled the strongest desire I had at the time of action might bring me no benefit at all.

These objections render completely implausible the idea that our welfare is necessarily maximized by the fulfilment of our strongest desires at the time of action (for further objections, see Overvold 1980; Parfit 1984: 494; Hooker 1991: 335–6). Fulfilling our strongest current desires need not maximize our own good.

If we reject the present-desire-fulfilment theory of welfare, then (whether or not we reject the theory of action I mentioned) we have the logical space to reject psychological egoism. This leaves the question of whether, even if psychological egoism is not logically necessary, it is empirically true—that is, whether, as a matter of plain empirical fact, people always do care about their extended future and always act in the way that is best for themselves in the long term.

So stated, this theory is ridiculous. For, clearly, people sometimes make mistakes about what will be best for themselves. And there are cases where weakness of will impels people to do what they know is not best for themselves. But we could build these concessions into our understanding of psychological egoism. So take psychological egoism to be the theory that, *except for cases of weakness of will*, everyone always intends to do what he or she *thinks* will be best from the point of view of his or her self-interest.

Note that, even if psychological egoism doesn't follow from philosophical theories about welfare and action, and even if we incorporate the concessions just mentioned into our conception of psychological egoism, the theory still has universal scope. In other words, psychological egoism isn't a claim about what *most* people do *most* of the time. It is a claim about *everyone's every* action, apart from cases of either weakness of will or mistake.

There seem to be real-life counter-examples to psychological egoism, particularly cases in which someone sacrifices his or her own good for the sake of other people. Actually there seem to be many such cases. I remember seeing an interview of a fisherman whose boat sank off the Great Barrier Reef. He had a friend with him at the time. Soon after they were in the water, one of them noticed he was bleeding badly. The bleeding man then said his good-byes and swam off away from the other so that the sharks would eat only him and not both of them. The bleeding man presumably would have personally benefited more from having some human company during his last minutes of life, some company to face the terror of the coming shark attacks. But he apparently was thinking of the other person's welfare, not his own.

The most common sort of counter-example to psychological egoism is the one of soldiers deliberately jumping onto a grenade. This was done so as to prevent their comrades from being killed. The ones who jumped onto the grenade could have jumped in the other direction. In so doing, they would have saved themselves. But they chose to sacrifice themselves to save their comrades.

Many sceptics remain unconvinced by such anecdotes. The unconvinced say such things as: 'We don't know what was going on in the head of the person who was to be eaten by the sharks, or in the heads of those who jumped onto a grenade. Maybe they thought such actions would get them tickets to Heaven. Or maybe the hero in the shark case knew he would be so miserable with guilt if he unnecessarily endangered his friend that he figured he would be more at peace swimming away. Likewise, maybe the soldiers who jumped onto the grenade thought they would not have been able to live with themselves if they hadn't.'

True, we can't be absolutely *certain* that in a particular case the person who did what seemed to be against his own interests was not actually doing what he thought best for himself. But what if we could ask him, rather than having to rely on the reports of a witness? Suppose, for the sake of argument, that subsequent events had gone better. Suppose that the man who swam away was unexpectedly rescued before the sharks arrived, and then we asked him what he was thinking while he was swimming away. Suppose he said he thought that he would personally benefit more from not swimming away, but also that this benefit was much less important than the survival of his friend.

Or, suppose the soldier jumped onto what he thought was a grenade about to explode, but it turned out to be a dud. Suppose we then ask him what he was thinking as he jumped into, instead of away from, what he thought was death. He will probably say what the man said who jumped off the bridge in Washington, DC to save the airline passengers drowning in the freezing Potomac. When asked why he risked his life for these people, he said he did not think about his own life, but only their desperate need.

Even such autobiographical reports, however, will not convince some sceptics that psychological egoism is false. These sceptics will say: 'Why take his word? We know that, because people want us to think well of them, they report that they were trying to benefit others when in fact they were trying to benefit themselves.'

True, people often misrepresent their motivations. But, given the huge number of apparent acts of intentional self-sacrifice, is it really plausible that in every case the appearance is an illusion? That in every case where someone thinks he or she is a witness of someone else's intentional self-sacrifice, the witness is mistaken? That in every case where someone claims to have acted against self-interest for the sake of someone else, the report is a lie?

I know the anecdotal reports do not convince everyone. So let me offer a second kind of argument against psychological egoism. Many people believe some form of hedonism is the correct account of welfare. That is, many people believe that something is a benefit to a person only if it gives pleasure to (or reduces the pain of) that person. On this view, the alternative course of events that is best from the perspective of my own welfare is just whichever course of events will bring me the greatest balance of pleasure over pain.

Given the above definition of psychological egoism, we can see that defenders of psychological egoism will claim that people who accept a hedonistic theory of self-interest will always do what they think will bring them the greatest balance of pleasure over pain. Now consider a thought experiment (adapted from Williams 1973: 262; see also Kavka 1986: 37). Suppose you are captured by an evil hypnotist who gives you the following options:

A. Your child will get some huge benefit but you will be instantly hypnotized and convinced that you just betrayed your child; and because you will never discover the truth, you will spend the rest of your life feeling guilty for what you believe you did.
B. Your child will suffer some terrible evil but you will be instantly hypnotized and convinced that you just benefited your child; and

because you will never find out the truth, you will spend the rest of your life getting pleasure out of the thought that you benefited your child.

After your choice, you and your child will never have any more direct or indirect contact, one result of which is that your child will have no way of rewarding or punishing you for your choice. Now isn't it clear that you might accept the hedonistic theory of welfare (i.e., think that pleasure and the reduction of pain are the only things that could benefit you) and yet, when faced by the choice the evil hypnotist gives you, choose A? If *any* proponent of the hedonistic theory would *ever* choose A over B in the example, psychological egoism is refuted. Actually, I believe that many parents would (at least sometimes) choose A over B.

And I believe this not just on the basis of my observations of parents. This brings me to the third kind of argument against psychological egoism. Evolutionary theory has deeply controversial elements in it. I by no means believe many of the claims put forward in the name of sociobiology. Yet I think that it presents reasons to believe that people would be disposed to sacrifice themselves for the welfare of certain others—in particular, their kin and those disposed to reciprocate altruism (Kavka 1986: 56–64).

Imagine two lionesses. The two are exactly alike except that one has a gene which results in her being disposed to fight to the death in order to protect her offspring, and the other has instead a gene which results in her being disposed *not* to sacrifice her life, even when doing so would save the lives of her offspring. Now, other things being equal, the genes of which lioness are more likely to be found in future generations of the species? The lioness with the gene for parental altruism will probably have a shorter life than the other lioness, but her cubs are more likely to survive, and thus pass down her genes to cubs of their own. And similar claims should be made about other animals, *including humans.*

Somewhat similar claims could also be made about reciprocal altruism, in particular the disposition to help others of the same species unless and until they fail to reciprocate (Kavka 1986: 62; Axelrod 1984). Think of dispositions to cooperate by sharing shelter and food, removing parasites from each other's backs, and hunting together. Groups with such dispositions are more likely to survive, and thus more likely to pass down the gene, than groups without such reciprocal altruism.

So there seem to be excellent reasons for believing that evolution fosters the development of some dispositions to make sacrifices for certain others. This sociobiological reasoning accords with our earlier arguments against psychological egoism.

3. PREDOMINANT EGOISM

On careful analysis, psychological egoism is clearly false. Why then have so many people believed it? Part of the answer is that they have confused the idea that *every intentional action arises from one of the agent's motivations* with the idea that *every intentional action aims at something for the agent*, construed as some benefit to the agent. Perhaps even more important is the fact that extremely often people really are motivated by self-interest. And very often when people claim to be doing something out of altruism or some other moral motivation, they are either lying or deceiving themselves. Some would go so far as to say that *most* human behaviour is motivated by self-interest. Thus some would say that psychological egoism, though not accurate, is close to the truth.

Let me use Gregory Kavka's term *predominant egoism* (1986: 68–80) to refer to the view that, apart from cases of weakness of will, most people *usually* do what seems to them best for themselves. Kavka himself is willing to soften this doctrine to allow for more altruism as 'basic material and security needs are satisfied' (p. 67). Predominant egoism also grants that there are some exceptionally altruistic people, in whom concern for self is not predominant. And it grants that many or even most people are willing to make repeated sacrifices for family and others to whom they are closely connected.

The main opposition to predominant egoism comes from, on one side, those who maintain psychological egoism, and, on the other side, socialists who believe that human nature is more variable and plastic than predominant egoism suggests. Some socialists would say, for example, that even if most people in Western societies are predominantly egoistic, this is a consequence of the individualistic culture and capitalistic economic system, and that different arrangements might make for more altruistic people.

Can we point to an actual example? Have the socialist economic systems succeeded in producing more altruistic people? Many people have their doubts (for examples of philosophers with such doubts, see Kavka 1986: 76–8; Nagel 1991: 91–2, 122, 123, 127–8). But even if people in a socialistic economic system would be more altruistic towards their fellow citizens, there is the further question whether the increase in altruism would be enough to get these people to do the hard work and innovation on which increasing prosperity depends. We know that appealing to self-interest—in particular, offering to individuals economic rewards—can elicit hard work and innovation and personal risk. We might well be sceptical, however, whether *in a successful economy* a wide-ranging altruism could take the place of the desire for personal gain (Hooker 1993: 91).

4. SELFISHNESS AND MORALITY

The concepts of self-interest and personal welfare can be understood independently of morality (for complications, see Hooker 1996). If I say that self-interest induced Joe to move house, I may not have made any moral judgement whatsoever. The concept 'selfishness', however, is inexplicable without reference to morality. To be selfish is to be wanting something for ourselves when we should be wanting something for others. Put another way, to be selfish is to have a concern for ourselves that is too strong relative to our concern for others. If I say that Joe was selfish to move house, the implication is that—because of effects on others, effects he should have cared more about—he should not have moved.

Let me provide another example. If I learn another language because of the benefits this will bring me, I have acted out of self-interest. I may have acted neither immorally nor selfishly. If there were no other moral obligations that I neglected in order to learn the language, my self-interested course of action was not immoral. However, if I knew that learning the language would (e.g.) prevent me from keeping a promise I'd made to do something else, or prevent me from attending to my needy parent, then my self-interested course of action was immoral and selfish.

Many business decisions are driven by the so-called 'profit motive'. The profit motive is usually understood as the desire for profits *for oneself*. Thus, we might think of it as a *self-interested* motive. But being concerned with one's own profits is not necessarily *selfish*. Just as my learning a second language might be motivated by self-interest without being at all selfish, so my selling to the highest bidder might be motivated by self-interest without being at all selfish.

Of course maximizing one's own profits *can* be selfish. If I dump deadly toxins down river from my factory because this will minimize costs and thus maximize my profits, I am doing a horribly selfish thing. I should be more concerned about the welfare of others, concerned enough so that I would not do what poisons them. Still, although acting out of the profit motive can involve selfish and immoral behaviour, pursuing profits for oneself is not necessarily selfish or immoral.

At this point, someone might object that my example about learning another language is misleading in this context. It can be debated whether my learning another language has any significant effect on other people. (Our answer will turn especially on whether we take into account what I could do to help others with the time I devote to learning the other language.) But there can be no debate about whether a person's business decisions typically have important effects on other people. Now, if my learning a language has no significant effects on others, then any concern I might have for others has no room here to oppose my self-interested motive for learning it. *In this sort of case*, acting out of self-interest cannot be selfish. But in a business context, where my decisions virtually always have some impact on other people, there will almost always be the potential for conflict between my self-interest and the concern I should have for other people. Whenever I wrongly resolve this conflict in favour of self-interest, I am being selfish. If business people usually resolve such conflicts in favour of themselves, and if this usually involves too little concern for the good of others, then selfishness pervades the business world.

However, in order to decide whether selfishness really does pervade the business world, we have to determine how much priority morality allows agents to give to their own good. This is a question very much at the centre of contemporary moral theory (see, for example, Williams 1981; Scheffler 1982; Kagan 1989; Brandt 1989; Nagel 1991; Singer 1995; Crisp 1996a; Cottingham 1996; Unger 1996). Here is not the place for an investigation of that topic. Let me simply take it for granted that agents are allowed by morality to give priority to their own good, except under certain conditions.

What are these conditions under which you are *not* allowed to give your own good priority? You may have promised (explicitly or implicitly) to do whatever is in the other person's best interest. Or you may be a parent obligated to give the good of your children greater weight than your own. Close friendships can impose similar obligations. And, in all these cases, the obligation can be to give the other person's good priority not only over your own, but also over that of other people with whom you have no such connection.

Neither the priority you are allowed to give yourself nor the priority you are required to give to family, friends, and those to whom you have made certain promises is absolute, of course. First, in the allocation of your own resources and time, you must give some weight to the needs of others even if they have no special connection to you. Again, I cannot take up here the large issue of how much weight you must give to the needs of such people (see the references above). Second, there are certain things you are not allowed to do even if they are best for yourself or those within your circle. I discuss this idea in the next section.

Now behind the legitimate prioritizing of yourself and those to whom you have special connections, there may be some sort of background moral impartiality that endorses it (Brandt 1989: n. 22; Powers 1993; Hooker 1994*a*: 234–5; also HARE). But whether there is a background impartiality is another debate too big to join here. The main point is that I am assuming, as most of us do, that some considerable degree of partiality towards oneself is permissible except in certain contexts. If this is correct, then acting on self-interest, even when this conflicts with the interests of others, need not be immoral.

5. MORAL RESTRICTIONS

Although pursuing self-interest need not be immoral, of course it sometimes is. Indeed, one of the main roles of morality is to prohibit people's pursuing their goals in ways that are generally harmful to others. Thus, we are not morally allowed to lie, or steal, or physically injure others, or break our promises, and so on, even if we would benefit from doing so.

What are the moral restrictions on people's pursuit of their goals in business contexts? In light of both the pervasiveness of business in modern life and the high stakes, this question is immensely important.

I cannot address it fully here (see LUCAS); but let me call attention to some considerations I have already mentioned.

The prohibitions on lying, stealing, injuring, and promise-breaking will of course apply in a business context, with important implications. For example, the prohibition on lying will forbid false advertising, lying in order to get or keep a job, making false promises, and much else. Likewise, the prohibition on stealing will forbid copyright infringement and industrial spying. And the prohibition on injuring will forbid selling dangerously shoddy products and poisoning people's environment.

The moral requirement to keep one's promises seems to me particularly interesting in the business context. This requirement applies to implicit as well as to explicit promises. Suppose employees either explicitly or implicitly promise to help maximize profits for the company that hires them. Given this promise, maximizing company profits is now a *moral* duty of these employees. (A promise to do something immoral cannot be morally binding. So this moral duty is not a duty to do *absolutely anything* that would maximize profits, but only a duty to do whatever is morally permissible to maximize profits.)

Now this moral duty to maximize profits notoriously can conflict with the employee's own self-interest. An employee's interest in job security, higher wages, and other benefits can conflict with a duty to maximize company profits. This might be mitigated to some extent by using stock options to tie what the employee earns to company profits. But this route raises problems of its own. Employees (especially managers) might manipulate company profits so as to maximize the value of their stock options at the time they plan to cash out. This will probably not be what maximizes long-term profits for the company. So much is extremely familiar to business people. Here I am simply pointing out that here is an example where a promise to maximize company profits creates a moral duty that can then conflict with the employee's own self-interest.

6. IDEAL RULES VERSUS ESTABLISHED RULES

Further complications arise from the disparity between the established code of rules in some field of practice and an ideal code of rules for that field. Certainly, in the past some businesses and professions seemed to have virtually no established ethical rules. And even where rules are established, they might be less than ideal in any number of ways.

Why might a company or profession establish rules that are less than morally ideal? For one thing, the morally ideal rules might be very difficult to identify. For another, the company or profession might not even be looking for rules that are morally ideal. They might instead be aiming at rules best for themselves. They might thus introduce a code of ethics as a public relations exercise—as a way of engendering the goodwill of people outside the company. Or they might introduce a code of ethics as a way of putting added pressure on people to do things that are in the best interests of that particular company or profession.

For example, a company may institute a code of 'ethical' rules for its employees which forbids any discussions with the press about company projects. But suppose the company is selling arms to terrorists or poisoning the water table or bribing city officials. Any rule forbidding whistle-blowing here is a bad rule, and should be ignored. No morally ideal set of rules would forbid whistle-blowing in such a case.

To take another example, suppose you belong to a profession with an established rule that clients must never negotiate directly with one another, or with one another's agents. All negotiation is supposed to be channelled through each client's agent. Are you then morally wrong to let your client negotiate directly with the other client's agent? No matter what the established rule says, your letting your client negotiate directly hardly seems immoral. What is wrong is the established rule.

Nevertheless, breaking an established rule can be especially costly in terms of your own welfare. The company for which you work, or the profession in which you work, may well have sanctions enforcing its established rules. These sanctions would be intended to give people a self-interested reason not to break the rules. And the self-interested reason supplied by the sanctions will often persuade people not to break the rules, even when these people think the established rules are unwise, unfair, or in some other way defective.

Arguably, there are limits to the amount of self-sacrifice morality can demand. Suppose the sanction enforcing some established rule is very severe. Then, the existence of this sanction might sometimes prevent people from being morally required to break the established rule. For if they did break the established rule, they would incur a cost that is just too high.

On the other hand, no one should think that complying with the best rules can never be costly to oneself. When the stakes for others are very high, one can be morally obligated to break some established rule even though this will be costly to oneself. Being moral isn't always easy.

There are just two more points I want to note here about the distinction between established and ideal rules (for further points, see Hooker 1994*b*). The first is that established rules may be so faulty that they should be abandoned immediately, even though this would upset people who formed expectations on the basis of those rules. The rule used to be that you could hire, sell to, and buy from whomever you want. People formed expectations on the basis of this conventionally accepted rule. But the rule was not ideal, at least in a place where many people acted in accordance with prejudices concerning race, gender, religious affiliation, sexual preference, etc. Rules forbidding such discrimination were best implemented immediately, even though this led to the frustration of many people's old expectations.

In other cases, however, we have to be careful about applying new rules to situations that developed under old rules. Suppose that in a given company there is no conventionally accepted rule prohibiting people from dating those who work under them, and thus there is no conventionally accepted rule against higher-ups asking the people under them for dates. Suppose that on the whole things would go better if there were such a prohibition, because the prohibition would combat sexual harassment and favouritism in the workplace. But now suppose two people in our office are dating happily and the higher-up was the one who initiated the relationship. Obviously, it would be seriously unfair to apply a new non-fraternization rule *retroactively* to this couple.

7. CONCLUSION

Prosperity depends on the economy, and our economy depends on the profit motive. Of course some things done in the pursuit of profit are immoral. But the pursuit of profit need not be immoral. And when employees have implicitly or explicitly promised their employers to help maximize the employers' profits, doing so is a moral duty. Often the maximization of company profits is in the interests of the employees, but sometimes of course it isn't. Further conflicts with self-interest can arise when the best set of rules governing business requires breaking an established rule that is enforced within a company or profession.

My discussion has outlined the concepts of self-interest and self-ishness, and focused on possible conflicts in business between self-interest and moral requirement. But let me close by stressing the communal benefits of trustworthiness and fairness in business. Anyone who has operated in a setting where people could trust one another without resort to legal measures will attest to these benefits.

REFERENCES

Axelrod, R. (1984), *The Evolution of Cooperation* (New York: Basic Books).

Brandt, R. (1989), 'Morality and its Critics', *American Philosophical Quarterly*, 26: 89–100.

Brink, D. (1989), *Moral Realism and the Foundations of Ethics* (New York: Cambridge University Press).

Cottingham, J. (1996), 'Partiality and the Virtues', in Crisp (1996*b*): 57–76.

Crisp, R. (1996*a*), 'The Dualism of Practical Reason', *Proceedings of the Aristotelian Society*, 96: 53–73.

—— (1996*b*) (ed.), *How Should One Live?* (Oxford: Clarendon Press).

—— (1997), *Mill on Utilitarianism* (London: Routledge).

Griffin, J. (1986), *Well-Being: Its Meaning, Measurement and Moral Importance* (Oxford: Clarendon Press).

Hooker, B. (1991), 'Mark Overvold's Contribution to Philosophy', *Journal of Philosophical Research*, 16: 333–44.

—— (1993), 'Political Philosophy', in McHenry and Adams (1993): 87–102.

—— (1994*a*), Review of M. Slote, *From Morality to Virtue*, *Mind*, 103: 232–6.

—— (1994*b*), 'Compromising with Convention', *American Philosophical Quarterly*, 31: 311–17.

—— (1996), 'Can Being Virtuous Constitute a Benefit to the Agent?', in Crisp (1996*b*): 141–55.

Hurka, T. (1993), *Perfectionism* (New York: Oxford University Press).

Kagan, S. (1989), *The Limits of Morality* (Oxford: Clarendon Press).

Kavka, G. (1986), *Hobbesian Moral and Political Theory* (Princeton: Princeton University Press).

McHenry, L., and Adams, F. (1993) (eds), *Reflections on Philosophy: Introductory Essays* (New York: St Martin's Press).

Nagel, T. (1991), *Equality and Partiality* (New York: Oxford University Press).

Nussbaum, M., and Sen, A. (1993) (eds), *The Quality of Life* (Oxford: Clarendon Press).

Overvold, M. (1980), 'Self-interest and the Concept of Self-sacrifice', *Canadian Journal of Philosophy*, 10: 105–18.

Parfit, D. (1984), *Reasons and Persons* (Oxford: Clarendon Press).

Powers, M. (1993), 'Contractualist Impartiality and Personal Commitments', *American Philosophical Quarterly*, 30: 63–71.

Scanlon, T. (1993), 'Value, Desire, and Quality of Life', in Nussbaum and Sen (1993): 185–200.

Scheffler, S. (1982), *The Rejection of Consequentialism* (Oxford: Clarendon Press).

Singer, P. (1995), *How Are We To Live?* (New York: Prometheus).

Unger, P. (1996), *Living High and Letting Die: The Illusion of Innocence* (New York: Oxford University Press).

Williams, B. (1973), 'Egoism and Altruism', in Williams, B., *Problems of the Self* (Cambridge: Cambridge University Press): 250–65.

—— (1981), 'Persons, Character, and Morality', in Williams, B., *Moral Luck* (Cambridge: Cambridge University Press): 1–19.

4

One Philosopher's Approach to Business Ethics

R. M. HARE

I MUST start by explaining two things in my title. I say '*one* philosopher's approach' because not all philosophers agree. There are a great many different ethical theories, nearly all of which have something to be said for them. One has to look at them all and see what truths they bring out, and also what mistakes they make, and try to find a theory which preserves the truths and avoids the mistakes; and that is what I have done. There has to be a theoretical basis for the rational discussion of moral problems in business, just as of anything else, and no one should think that we can do without it. That would leave us at the mercy of whatever prejudices we started with. My own theory is in the main a combination of the insights I find in Kant and in the utilitarians—two sorts of philosophy that are thought to be quite irreconcilable but which actually fit together very well if we understand what is going on in them (Hare, 1993).

I have next to explain what I think philosophers should be doing: what philosophy is, and what good it does. There are different views about this too, and I can only give you mine. I shall be content if you think that philosophy, as I understand the word, can help with problems in business ethics; I leave it to others who mean something different by 'philosophy' to show, if they can, that their kind of philosophy can help too.

So what is philosophy, and what good does it do? When I am asked this question, the answer I always give is that it is the study of *arguments* to find a way of telling good from bad ones. In short, philosophy, broadly speaking, is *Logic*. By 'Logic' I mean not just the mathematical kind that is done in ps and qs, but any study that casts light on what are good reasons for holding opinions that we hold, or what would be good reasons for abandoning them. If there are good reasons, then we ought to be able to defend them in argument; and that is what philosophy is about.

Obviously, in order to study arguments, we have to ask what implies what or what follows from what. And this takes us straight into the study of *language*. For what follows from what somebody says depends on what his words mean. Their meaning is intimately bound up with what they imply; if they implied something different they would mean something different. So you cannot study arguments without studying the meanings of words, and the logic that that meaning generates.

All study of arguments leads us into the study of the language that we are using when we argue. So then, what use is it to study this? I think you will understand what use it is if you consider how, every few weeks in most large and many small colleges, some famous guru comes on to campus and talks to the students, and how they often hang on his (or her) words, so that what goes for gospel in the student community, and sometimes even among their elders, is what has been made fashionable by such people. To add insult to injury, some of these people even call themselves 'philosophers'. What distresses me as a philosopher is that hardly anybody ever seems to ask what the arguments are for holding these opinions, or whether they are good ones. If we had more, and more serious, philosophers on campuses, it just might happen that the purveyors of fashionable rhetoric would get asked, more often than they do, to justify what they say. Perhaps some of what they say is good sense; perhaps some of it is the most poisonous rubbish—hazardous waste. But we shall never know which is which until we have learnt to sift good arguments from bad. So, for want of good philosophy, the intellectual pollution will go on.

This present situation is not new. It has all happened before; and the first time in history that it happened was when philosophy began, as an attempt by its founder, Socrates, to come to grips with the gurus of his day, the sophists. The Greek word 'sophos' means, in this context, not 'wise' as it is often translated, but 'clever'; and these people were tremendously clever, like many of our modern gurus. They were clever above all in making a great name for themselves, and as a result amassing huge amounts of money. Socrates did not claim to match their cleverness, and did not seek their wealth; but he had a move to put them all down. This consisted in asking what they meant by some key *word* in their discourses. Aristotle says of him in the *Metaphysics* (987b 1) that he was concerned with moral questions, and was the first to turn his attention to definitions. If we are going to sift good arguments from bad, the first need is to make absolutely clear what is being claimed and what the premises, on which the arguments for it are based, mean. Unless we know this, how can we tell whether they are in fact true or whether the position that is being defended actually follows from them?

My own particular interest, like Socrates', is moral philosophy. I have therefore devoted most of my working life to elucidating the meanings of the words we use when we ask and try to answer moral questions. Such words are 'ought', 'right', 'wrong', and also 'good', as they are used in moral discussion. I think that the understanding of the logic of these words casts a flood of light on moral arguments. It often enables one to spot false steps in them, such as suppressed premises which have not themselves been argued for, ambiguities or equivocations, and so on. It is also helpful in revealing what the structure of a good argument on a certain question would have to be like.

Although I do now spend about half my time on the study of practical issues (the other half being still devoted to theory), I do not want to set myself up as an expert on the issues themselves. A philosopher, interested in many different practical issues, is bound to get much of his information about them from secondary sources like the newspapers (which I spend a lot of time reading). Nobody can become an expert on the facts involved unless he is immersed in the practicalities of a particular field, as business people are in business, doctors in medicine, planners in environmental planning, and so on. It might be thought that the philosopher, who will always know less about such subjects than the practitioners, cannot contribute much. But he has his own contribution to make, namely the study of the logic of the arguments; and the experts in the field are often not so versed in this as they might be.

I have sometimes, but rarely, tried to go deeply into the facts relevant to a practical question. I used to do it on urban planning, especially the location of new roads. I even got to the stage at which papers of mine were accepted in a technical journal. That was a long time ago, before the subject got computerized. But generally speaking there is a better way for the philosopher. What I recommend is that he should do enough study to see what the problems are. This will include mainly reading, but also observation. For example, if he is interested in racism, he can usefully pay a visit to South Africa, but he will not try by himself to arrive at solutions. If he is lucky, he will have the opportunity to talk with practitioners of the relevant disciplines, and thus acquaint himself more deeply with the problems.

After that, the philosopher will not, if he is wise, lay down the law about what should or should not be done. What he will do, instead, is to say what facts would support what conclusions. That is, what *would* the facts have to be to justify a certain policy, and what *would* they have to be to justify rival policies? When that is understood, the practitioners themselves can go on to establish what the facts actually are (which they are better at doing, normally, than the philosopher), and so determine, by sound arguments in the light of these facts, what ought actually to be done. This kind of collaboration between the disciplines is the most likely to be fruitful.

There is another reason for philosophers to be hesitant about arguing themselves for conclusions about practical issues and policies. Since the relevant facts are often so complex, ramified, and hard to come by, there is a great temptation to *select* those facts which suit one's own prejudices and ignore the others. Then one will be at the mercy of some opponent who selects a set of facts which support the opposite point of view. Philosophers can seldom spare the time (certainly if, as they should, they try their hand at a number of *different* practical issues) to make a really comprehensive study of the facts; so such disputes may well be inconclusive. Perhaps, therefore, it is better for the philosopher to stick to his last and study the structure of the arguments. There may be exceptions to this: some philosophers have done good work by devoting themselves to the facts about a particular restricted topic. Or the relevant facts about some topic may be sufficiently clear for there to be no argument about *them*, but only about the nature of the argument itself—this being what has generated the difficulties. In that case the philosopher can perhaps sort things out without much more fact-finding. I think that this is true of the disputes about abortion, for example. But usually the philosopher will be of most help if he tries to clarify the issues without coming down on one side of them.

The best way I can illustrate for you what philosophy is and how it can help is by taking some problems in business ethics and talking about them in a philosophical way. I said just now that I shall be applying a particular ethical theory which I think is well supported, being, as I said, a combination of the true insights in the utilitarians and Kant. It is also consistent with the Golden Rule, the foundation of Christian morality and other moralities too: that we should do to others as we wish they should do to us if we were in their situations. In effect this will lead us, as Kant said, to treat their ends as our ends, or, as the utilitarians say, to do the best we can for them, treating them all impartially.

I have got this theory by selecting the best bits from other people's theories. My own contribution, if there was one, was to put the theory on a firmer logical basis. I think, unlike some other moral philosophers nowadays, that there is a logical structure for moral reasoning implicit in the very meaning, and thus in the logical properties, of the words or concepts we are using when we ask moral questions. So long as we go on asking the same questions, we are stuck with those concepts and with that logic; if we altered the concepts and the logic, we would be asking different questions. But this is not an appropriate place to argue that issue. I will merely say that if we want to be rational in our moral thinking, we must have something to control the thinking, that is, a logic, and that this can only be determined by the meanings of the words we are using.

All the theories that I am drawing on face a well-known difficulty which their opponents try to exploit. But it is not hard to avoid this difficulty if one understands what is going on in our moral thinking. The difficulty is that all these theories seem to have counter-intuitive consequences. Many of these concern special duties that we think we have to those close to us in various ways: our family, our patients if we are doctors, our firm if we are in business. Taken strictly, both the Kantian prescription to treat all humans as ends, and the Christian command to do to all of them as we wish should be done to us, and the utilitarian principle of furthering the interests of all impartially, would, it is said, lead mothers to pay equal regard to the welfare of all children without favouring their own children; lawyers to try to do as well for their clients' opponents as for their clients; doctors to pay no attention to the fact that their patients are *their* patients; and employees or managers to give no more weight to the interests of their own firms and their shareholders than to the interests of their competitors. And it is held that this is absurd.

However, this is not a real difficulty. The only people who now raise it are those who have not understood what has been written on the subject in the last ten years or so, and indeed for many centuries if one looks at the literature. The solution is to recognize that moral thinking takes place at two levels at least. There is, first of all, the intuitive level at which we do, and should do, most of our moral thinking for most of the time. At this level we apply fairly simple and general principles which have proved best on the whole in our experience and in that of our forebears. These are the principles that one follows if one has the common virtues of honesty, for example, and truthfulness, and fairness, and kindness, and courage, and determination, and so on.

Loyalty is one of these virtues, and so are other kinds of partiality such as I listed just now. So, *at this level*, we do expect mothers to give their own children's interests priority over those of other children, and lawyers to seek the advantage of their own clients to the possible detriment of other people's clients. But the principles which we employ, or the virtues that we commend, at this level need some justification. How do we know, when we are bringing up our children, whether the virtues that are now commended are the ones we ought to cultivate in them? Perhaps more vigorous aggressive devil-take-the-hindmost principles would be better for them to have.

In any case the principles I have mentioned will certainly come into conflict with one another in difficult cases. No business person will need reminding of this, for these conflicts are obvious in business. The duties of honesty and truthfulness and fairness and public responsibility can certainly, and often do, conflict with the duty of loyalty to one's firm. There has to be some way of resolving these conflicts of duties; that is what business ethics is all about.

The task of resolving the conflicts, and of justifying the principles in the first place, belongs to a higher level of thinking which I am going to call critical thinking. The expression is used in a number of related senses; but what I mean by it is the thinking which criticizes and assesses the principles which are appealed to, and the decisions which are made, at the lower intuitive level. In order to decide whether ruthlessness, for example, is a virtue in business, we have to ask whether it is a good thing to cultivate it. Or would we do better to cultivate other gentler virtues? The answer to this question will depend on what we are after when we are educating our children, or for that matter students in business.

It is at this higher critical level that the theories I mentioned earlier—Kantianism, utilitarianism, and Christian *agapē*—come into their own. It is perfectly consistent to say that *at the intuitive level* there are virtues and principles which we ought to follow, often without much thought, like the principle that we ought not to tell lies, or that we ought to look after our firm's interests, or alternatively that of the public; but to go on to say that when we examine these principles in the light of critical thinking we are not appealing to those principles themselves—that would be arguing in a circle. So, for example, it might be the case that it was good to have, at the intuitive level, principles requiring partiality to one's children or clients or firm; but that in justifying such principles we can appeal to impartial principles.

Let me illustrate how this could be done. We might say that it is a very good thing that employees think in general that they ought to serve the interests of their own firms. This is a good thing, not just for the firms themselves, but also for the public in general. If firms are to operate efficiently and successfully they have to be able to rely on loyalty; and if they do not operate efficiently and successfully, the interests of all—not just the firms' shareholders, but also their customers and the public in general—will suffer. That is a feature of the economic system by which we operate in capitalist economies, and I believe myself that it is the best way, in the general interest, of organizing things. That other types of economic system do not do so well for people in general has, I think, been amply shown by what went on in the Soviet Union and Eastern Europe during the Cold War era, and in other parts of the world. So the typical business virtues *are* a good thing. And they include the virtue of loyalty.

So this *partial* virtue can be justified by critical thinking, which appeals to the *impartial* principle of doing the best for people in general. An impartial critical thinker will recommend the cultivation of these partial virtues. We can see how in this way the difficulty I mentioned earlier can be got over. We should indeed cultivate the virtues and principles to which the opponents of Kantianism and utilitarianism appeal; in our ordinary dealings we should, for example, be partial and loyal to our firms and our clients and our patients and our children; but the reason is that the cultivation of these partial virtues is justified by an *impartial* appeal to the good of all, of which these theories are expressions.

The same can be said about the other virtues. The reason why honesty is rightly called a virtue is this: its cultivation by all, which leads to the firm acceptance of it, so that people feel awful if they have been dishonest, conduces on the whole to the good of all treated impartially. One can say the same about truthfulness, consideration for others, and all the rest.

So the objection that Kantianism and utilitarianism and Christian morality yield absurd results is easy to get over. The results seem absurd only because we are mixing up the two levels of moral thinking. The apparent difficulty is created by appealing to our common intuitions or moral convictions, and claiming that the theory yields results inconsistent with them. But these common convictions are implanted in us for use at the everyday intuitive level. At that level we ought to follow them; and the reason is that, as the theory itself shows, critical thinking would recommend the implanting of these convictions, as being for the best. So, for example, Christian *agapē*, founded on universal love, would bid us teach to business students the virtue of loyalty to their own firms (which is far from universal—that is, it requires us on occasion to fight against the interests of rival firms); but the reason for this is that the cultivation of this virtue by all will lead, in a properly functioning market, to the maximal furtherance of the interests of all.

Mention of the market brings me to my main illustration of what I have been saying. It is sometimes claimed that the market is a substitute for ethics. It would be, in a way, nice for business people if it were so. By operating in the market, and doing the utmost to secure their own advantage (which may mean damaging other people), they would be doing all that a good business person can be expected to do. They would not have to bother about moral considerations, and that would be a weight off their minds. The most important thing I have to say in this paper is that this is a simple mistake. I owe the point I am going to make now to Mr Tim Congdon, who is an excellent economist working in the City of London, and writes occasional brilliantly clear and I think very sensible pieces in the London *Times*. But I learnt this point not there, but from a talk he gave to a dining club to which we both belong.

The point is that the market is no substitute for ethics, because the market will not function without ethics. I could give examples from modern business life; but history provides us with a simpler one. The same thing has happened in all civilized economies, but I will take my example from China, because that is more picturesque. In front of the main audience chamber in the Forbidden City, the Imperial Palace in Beijing, there are two pillars. The one on the right as one faces the palace supports a sundial. I do not know whether this symbolizes the constancy of the heavenly motions, or the virtue of punctuality, or what. The other contains the standard set of weights and measures. This was put in that prominent position, many centuries ago, to symbolize the truth that honesty in trade is the foundation of prosperity. What does this teach us about business ethics? It teaches us that there could be no efficient market unless people could trust one another. Suppose, for example, any trader could sell what he called pound loaves of bread, but which actually weighed a fraction less, so that he would make an immediate gain. But then, if he got away with it, everybody would start doing the same.

The result would be that nobody would know how much bread they were getting for their money, and the market would function far less efficiently, if at all. However oriental the bargaining, it would be no use going from stall to stall seeking the best price, because you simply would not know what price you were getting *per pound*; indeed, the very word 'pound' would have become meaningless. The same applies with even greater force to the currency; if people start making counterfeit coins and notes and get away with it, the time will soon come when we don't know what 'dollar' means either.

That is what I mean by saying that the market is not a substitute for ethics, but depends on it. If I were more versed in these matters, I could have used modern examples like market-rigging, insider dealing, misleading advertising and packaging, and the like. But although I do follow the careers of Boesky and his kind in the newspapers, I should probably slip up on the technicalities if I got involved in them. The point is perfectly well illustrated by my simple model from Beijing. To generalize: unless certain minimum standards of honesty, truthfulness, fair dealing, and so on are observed in the market, the market will not function efficiently, or even at all, and the good that the market is supposed to bring about will not be achieved. I shall come in a moment to the question of *how* people are to be got to observe these standards.

The standards are for use at what I called earlier the intuitive level. Their inculcation can be amply justified by thinking at the critical level, as is shown by what I have just been saying. If they were not inculcated, the whole fabric of society, including business society, would collapse. We have here an example of the phenomenon known as the 'prisoners' dilemma'. Here too, I need not go into the technicalities. Because the phenomenon is a commonplace of game theory, I am sure that it will be familiar. For an up-to-date account of how dilemmas of this sort work, with many examples from different fields, I do not know anything better or clearer than the one in Parfit (1984: ch. 2).

The essence of these dilemmas is that, of two or more parties, each knows that whatever the others do, it will be to his (or her) individual advantage to take a certain course; but if all take that course, they will collectively do worse than they would if they had all taken some other course. Our present example illustrates this very well. It is to the individual trader's advantage to file a bit off his 'pound' weight, provided that he can get away with it; and this will be so whatever the others do. If they remain honest, he will get more money for less bread; but if they do the same as he has, he will still get more money for less bread than if he had not filed down his 'pound' weight. If everybody does it, or even just a few people, the market will start operating inefficiently and all will suffer. But all the same, the dishonest will suffer less than the honest.

How then are we to set about avoiding this decline of the market? There are three ways that are canvassed. They are not mutually exclusive, and various mixtures of them are possible. They can also be used concurrently to prevent different malpractices, or even the same malpractice. But for simplicity I will consider just the three. I am going to call these three ways 'custom', 'self-regulation', and 'legislation'.

I can explain these words in terms of my simple example. It might be the case that merchants just did not file down their pound weights—it was simply 'not done'. Morality might come into it: they might have been brought up as children to be honest, and taught that it was dishonest to tamper with one's weights. So they might be using this principle in their intuitive thinking, and they might have been so well taught that they simply could not live with themselves if they did any such thing.

They might even, if they were more articulate, have done some critical thinking, in which they would have seen the results that would follow if people tampered with weights. They might have concluded from this that they could not will weight-tampering as a universal law for others to follow as well as themselves; and they therefore might have been unwilling to subscribe to a universal principle permitting this, and so they might have become sure that it was wrong to do it. But however they had come to have this principle, it might work very well if everybody had it.

I think that there have been some business communities in which most people are induced in this way to be honest. One of the main conditions for this is that people should know what other people are doing. If a malpractice is evident, those who are committing it will sooner or later come to grief in their business, even if the malpractice is not against the law. People will just stop trading with them. This condition can perhaps be realized in a fairly close-knit business community. It is sometimes claimed that the City of London was once such a community, when everyone was a gentleman, everybody knew everybody else, and there were not many foreigners in the market. I suspect that this is a pleasing legend; but it certainly does not hold of the City of London now, nor of any other big market, let alone of the world market as a whole.

However, we must not think that, if morality by itself, unsupported by self-regulation or legislation, cannot keep enough people straight to make the market work, it is no use at all. This is obvious in my simple example from Beijing, and also in more modern examples. It will be much easier to keep people straight if *most* of them want to keep straight anyway. Then if you have self-regulation or legislation, the authorities, whoever they are, will have a much easier time enforcing the rules or the laws. They will only have to keep their eyes open to catch the delinquents, who in such a fundamentally moral community will be few. If they had to keep tabs on everybody, there would have to be much more paperwork, many more inspectors, many more court cases and lawyers to manage them, and so on. So the market would be, again, less efficient than it could be, and the costs would be huge.

I cannot forbear giving an example from my own line of business, academic life. In Oxford, where I used to work, people trust one another. In Florida, where I work now, and I suspect in most big American academies, they do not. In Oxford, when I went to speak at a conference, I got the journey approved in the relevant committee— usually on the nod, because I never asked for anything unreasonable. It went in the minutes, with the amount I asked for. When I came back from my journey, I wrote on a blank sheet of paper the amount I had spent, signed it, gave it without any documentation to the secretary of the committee, who sent it on to the University Chest, as our financial office is called, and I would get the money within a few days. In Florida by contrast, although I have not one but two large personal funds for my travel, actually getting the money is a formidable business. One has to fill in the details on enormous forms in many copies (a task which I am incompetent to fulfil correctly; the department secretary has to do it), and elaborate documentation is required; and one often does not get the money for months. Huge costs are incurred in paying people to prevent me being dishonest. All this is because in the University of Florida they are not gentlemen and cannot trust one another. And they still do not catch any real culprit who has the minimum of criminal expertise—how could they? I suspect that the New York and London business communities now are like the University of Florida writ large.

So it is certainly a help if people are moral, but not enough. The first step towards regulation, if regulation is needed, is usually called self-regulation. What happens is that various professional bodies are set up with the job of making rules and securing compliance with them. They usually have powers of inspection or at least power to investigate complaints. In the weakest case—the nearest to unaided morality—these bodies have no real teeth except publicity. For example, we have in Britain a body called the Press Council. This can hear complaints against newspapers which, it is alleged, have reported unfairly or untruly and so damaged individuals or companies. There are many cases when a complaint is upheld, although there is no *legal* redress because, for example, the law of libel does not cover the offence committed. This body has no teeth; all it can do is to blacken the name of the offending newspaper in its reports. But even this may do some good, and I think that standards are a bit higher as a result of the Press Council's activities—but not much.

The next step, obviously, if needed, is to give such bodies teeth. This can only be done—short of bringing in the law—by having professional associations whose members are bound by the regulations made by their ruling bodies. If they break the rules, they can in the last resort be slung out, as lawyers and doctors can be if they commit recognized malpractices. This is obviously a more powerful engine for securing good conduct. It is preferred by many practitioners to statutory regulation, because they like to be governed by their own peers and not by the legislature. The votes, and even the strenuous lobbying, of doctors or lawyers cannot much influence the success of bills before legislatures; but they are much more likely to influence the decisions of their own professional bodies. So it is obvious why they prefer self-regulation.

However, the system has one obvious disadvantage, which is frequently alleged against the medical and legal professions, and will be against whatever self-regulating bodies we have or may have in financial centres. The objection is that these bodies, because they are not directly responsible to the public, do not sufficiently protect the public interest, whatever they may do for the interests of their own constituents. For example, suppose we have an Advertising Standards Authority to enforce a code of practice among advertisers, and suppose that this body is elected by, and responsible to, the members of that group (let us say the advertising agencies or their clients). Then the body may ban practices which are detrimental to its constituents (knocking copy for example), but may do nothing about practices which are to the advantage of advertisers themselves but harm the public in general. This may be so even if the self-regulatory body is given legal teeth, and can not merely expel or disqualify any delinquent members of a profession, but take them to court, or themselves impose penalties.

For these reasons a call will arise for the legislature or the government to step in itself and *appoint* regulatory bodies enforcing, not their own rules, but laws laid down from above in what is thought to be the public interest. The disadvantage of doing this is often said to be that the legislators, not being members of the profession in question, do not always have the knowledge to make the best rules; and that therefore the system, besides becoming cumbrous and unworkable and even easy to circumvent, may fail to achieve the desired objects in the public interest. I would say that this is especially likely to be true in the financial area.

In most financial centres and other walks of life where regulation is attempted, we can see examples of all these methods, and indeed there are many different variants of them which I have not had time to describe. As I said, they can be used concurrently. What are we doing when we are deciding between them in a particular field? Reverting to my distinction between intuitive and critical thinking: just as, there, the best intuitions are the ones whose inculcation does the best on the whole for everybody treated impartially, so here the best rules and regulatory systems are the ones which do the best for those affected. Those affected in the first instance are the members of the profession in question or the participants in the market. In some areas they are the main people affected. Some financial malpractices, for example, may do enormous harm to individual people or firms, but not harm the public much except by damaging the operation of the market. In such cases self-regulation is perhaps all right; the main interests are protected.

But in other cases malpractices may harm a wider public (for example by precipitating a stock market crash). When that is the situation, the public through its representatives in the legislature will rightly call for legislation to take the matter out of the hands of cosy professional bodies and subject it to the law of the land, in the public interest. But, as I said, the legislators may get it wrong.

The best advice I can give is that everybody in a particular walk of life, be they doctors or lawyers or business people, would be sensible if, first of all, they cultivated sound *moral* principles, so as to avoid even self-regulation and the bureaucracy that it brings with it; and that if recourse has to be had to self-regulation, the bodies that do it should conduct themselves in such a way that the public does not think that the professionals are feathering their own nests, but have the interests of the public primarily at heart. In this way we shall avoid legislation, and get an efficient market with the minimum of regulation. But I know that I am asking for a lot.

I will end with another example of a question that often troubles business people. What difference to the *morality* of an act does it make that it would be against the *law*? Cases like this are familiar. The actual case I am thinking of concerned a firm called the Beech-Nut Company, but I do not have all the details. An executive of this company ordered a product from its inventory to be kept on the market; the product claimed to be apple juice, but was in fact mostly sugared water. The company had innocently bought this from fraudulent suppliers and had an enormous stock of the stuff. Let us suppose that the executive knew that to sell the product was illegal. The executive, however, thought he was *morally* obliged to sell the product and try to get away with it, because of the loyalty he owed to his company and its shareholders, who would lose a lot of money if the company went out of business. He thought the public would not come to any harm by drinking sugared water.

I will answer this question as briefly as I can. There are two ways in which the unlawfulness of an act affects its morality. The first way is this: it may be that the legal consequences of the act are such that people (for example the shareholders) will be harmed. In the present case, if the firm were sentenced to a large fine, the shareholders would suffer, and this would be a consequence, or probable consequence, of the illegality of the act. That is why wise firms employ attorneys. It is simply an example of the truth that the consequences of acts are relevant to their morality.

In case anybody should, through confusion, reproach me for being what is called a 'consequentialist', I must point out that to be a consequentialist, in the sense in which I am one, is inevitable. Our acts are what we do, and what we do is the difference that we make to the course of events, that is to say the consequences that we bring about. So if this executive gets his shareholders into legal trouble, we shall say he has harmed their interests; that is one of the things he did. In this sense consequences are part of the act, and may be a morally relevant part.

That then is the consequentialist reason for keeping on the right side of the law. It may tell against other consequentialist reasons for *breaking* the law. If the executive thought that the probable balance of advantage for his shareholders lay with breaking the law, then, so far as this reason goes (namely the reason of loyalty to shareholders, which, as I have said is *one* moral reason) he morally ought to break it.

This first reason for keeping the law may sound cynical, but it is a moral reason all the same, to be appealed to in appropriate cases at the intuitive level. But there is another reason which may be thought less cynical. I said that there were these two levels of moral thinking, and that at the intuitive level what we do is stick to the sound moral principles in which we have been raised. Loyalty to one's company is one of these principles, but only one. Since we are here operating at the intuitive level, and there are other principles (honesty to the public in this case), we may, and do, have a conflict between these principles. But the relevant thing here is that one of the principles that may come into conflict is the principle that we ought to keep the law. This is an intuitive moral principle in which most of us have been raised, and it is a good thing that we have. Things would go worse not only for others but for us if we had not been raised in this way.

But what we have here is a possible conflict between this principle and the principle of loyalty. I said earlier that there would be these conflicts of principles, and that in such cases it was the function of critical thinking to resolve the conflict so as to get the best outcome, morally speaking, in the particular case. So, faced with such a conflict, we shall give a great deal of weight to our duty to keep the law, and shall break this principle only with repugnance, if we have been well brought up. But in some cases we may think that, all things considered, we ought to break the law, because to do so is required by some other principle which also has great weight. *Which* principle we ought to allow to override the others in a particular case is a matter for critical thought.

I shall not have time to tell you in detail how I think that such critical thought should proceed. That is the stuff of ethical theory, of which the theory of business ethics is a part. All I have been doing is to sketch my approach to the subject, and not to deal with it exhaustively. Anyone who wants to know what I think about ethical theory in general will have to read my books (especially Hare 1981); and in fact it is not difficult, if one gets the hang of the general theory, to apply it in particular fields like business. Ethics is ethics whatever one's vocation.

REFERENCES

Hare, R. M. (1981), *Moral Thinking* (Oxford: Oxford University Press).
—— (1993), 'Could Kant have been a Utilitarian?', *Utilitas*, 5: 1–16. Also in Dancy (1993): 91–113.
Dancy, R. M. (1993) (ed.), *Kant and Critique: New Essays in Honor of W. H. Werkmeister* (Dordrecht: Kluwer).
Parfit, D. (1984), *Reasons and Persons* (Oxford: Clarendon Press).

5

The Responsibilities of a Businessman

J. R. LUCAS

I

MANY thinkers deny the possibility of businessmen having responsibilities or ethical obligations. A businessman has no alternative, in
view of the competition of the market-place, to do anything other
than buy at the cheapest and sell at the dearest price he can. In any
case, it would be irrational—if, indeed, it were possible—not to do
so. Admittedly, there is a framework of law within which he has to
operate, but that is all, and so long as he keeps the law he is free to
maximize his profits without being constrained by any moral or
social considerations, or any further sense of responsibility for
what he does.

This view is mistaken. Economic determinism is false. The iron
laws of supply and demand are not made of iron, and indicate
tendencies only, without fixing everything, leaving no room for
choice. In economic affairs we are often faced with decisions, and
often can choose between a number of alternative courses of action.
It is up to us what we do; we are responsible agents, and may fairly be
asked to explain why we did as we did.

Nor do canons of rationality pick out one single course of action
as the only rational one to take. They do not show that it is irrational
to do anything other than maximize our profits. It is a mistake to
construe rationality in terms of maximizing. Even though some
economists, influenced by the Theory of Games, offer it as a definition, it is, as the prisoners' dilemma shows, an incoherent one. For
individuals each to seek to maximize their own pay-off can lead to
sub-optimal outcomes assessed in maximizing terms. It may seem
like a good idea for me to maximize irrespective of what others do,
but if it is really a good idea for me, it is a good idea for them too,
and then we shall all be worse off than if we had each pursued a
policy that considered others as well as ourself. Rationality requires
us not just to maximize, but also to widen our range of concern. We

accept that it would be foolish to be guided only by immediate pay-offs without considering future ones; we need to extend our vision not only over times, but over persons, identifying with certain groups, and thinking not only of my individual good, but our collective one as well.

It is a mistake, finally, to think that once the law has been laid down, the businessman is free to pursue profits within the limits laid down by law. The standards enforced by the law can only be minimal ones, not replacing moral standards, but needing to be supplemented by them. We generally acknowledge that there is a moral obligation to obey the law, and that almost every legal system enshrines much moral teaching, and that moral considerations have an important influence on the interpretation and development of the law. The legal system would break down unless most people obeyed most laws most of the time, and unless witnesses told the truth, and judges and juries reached honest verdicts, without being made to by the threat of coercion. We need the law to be enforced on occasion because civil society, unlike some voluntary associations, is unselective, and contains some members who are not minded to abide by the law, and would flout it if they could; and if they got away with it, others would follow suit. The law therefore needs to be backed by the threat of coercive sanctions, but just because these sanctions are severe, their use has to be subject to many safeguards. We need trials and burdens of proof, and often are chary about legislating against some admitted evil on account of the difficulty of actually enforcing the law, or of the dangers of blackmail, or for many other cogent reasons. Hence the standard required by the law is necessarily a minimal one, well below what is tolerable in social or commercial life.

Businessmen do have some, although only limited, room for making decisions; they are not being irrational if they take into consideration a wider range of concerns than simply maximizing immediate individual profit; and their legal duties do not exhaust their obligations generally. In deciding what to do, and justifying their decisions afterwards, there are a variety of reasons, for and against, the different courses of action open to them, these reasons not being necessarily confined to maximizing profits while keeping within the law.

Many businessmen are shy of moral argument. It is partly because moral philosophy seems remote from practical decision-making, partly because the claims of morality seem insatiable, and if once allowed a foothold will end up by demanding that the business-man sell all his plant to buy low-cost housing for unmarried mothers.

Much moral philosophy is, indeed, remote from practical decision-making, and often is unduly *simpliste*. Many of the questions we have to decide are ones where there are weighty considerations on either side, and it is a matter of weighing the *pros* against the *cons*, and striking the best balance we can. Some of the considerations may be said to be moral, but there is a wide variety of reasons for action covered by that term. An existentialist may find himself impelled by his authenticity to abandon everything, and go off and stage an art exhibition in Paris; a young man may be called to give away his possessions and follow St Francis; a middle-aged woman to throw up her job and devote herself to caring for a sick relative: but these vocations are not ones to which a businessman is called. Corporations have no souls: they cannot be called to witness to artistic integrity, the monastic ideal, or altruistic devotion to another's good. But it does not follow that the ordinary universal obligations of communal life do not apply to them. These obliga-tions arise from the activities we engage in and the context in which we carry them out, and apply to businesses as much as to other undertakings not because they have souls, but because they are centres of decision-taking.

It would still be possible for a businessman to remain sceptical. Scepticism is always possible—at a price. The tough-minded can dismiss all concern for the environment as unrealistic woolly-mindedness, and may defer payment to his suppliers until the last possible moment: but when the Mafia call, and suggest that he might like to purchase protection from arson attacks, he is likely to be indignant. He believes vehemently in the rule of law, and that vio-lence has no place in a civilized society; his scepticism, in short, is selective. And each selection of sceptical theses is likely to turn out incoherent. Different arguments are needed to show the untenability of different positions, and with each position there is a contrast between immediate self-interest, narrowly conceived, and wider-ranging reason, conveniently termed moral. Morality and self-interest remain opposed, but each version of self-interest is seen ultimately to be lacking in enlightenment. Scepticism is always possible, but never in the long run reasonable.

The positive grounds of obligation for a businessman arise from the nature of business. Contrary to present perceptions, business is fundamentally a cooperative activity. Business transactions would not take place unless there were fruits of cooperation that could, perhaps by means of some pecuniary adjustment, benefit both parties. Business transactions are essentially two-sided, with both parties benefiting as the result of the transaction. Cooperation, not competition, is the most fundamental aspect of business, and though competition remains important, the cooperative setting constitutes grounds for many obligations which a businessman should recognize. Moreover, the cooperation is normally long term and wide-ranging; the one-off transaction is the exception rather than the rule. Business is typically a process continuing over time and set within a definite social system of mutual understanding. I sell to customers who are in the habit of buying the sort of goods I sell, and buy from suppliers, who make their living by regularly and reliably supplying goods or services to those who want them. The obligations of a businessman arise from the cooperative nature of business, and the shared values and mutual understanding of the cooperative associations within which business transactions take place.

In many cases the cooperative setting is obvious. It is only because shareholders, superiors, colleagues, and employees cooperate with him that a businessman is able to do business, and the shared values on which that cooperation is based constitute considerations he should have in mind when reaching his decisions. Exactly what duties he has to shareholders, superiors, colleagues, and employees, and, more problematically, how conflicts of duties are to be resolved, still remains to be seen. But it is hardly controversial to claim that he does have duties to them, and that these duties arise from their being fellow members of the same business enterprise. It is, however, controversial to argue that a businessman has duties also to his customers, suppliers—and even his competitors—for in these cases we are more immediately aware of the adversarial, competitive aspect of the relationship, which seems altogether external. And, indeed, these relationships *are* more external. There *is* an adversarial element in bargaining with suppliers or customers, and competitors *are* competing. But bargains cannot take place unless there is some cooperators' surplus to bargain about, and nobody will do business with me in order to make me better off. Only if I hold myself out as meeting the other person's wants or needs will that person want to do business with me, so that if I am a person people want to do business with, I must see myself as others see me, and see to it that my business is good from their point of view. Although I may, for a season, be successful in ripping customers off, I cannot construct a coherent account of what I do in those terms alone, as I cannot offer any reason why people should want to do business with me. Much as we distinguish what it is to be a good doctor from what it is to be a successful one, so we can, following Plato's lead in the first book of the *Republic*, argue that the role of the businessman is socially defined in terms of the services he offers to others. These provide the criteria for judging whether he performs his role well or ill, and constitute grounds for his obligations to those he does business with. My competitors share these, and we collectively may need to uphold standards, and ensure that the public is well served by members of our trade generally. Beyond these shared values, there is the further bond of a common humanity, which enjoins us to recognize other people as fellow human beings; so that even where I have no common interest with my customers, suppliers, or competitors, I still need to treat them as persons, each with his own point of view, to whom I have, as a matter of justice, certain obligations of fair dealing and honesty.

III

C. B. Handy distinguishes six different sorts of 'stakeholder', whose interests ought to be considered by those taking decisions: financiers, employees, suppliers, customers, the environment, and society as a whole; he argues that these six classes constitute a hexagon, within which a decision-maker has to balance different, and sometimes conflicting, obligations (Handy 1995: 130–1, 143). Further distinctions may be drawn. Shareholders are in a different position from other creditors. Employees have obligations to employers, as well as vice versa. Obligations to society comprise obligations to the local community, to the nation and perhaps to the international community and the whole of mankind. Many firms also recognize some obligation to their industry or trade. There are certain obligations of honesty and fair-play to competitors. We may summarize:

(1) shareholders
(2) employees and employers
(3) customers
(4) suppliers
(5) creditors
(6) competitors
(7) trade or profession
(8) the local community
(9) the state
(10) the international community and mankind generally
(11) the environment

It is tempting to describe these as duties. Certainly, we could tax a businessman to explain why he had failed to consider his shareholders, employees, locality, country, or the environment, and if the question were brushed off with a 'Why should I? It is none of my business', his reply would sound hollow. But the word 'duty' denotes a stringency of obligation that often does not obtain. The duties of avoiding violence and of honesty are stringent, but many obligations are *prima facie* only, and may be overridden by others. A business has to survive, and that may require sacking not just an incompetent, but even a hard-working, employee. Faced with the apparently insatiable demands of morality, a businessman may feel inclined to follow Machiavelli and relegate morality to a private world, as not being practicable in the serious conduct of affairs. That is a mistake. We can guard against that mistake by talking not of peremptory duties, but grounds of obligation. I do not always have to keep redundant or incompetent employees in work: but I have some obligation towards them. If the survival of the firm depends on it, I must take the hard decision: but I am not usually in that extremity, and may be able to postpone the sacking, giving warnings in the case of incompetence, and long notice in the case of redundancy. It is not a matter of hard-and-fast rules. A businessman is not required always to be soft. But neither need he be always ruthless as a matter of course.

Obligations to shareholders and employees, as well as obligations of shareholders and employees, are primarily internal obligations, arising out of shared concerns. Obligations to customers, suppliers, creditors, and competitors are primarily external obligations, arising from our recognition of the validity of the other person's point of view as a necessary condition of making coherent sense of business activity. But in each of these cases some of the other considerations also apply, and the remainder are evidently mixed cases.

IV

It is often thought that public limited companies are owned by their shareholders, and that in consequence obligations towards shareholders are paramount. But, strictly speaking, shareholders do not own their company. Public limited companies are artificial creations, in which shareholders have certain rights, but as their liabilities are limited, so their rights are limited too. Their directors have certain specific obligations, spelled out by law, particularly in relation to take-over bids, and more generally to make the company prosper, but the latter does not override all other obligations. Managers are not under an obligation to drive the hardest bargain possible on each and every occasion so as to maximize dividend payments. Although they have a commission to seek profits, they have, as in all cases of people acting on behalf of others, some discretion as to how they carry out their commission, and are empowered to take other factors into consideration. Paying employees more may mean less money immediately available for dividends, but may prove more profitable in the long run, and may also enhance the standing of the company. Although the shareholders might instruct their board to go for immediate profits and to screw their employees as much as possible, it is not to be assumed as a matter of course that shareholders want to be Gradgrinds. The natural assumption is that they want their company to be one they can be proud of, treating its employees fairly and doing its bit for the locality in which it operates and the wider context in which it carries on business. It is a matter of degree: Pilkington, an exceptionally generous and community-minded firm, gave just over 0.4 per cent of its profits in charitable donations in 1983 (Sorell and Hendry 1994: 160). Only the most exacting shareholders could insist on their dividends being increased by a negligible amount rather than their company play its part in its sphere of operations.

Shareholders have duties. Some are spelled out by law—mostly concerned with treating other shareholders fairly if acquiring a majority of the shares. Others arise from the fact that each shareholder derives some benefit from the operations of his company, and can make his voice heard at the annual general meeting. Many modern thinkers deny that shareholders are under any obligations—their motive for buying shares is to make money, and that is their sole concern. But the argument is a *non-sequitur*: there are many things I do in order to make money, but that does not abrogate my responsibilities in the matter. I may have invested money in land or houses, but am still open to criticism if the land becomes a public nuisance, or the houses are used for immoral purposes. Some pension funds have invested in works of art, but if the works of art went out of fashion and were consigned to the scrap heap, we should think that the fund had not only made a bad investment, but acted irresponsibly. Equally, if I own shares, I cannot escape from the obligations of ownership on the grounds that I had only owned them in order to make money.

But the obligations are different. Although I have a voice, I have only one voice among many others. I can call attention to gross breaches of reasonable behaviour, but I cannot exercise much control. Moreover, all business is conducted on the basis of my not being my brother's keeper, and not being answerable for all his actions. Much criticism of the conduct of particular public limited companies is based on unreasonable requirements of moral purity— if they are in business, they are going to do business with the Soviet Union, South Africa, South America, and other (erstwhile) unsavoury places. A shareholder is—slightly—responsible for what his company does, and can—and occasionally should—criticize, but his criticisms should be reasonable and realistic, and not based on fashionable prejudice or idiosyncratic ideals.

v

One reason why thinkers recently have been anxious to emphasize the duty of managers to maximize the shareholders' profit is that other competing claims have been advanced, and they fear that companies were coming to be regarded as milch cows to be run for the benefit of other parties, most notably of their employees. Businessmen do have obligations to employees, but not unlimited ones. The obligations arise from the common enterprise in which the employees engage to do what the employer tells them in return for a wage. There are two aspects to this relationship: not only the external, adversarial one in which their interests are opposed, but an internal, cooperative one, arising from the common enterprise that generates the surplus available for division between them.

The employer tells the employee what to do, and therefore shares responsibility for what he does. Both have responsibilities, but the employer has the greater one. He owes it to the employee to give him the amount of direction appropriate to the job, neither depriving him of all autonomy nor leaving him without clear objectives; and to ensure that he does nothing illegal, imprudent or immoral. Many of these obligations have been hammered out in the law of master and servant and in Workmen's Compensation Acts. Equally, the employee owes it to his employer to carry out instructions efficiently, and to exercise his discretion responsibly.

Conflicts arise when explicit instructions run counter to the general policy of the firm, often now articulated in a mission statement, or are manifestly illegal or immoral. The general duty of obedience and confidentiality may be overridden in such cases. This is nothing new. In the Middle Ages the servants of the King sometimes disobeyed the explicit orders of the monarch out of loyalty to the Crown. But only in extreme cases is such behaviour warranted, and even then not in some jobs: confidential secretaries, like solicitors and priests, have a duty to keep silent even in the knowledge of grave legal or moral wrongdoing.

Because the employer has greater responsibility, it is reasonable for him to shoulder greater burdens and have more of the benefits resulting from the enterprise. Although most contracts of employment are short-term, the reality is that most employment is fairly long-term. Employers could not train a new workforce each week, and employees value the security of a job. It is reasonable for the employer, in the absence of welfare provided by the state, to carry some of the risk of ill health, because the cost of an absentee is a small part of his budget, and can be averaged out over the whole of the workforce, whereas the loss of the weekly wage is calamitous for the individual; and in the same way, though both parties should give long notice, it is more incumbent on the employer to do so. But these obligations, though real, are not indefinitely extensible. Not only the idle and incompetent, but even the hard-working but redundant employee may have to be sacked, if the firm can no longer employ him profitably. It is not the employer's business to provide employment—and recent history makes it very doubtful whether it can be the state's responsibility either.

Many people think that employees should have a share of the profits, and that this would remove the adversarial element. It is a possible arrangement, adopted by a few firms, but it has difficulties. There is still an adversarial aspect in the determination of what share each employee should have. Moreover, profits are uncertain, and can well fail to materialize in bad years; few employees can withstand a prolonged drop in earnings. They are rationally risk-averse, and just as widows were encouraged to take preference shares with a lower but more reliable yield, so it is natural for employees to want a fixed return rather than a greater, but less certain, share in the profits. Again, the holders of tradable shares can be fairly relaxed about forgoing immediate dividends for the sake of future growth, whereas an employee approaching retirement, or thinking of moving jobs, has no incentive to support policies of ploughing back profits into the firm. These objections are none of them conclusive, but together suggest that the current practice of paying employees fixed wages rather than some share of the profits is a reasonable and fair one.

In negotiating wages the employer's and employee's interests are opposed; but the immediate opposition is largely subsumed under a longer-term profitable partnership. It is in the interests of each that the other, and others similarly situated, should want to continue the relationship; and that therefore that it should be a profitable relationship from the other's point of view. These considerations do not suffice to determine an exact just wage or just price: usually we leave it to the market to determine the going rate, and normally to pay the going rate is fair enough. But the market is imperfect, and the market rate can be unfair; we can justly criticize the employer who pays starvation wages, even though he can find desperate workers ready to work for a pittance, and trade unions which drive industries into bankruptcy through their exorbitant wage demands.

VI

The relationship with customers and suppliers is much more external than that with shareholders or employees, and the obligations arise from the other-directedness of the business transaction rather than from a long-term association. Traditionally the responsibility has been on the purchaser to make sure that the transaction suits his purposes: *caveat emptor*, for only the purchaser can know what his priorities really are, and only he can decide whether to buy or not. But even in the Middle Ages there were qualifications of this doctrine, and the Crown took responsibility for hallmarking precious metals and monitoring weights and measures. The Sale of Goods Act 1893 laid on sellers the responsibility of seeing that goods were of a merchantable quality, but the motor manufacturers used to evade its provisions by getting purchasers to sign an order form waiving their statutory and common-law rights. At length this practice was disallowed under the Unfair Contract Terms Act, 1977, and a further Sale of Goods Act, 1979, which was extended to cover services as well under the Supply of Goods and Services Act, 1982. Most recently the insurance companies have been brought to task for the sale of unsuitable pensions by over-eager salesmen, and Lloyds Bank for encouraging a couple to borrow unwisely, and one might think that instead of *caveat emptor* we now have *caveat vendor* (strictly speaking, *caveat venditor*, but that is ugly and unnatural).

In reality the situation is more complex. It remains true that only the purchaser can decide what his priorities are, and that the final decision is his. But we now recognize that in deciding to buy he is not exercising an arbitrary whim in a particular case, but is to be presumed to be making a rational choice to buy some good or some service of a suitable type, whereupon the onus is on the seller, who is in a position to know what he has to sell, to supply what the purchaser may reasonably be supposed to want. *Caveat emptor* represents the ultimate responsibility of the unique individual who alone can decide what he shall do: *caveat vendor* the ensuing responsibility of the seller to meet the requirements of the sort of purchaser that someone who holds himself out as providing goods or services must expect to satisfy.

Those who sell get paid standardized units of accredited value. Since they can be sure that one man's money is as good as another's, they should be ready to treat all comers equally, and not discriminate against some or charge them extortionate prices. In some jurisdictions discounts may not be given at all, without prior permission, even to long-standing and valued customers, but usually discounts are allowed, provided the outsider is not greatly disadvantaged. Taxi drivers in St Petersburg or Prague, who charge exorbitant prices to vulnerable foreigners, are acting unfairly. If I can rely on being paid in standard coin of the realm, others should be able to rely on me to ask only standard charges for standard services.

Many modern businesses, some of them household names, cheat their suppliers by not paying them on time. It is thought to be clever financial management to defer payment until the last moment before a writ is issued, so as to increase cash balances or avoid paying interest on overdrafts. Many small firms have been bankrupted in consequence. The fact that the practice has not been effectively outlawed shows a shoddiness in British business culture of which all businessmen should be ashamed. Of course, it is open to a firm, and in some cases reasonable, to negotiate long terms of credit. The contract price will then reflect that fact. What is indefensible is to agree to pay at a certain time and then not pay. For the reasons already given, the law is difficult and expensive to invoke. The obligation is to pay on the date agreed, not when ordered to do so by a court.

The business world needs to set its house in order, and create a climate of opinion in which no businessman could hold up his head if he failed to pay his suppliers on time. It could be done by government action, but it would be better if it were undertaken by the Confederation of British Industry (CBI). The CBI could investigate firms suspected of late payment, asking to see invoices and cheque stubs, checking up with the suppliers concerned, and publishing a black list of those who refused to supply details or were found to be in default. A few firms might try to outface the black list, but soon compliance would be seen as the easier course.

VII

It may seem strange to say that we have duties towards our competitors, because on the classical view we are locked in cut-throat competition with them in a zero-sum game, where their gain is our loss. But, as the analogy with games, competitions, and the law courts shows, the fact that the exercise is adversarial does not mean that there are no obligations, only that some do not obtain in these situations. The obligations of honesty and fair dealing hold good both in competitive sports and in the market-place. Although there is a natural opposition of interest, with each party striving to succeed, even though it will be at the expense of its rivals, there are different ways of competing, and we have a strong intuitive sense of which are fair and which unfair. To provide a better product or render a better service at a lower price is fair: but when British Airways got hold of the names of those intending to fly with their rival, Virgin, and telephoned them offering a comparable flight at a reduced fare, it was properly seen as unethical conduct. They were not competing on a level playing-field, but were using information they should not have obtained in order to make special offers, not open to the general public, to persuade just those who had made up their minds to fly with Virgin to change their minds. Many people buy the *Independent* newspaper, just in order to frustrate what they believe to be Mr Murdoch's attempts to drive it out of business by selling *The Times* at a loss.

Less controversial than the claim that a firm has duties to its competitors is that it has duties to its trade, or line of business. In some modern industries, especially in newer science-based ones, research will benefit the industry as a whole, but is too expensive to be undertaken by any one firm. Many firms help to provide education for new recruits to the industry. In both cases a partial justification can be made out in terms of enlightened self-interest, but it is evident that this is often only a rationalization. When a new product is being launched, or a new factory built, very careful estimates are made of the return on the expenditure. But no such analysis is made of likely benefits from contributing to a research centre or providing scholarships for students. Sometimes the research pays off, sometimes the students supported subsequently take jobs with the company. But the connection between money laid out and benefits obtained is tenuous. We cast bread upon the waters, hoping that in many days the return will justify the deed, but reckoning that anyhow it behoves a firm in a particular trade to make some contribution to the good of that trade.

Trades often also seek to maintain standards, to police themselves, eliminating cowboy operators who cheat the public and bring the whole trade into disrepute. They are right to do so, but care is needed. The mediaeval guilds kept up standards, but tended also to restrict competition. Doctors in the United States manage to be very well remunerated, with the result that medical attention is usually difficult and always expensive to obtain; so much so that it is beyond the reach of the poor. Many economists have argued that all restrictions in the name of quality control are against the public interest, and that members of the public should be left free to make their own choice. But that is unrealistic. I do not have the knowledge to choose a good doctor, and having only one life, cannot afford to discover by trial and error who is competent to look after my health. Although at first it might seem that an absence of regulation would extend competition by opening the industry to new competitors, if there were a general perception that many operators were shoddy, the end result would be to put a great premium on having already acquired a reputation for reliability. Some degree of regulation and certification not only gives the public information that it needs about quality, but also can enable new firms to compete with those already established. But the dangers remain. There is a standing temptation to raise standards, ostensibly for the benefit of the public, but actually to restrict competition and increase the remuneration of those already practising. Although it is good to have a very highly trained doctor to attend me, it is better to have some less highly qualified medical auxiliary than none at all. Many occupations are over-qualified and too expensive. Moreover, by setting a long obstacle race for would-be entrants, they not only restrict the number of those who actually qualify, but ensure that nobody can qualify until he is past the first flush of youth, and no longer liable to have new ideas. Lawyers and chartered accountants, in particular, have a reputation for being staid, dull, and obstructive: the air of middle-aged mediocrity of these professions is at least partly due to the way their governing bodies demand an over-long period of deadening training.

VIII

Firms have duties to the local community and to wider ones. The underlying argument is the one already given, that a firm is a corporation, a centre of decision-making, and hence able, and needing, to take into account a wide variety of considerations in arriving at its decisions. In particular, a firm can reasonably be said to be located in the place where it operates. It has the power to alter the way things happen in its locality, just as I have in mine, and questions can be asked about the things it does, which a responsible businessman will want to be able to answer satisfactorily, and show thereby that business is, indeed, a cooperative exercise, and not merely a matter of self-interest. Three different sets of neighbours may be identified: the local community, the national state, and—perhaps—the whole of mankind. In addition, we can identify a non-personal neighbourhood, the environment, as being also a focus of concern. To a considerable extent the firm's responsibilities to the local community are commuted into the payment of rates and taxes. But sometimes there are special needs which the local community is unable to meet, or opportunities open only to the firm, and then there may be good reason for further action. As in other cases, the action can be justified on grounds of enlightened self-interest—if the locality is a good one and the local community flourishing, people will want to work for the firm and to do business with it—but in many cases the underlying motivation is purely moral.

Economic activities often pollute, and businessmen are often asked to take into consideration the effect they are having on the environment. Some feel obscurely guilty, and wonder if there is any way they can obtain a clean bill of health: others are robustly defiant, and say it is up to the legislators to lay down acceptable standards of emissions, and within those limits they are free to do whatever will maximize profits.

Both views are wrong. While it is true that all human activity impinges on the environment, it is not the case that it is necessarily for the worse. The English countryside is the result of centuries of human interaction with the land. Sometimes it is right to take steps to keep some areas in their pristine state: in Brazil almost all the Atlantic seaboard has been brought under cultivation, and it is right to protect the remaining virgin forest. The Amazon rainforest needs protection because of the extremely destructive exploitation to which it has been subject hitherto. But not every exploitation is malign: to eliminate malarial swamps or the very existence of the smallpox virus is to make the world a better place, even though a less natural one.

Many industrial processes, however, do have bad effects. Waste products pollute the atmosphere, the water table, or landfill sites. Each ton of coal burnt contributes to acid rain, eroding ancient buildings and destroying forests, and to the greenhouse effect, which may, for all we know, have disastrous consequences in the twenty-first century. Such considerations should weigh with anyone taking decisions. The view that it is up to the law to set limits to what may be legitimately done, and that within those limits the businessman is free to do whatever seems most profitable is, as we have seen, a mistake.

The law is too crude an instrument to define accurately what may or may not be done, and often considerations of enforceability or public policy will make it impracticable or inexpedient to enact a law which, on the merits of the case, ought to be enacted. The fact that there is no law against sending out sulphur dioxide into the atmosphere is no reason for thinking that it is perfectly all right to do so. Considerations of practicality often also prevent laws actually in force from being enforced. Adverse neighbourhood effects are covered by the law of nuisance, but it is often difficult and expensive to invoke the law. Can an angling association prove in court that the dearth of fish in its stretch of the river is due to the effluent from my factory and not to that from another one higher up the stream? But the doctrine that one can damage one's neighbour so long as the damage cannot be provably laid at one's door is a doctrine that few responsible people would care to endorse.

The absence of legally enforced restraints is relevant. It determines the context in which the businessman operates, and the competition he has to meet. If everyone else is spewing out sulphur dioxide, I cannot afford to put in expensive apparatus to scrub my emissions— and anyhow it will not make much difference to an atmosphere already much polluted. My customers are not prepared to pay for the privilege of being environmentally pure, and the actual benefit will be marginal. And even if there were laws imposing strict controls on emissions, we should merely lose business to Third World countries that were not so pernickety.

There is force in these arguments, but they do not conclude the matter. At any one time we are caught up in a situation not of our own devising, and must live in the world as it is, not as we would like it to be. But we need not be completely conformed to the world. Some moves are open, at least to monitor, and perhaps to mitigate, the adverse effects of our activities. Carelessness, rather than economy, is often responsible for the worst pollution. Many effluents can be recycled, or made less noxious before they are released. Often, indeed, they can be degraded biologically, if only we allow time and take trouble to find the bacterium with the right appetite. And the pressure of the best practice is effective over time in raising standards in the locality, or industry, as a whole.

Because some environmentalists are woolly-minded idealists, anxious to save the whale, but altogether unaware of the realities of industrial life, and because the neighbours who suffer from neighbourhood effects are manifestly only neighbours, many businessmen and politicians have responded by rejecting environmental concerns, even against their own interests. But often they need to employ woolly-minded idealists as researchers, or sell to them as customers: one of the key factors in the rehabilitation of the North of England has been to make it a place where managers and those with rare abilities are willing to have their families grow up. Britain and the United States have been scandalously complacent over their emissions of sulphur dioxide and nitrogen oxides because Members of Parliament and Congress think that Norway and Canada are good places for acid rain to fall, but forget that most of the damage is done to their own buildings and their own woods and lakes. The communists cared little for the environment, and one of the factors that undermined the morale of their ruling élite was the evident mess they were making of the world, and the coughs and asthma of their families.

IX

We find it difficult to think clearly about the state. At times it seems an alien, even a hostile, power, which makes us obey its laws, pay its taxes, and fight its wars: but then, especially at times of national crisis, we—the businessmen among us very prominently—identify strongly with our country, and reckon its failures our failures, its successes our successes, and its values constitutive of our own individual identities.

Many thinkers hold that the state is omnipotent. Some, mostly in the Anglo-Saxon tradition, extrapolate from its having a monopoly of coercive power, and suppose that since its commands cannot be successfully flouted by any individual, it is able to issue whatever commands it pleases. Others, often influenced by Rousseau or Hegel, hold that the state is entitled to whatever it thinks best on account of its being that with which we all identify. Both views are wrong. Although the state can overpower any recalcitrant individual, it can do so only with the aid of other uncoerced individuals. As we have seen, it needs the unforced cooperation of witnesses, judges, and jurors, if it is to function effectively, and therefore needs to have their allegiance, and hence be worthy of allegiance. For similar reasons the state is not entitled to do whatever it thinks fit. Although many individuals identify with the state, it is not constitutive of their identity, and each individual finds himself in membership of many other groups, and having a mind of his own that he can make up for himself. If he finds the state worthy of his allegiance, he may make great sacrifices on its behalf, and be willing to obey its laws and pay its taxes at great personal expense. But it needs to be legitimate in his eyes, and legitimacy has to be earned and can be forfeited. Even democracies can err, and issue commands that ought not to be obeyed.

As far as businessmen are concerned, the state exacts taxes and demands compliance with various laws and regulations. Whether the taxes are paid or evaded, and whether the regulations are complied with or circumvented depends on the legitimacy of the state and the reasonableness of its demands. Heavy and complicated taxes, absurd and inappropriate regulations, are less likely to command respect than simple and uniform taxes, and regulations whose rationale is clear and which are adjusted to the actual circumstances of the case. Under these conditions a businessman has a clear obligation to abide by the enactments of the state. It is unfortunate that many states have abused their power, and lost the legitimacy that would lead businessmen and other citizens to obey them wholeheartedly.

x

The considerations a businessman has to bear in mind are structured by the role he occupies as employee, colleague, manager, or director. He has duties to his superiors, to his directors, to his shareholders, which certainly restrict his freedom of action, and which may seem to leave him with no alternative. But often he is the victim of false images which distort the picture he forms of himself and his situation. He is led to believe that he has no freedom of action, or that his one overriding duty is to maximize the profits of the shareholders. Yet he feels that the arguments are not all one way, and would like to be able to think clearly through a maze of conflicting responsibilities. It can be done, but is not easy. Often there is no clear-cut path of duty, and the businessman has to balance conflicting obligations. But that is nothing new. We are familiar with the dilemmas of private life, and though their resolution is not easy, we are sometimes able to discern what we ought to do. The same is true in business life. If we can understand, without distortion, the true nature of business transactions, we can try to think out the differing obligations that flow from them. The aim of this article is to help the businessman do that; not to give him easy answers, but help him in the difficult task of working out his own answers on his own.

REFERENCES

Handy, C. B. (1995), *The Empty Raincoat* (London: Arrow Business).
Sorell, T. and Hendry, J. (1994), *Business Ethics* (Oxford: Butterworth-Heinemann).

6

Armchair Applied Philosophy and Business Ethics

TOM SORELL

IN this paper I shall consider some of the difficulties posed by writing
and speaking as a philosopher about business ethics, especially in the
UK in the 1980s and 1990s. Some of these difficulties are local and
perhaps temporary; others arise whenever one tries to apply philosophy; and still others crop up when philosophy is applied in the
wrong way. I am very far from clear about the solutions to these
problems; but I have been trying to confront them in my own writing
and speaking over a number of years, and I can at least explain why I
have written or spoken in one way rather than another. To make my
discussion manageable, I am going to restrict it in three ways. First, I
am going to concentrate on applied *ethics*, ignoring the very wide
range of non-moral questions that belong to applied philosophy.
Next, in trying to describe how philosophy can be applied in the
wrong way, I am going to concentrate on approaches followed in
published work, rather than, say, conferences, or visits to companies.
Finally, I am going to concentrate on published work by people who
have academic jobs as philosophers. These are by no means the only
people who misapply philosophy, in my opinion, but they do
dominate the business ethics literature, and maybe also business
ethics activity outside that literature.

I

I want to begin with the intended audience for business ethics. To
identify this audience, and also the special difficulties it poses, I
propose to contrast writing in business ethics with writing in medical
ethics. When people produce writing in medical ethics, for whom are
they writing? It is possible to think of examples that are intended for
the general thinking public, and that are produced by publishers who

have access to this public. Jonathan Glover's *Causing Death and Saving Lives* (1977) was for the general public; and it had the right publisher in Penguin. John Harris's *The Value of Life* (1985), even though introductory, was probably directed at a narrower, largely student and academic audience; articles on medical ethics in *Philosophy and Public Affairs* have probably always been intended primarily for professional philosophers and other academics; while the audience of the *Journal of Medical Ethics* is probably doctors and other health care professionals. Whatever the intended audiences, I take it that the actual audiences of all of these journals and books have always included people from the health care professions, as well as people studying to enter these professions. I take it further that these people are *willing* readers of writing in medical ethics by professional philosophers, even if they do not find this writing spellbinding. Some medical professionals even have a sideline producing this writing themselves. And a number who do not follow the literature are keen to *discuss* the ethical problems raised by their clinical practice with medical ethicists who visit or are permanently based in hospitals. I have only anecdotal evidence for all of these claims as they apply to medical and other health care people in the UK, but I hope they will at least be taken as plausible.

If there is some sort of willing audience for applied ethics among medical professionals, this may be connected with the fact that applied ethics writing is broadly sympathetic to what health care professionals do, and sensitive to the difficulties of solving the ethical problems that confront them. Writers of medical ethics books and articles may disagree with what doctors and nurses have done in particular cases, or they may disapprove of the policies of regulatory and disciplinary bodies in the professions, but they tend to approve of doctoring and nursing, or certainly of some of the practice of particular doctors and nurses. As for the medical people themselves, some of them seem to have an appetite for a specifically theoretical approach to ethics, as against a case-by-case approach, which they think they can work out for themselves. This appetite, I believe, produces a tolerance on the part of medical people for a wide variety of theoretical literature from professional philosophers, a variety that includes, at one extreme, what I would call armchair applied ethics, and, at the other extreme, full-blown decision procedures and 'expert systems' geared to medical conditions that pose problems of rationing treatment, or confidentiality, or whatever it happens to be.

I can summarize this highly impressionistic sociology of medical ethics by saying that in the case of health care professionals one finds a broadly sympathetic applied ethics literature meeting a pre-existing appetite for theory. In the case of business ethics, as far as I can tell, things stand, or at least have until very recently stood, very differently. Business people, the counterparts of the health care professionals, have by and large been unwilling consumers of business ethics literature, and students at business schools have been, for the most part, unwilling consumers of business ethics courses. My evidence consists of personal observation, as well as the testimony of people who have tried to teach business ethics in the USA, the UK, and Western Continental Europe for many years. Business ethics tends to be relegated to sometimes sparsely populated elective courses, or to be treated in passing in core courses. In the UK in particular, there has been relatively little appetite for the problem-solving techniques or the theories of ethicists, whether they be academic philosophers or seasoned business people. And the business ethics literature itself can be unsympathetic to, even censorious of, routine business practice. It can also be ignorant and ill-informed—that is to say, written without the benefit of the legwork most academics need to do to find out a little about how markets and businesses work. In short, it is not unusual to find business ethics writing that has been composed without any travel from an armchair or a desk chair. Where credibility among the practitioners is at such a premium, armchair applied ethics is particularly objectionable. It gives business ethics a bad name in business, and so connives at limiting the influence that the best applied ethics always exercises on the practices it discusses.

Before giving some examples of armchair business ethics, and indicating in more detail how it squanders the opportunity to appear relevant, let us consider whether it matters if philosophical business ethics has no credibility or not much credibility among business people. Mightn't the subject still be worth pursuing out of an interest in increasing the range of moral theories in philosophy? Mightn't the rationale for business ethics be a little like the pure research in science that comes to be applied when the time is right, but that is worth developing independently of its application? Or, differently, might not even a business ethics without credibility among business people be picked up by institutions whom business people do take seriously—legislatures, say, or regulatory agencies, or the media? The answer to both of these questions is 'Yes'. The possibility that it might develop a moral theory *is* a reason for pursuing even a resolutely sedentary applied ethics. But the same reason could be a reason for pursuing a style of business ethics that is informed by legwork. Similarly, while it is *possible* that an armchair applied ethics will be taken up by legislatures, regulatory agencies, and newspapers, it is even more likely that an applied ethics with street cred will be seized upon.

It is time to say in a little more detail what a piece of armchair applied ethics is like.[1] An illustration that concedes something to the idea that armchair applied ethics can advance theory is Judith Jarvis Thomson's 'A Defense of Abortion' (1971). This paper does not mention a single abortion procedure, and it says nothing about what it is like to undergo such a procedure or carry it out. It does not talk about foetuses, or about abortion clinics, or abortion advisory services, or hospitals. Instead, it tests intuitions about the rights of foetuses. It tests these intuitions by means of some analogies. There is an analogy between the foetus and a violinist plugged into a woman who is forced to act as life-support machine, and an analogy between foetuses and seeds that penetrate the defences of houses and grow into people wherever they take root. Although the examples it uses are very contrived, Thomson's paper does argue persuasively that if a foetus is carried to term by a woman who is pregnant without her consent, or who becomes pregnant despite conscientious use of contraceptive methods, then the woman does more than is strictly required by the supposed status of the foetus as a person in carrying it to term. This is a valuable conclusion given the rhetorical force of appeals to the rights of the person, and since the force of that rhetoric is likely to be felt by doctors, there is a lesson for them in Thomson's paper, devoid though it is of facts about abortion.

Another example of armchair applied ethics comes from the ethics of war, where the question of whether it is morally permissible to kill non-combatants is sometimes made to hang on intuitions about the supposedly parallel case of a man who cannot repay his loans from criminals, and who is offered the chance to carry out a killing of an innocent person instead (Fullinwider 1975). As in the case of

---

[1] For a collection made up entirely of pieces of armchair applied ethics, see Singer (1986).

Thomson on abortion, the conclusion and argument based on this example, as well as the example itself, can be arrived at by someone who is quite ignorant of military affairs. This may or may not matter. Certainly the literature identifies a clear ethical issue that arises from what everyone knows about war. Certainly this issue is worth discussing. But there may be other issues that are missed, and the clarity of the issue being pursued may result from ignorance of war. Perhaps it takes military experience or at least investigation of incidents in war to understand the variety of non-combatants and the relations between non-combatants and civilian collaborators or between civilian bystanders and civilian workers in a munitions industry.

Finally, examples of armchair applied ethics concerned with business are not hard to find. In the literature from the early days of the subject, that is to say, the 1970s, a significant number of papers consisted of *a priori* analysis of the concept of corporate social responsibility. One question asked was whether it makes sense to hold companies responsible for things, a question that had been foreshadowed in more mainstream philosophical literature about collective responsibility. Though the question is not without philosophical interest, and though it is relevant to discussions of social responsibility, answers to it are likely to matter as much to business practice as questions about the ontological status of states and nations matter to parliamentary politics.

II

One piece of armchair applied ethics can provoke another. Thus there have been many, many responses to Thomson on abortion, and a whole series of more or less similar papers on innocents in war. The pressures on academics to publish being what they are, this is likely to remain a familiar pattern, with the possible result that the ethical questions generated by clinical practice or military experience will diverge more and more from those being pursued in a specialist, armchair literature. In the case of business ethics, the likelihood of a divergence is increased by the low status of business ethics within professional philosophy. In order to prove its academic credentials, some writers of business ethics have felt obliged to pursue the subject with as much theoretical apparatus as they can bring to bear, with the result that few business people can follow what is being said.

Then there is the moral distrust that some academic philosophers feel in relation to the profit motive, and their tendency to suppose that the ruthlessness of some business practice is typical of all business practice. In short, there is a difference of culture between business and academia in general, and between business and academic philosophy in particular. Perhaps this difference of culture is being eaten away as universities themselves are turned into businesses, or perhaps the commercialization of the university sector is seen as an encroachment by business that has to be resisted by resisting business in general.

Either way, it is not surprising that some writing in business ethics is remote from business itself. The remoteness has not gone unnoticed in recent literature. Andrew Stark (1993) sums up the unfavourable impression of academic business ethics that has become widespread in the USA, where the subject was invented:

Far too many business ethicists have occupied a rarefied moral high ground, removed from the real concerns and real-world problems of the vast majority of managers. They have been too preoccupied with absolutist notions of what it means for managers to be ethical, with overly general criticisms of capitalism as an economic system, with dense and abstract theorizing, and with prescriptions that apply only remotely to managerial practice. (Stark 1993: 38)

Stark backs up some of these charges with some effective quotations from a number of very recent business ethics textbooks by academic philosophers. Some of the quotations express the view that morality excludes self-interest as a motivation in business; others insist that the requirements of morality are overriding, so that they need to be fulfilled even if it means the collapse of a business.

Given my own worries about armchair applied ethics, I can sympathize with Stark's criticisms (see also Sternberg 1994). But I think some of the criticisms can be met without abandoning moral philosophy in business ethics, and I think other criticisms run together an objectionable ivory-towerism in business ethics with an unobjectionable interest in moral criticism of business. Take, to begin with, Stark's disagreement with philosophers who maintain that moral motivation excludes self-interest. Stark rejects the views of these people, but he gives the impression that they are the *only* views that moral philosophy can justify, or that moral philosophers are willing to justify, and of course he is wrong about this (see HOOKER, for example). Utilitarianism and Aristotelianism both make room for mixed but moral motivations: they do not exclude self-interest; and breaches of conventional morality are permitted by utilitarianism if enough well-being results. Some of the approaches in business ethics that Stark thinks are new, and of which he approves, are no more than applications of Aristotelian theories. It is true, of course, that writing in business ethics that makes use of Aristotelianism or utilitarianism does not always take advantage of the room they make for self-interest, but this is no criticism of the theories. Yet Stark's survey of the excesses of the business ethics texts comes in a section of his paper headed 'The Myopia of Moral Philosophy'. A fairer heading might have been 'The Myopia of a few Moral Philosophers who do not understand the audience of business ethics'. And even this may be unduly harsh.

It might turn out that the unreality Stark complains of in some business ethics writing is in fact a clumsy attempt at upholding the distinction between 'ought' and 'is'. Unless everything is morally all right in the business world, one *expects* to find business as usual falling short of what is morally required. Taking this view is not a matter of occupying a moral high ground, or a particularly rarefied moral perspective, but of occupying any moral perspective. This perspective is available in life as usual just as much as business as usual, and it is expressed by the background thought of participants in life and in business that 'we're no angels'. This background thought is not usually associated with the question of why anybody should bother to be an angel: usually people accept that they can and should aspire to better behaviour than they display. Now there is no reason to think that this background thought from life—that 'we're no angels'—is inaccessible in business, and it is one of the things that gives business ethics its point within the context of business. Of course it may be a strategic mistake to engage the background thought with an absolutist or purist moral theory—one that maximizes the distance between the ideal and the actual, one that takes the angel's rather than the decent person's point of view of business—but some distance is required for even a moderate and sympathetic moral message. The perspective that gives moral distance from business life is not the special preserve of theorists or academics: it is latent in life, and therefore in business. In calling for realism there is always the danger that one is trying to get rid of this perspective, rather than exaggerations of the moral distance that the perspective makes available. In calling for realism one may be calling not only for the end of moral haughtiness, or preachiness, but for the end of moralizing, and this is not a legitimate cost of making business ethics user-friendly.

The truth in Stark's point of view is rhetorical, not moral. In order to get business people to engage with business ethics, philosophers have to be able to present choices in business in a way that business people will recognize and in a way that will influence them, and this means, above all, coming to terms with self-interest. There are many different ways in which this can be done. Perhaps the best way is to begin with real-life ventures in corporate social responsibility that the corporations themselves justify partly by appeal to self-interest and partly by appeal to the public welfare. Then one can ask whether a normative ethical theory bears out or fortifies these justifications, and if so, whether there are any independent reasons for accepting or rejecting the normative ethical theory in question. This is the strategy I adopted in a textbook I have written with John Hendry (Sorell and Hendry 1994: ch. 2). I take some of the initiatives of two successful UK businesses, Grand Metropolitan and Kingfisher, consider how executives from those companies justify those ventures, and then get moral theories from philosophy to engage with those justifications. Although the moral theories I bring to bear are the usual ones, that is, Kantianism, utilitarianism, and Aristotelianism, all are introduced by way of their pronouncements on the compatibility of morality and self-interest, and not as moral philosophy textbooks introduce them. That is, they are not introduced by way of the difference between teleology or deontology, or the use they make or don't make of the concept of justice. Because self-interest rather than some other concept is used to introduce the three standard moral theories, there is no great difficulty about adding an unorthodox moral theory, namely egoism, to the orthodox ones. Egoism is introduced not because I endorse it, or because its status as a moral theory is unproblematic, but because its handling of self-interest is different from that of standard moral theory and close to at least some ordinary thought within business itself. Once egoism is in the picture, business people are at least able to identify with thinking behind a theory from moral philosophy, and are able to see how social contract theory or virtue theory might be a sort of halfway house between egoism and the, to business people, alien rigorism of Kantian theories. On the other hand, egoism is seen to fit the rhetoric of the Grand Met and Kingfisher executives less well than theories which are more pluralistic about moral motivation.

There are other ways in which the distance between business ethics and the business world can be diminished. In choosing the topics one writes about one can be led by the current preoccupations of the business world, rather than by the last number of the *Journal of Business Ethics* or the current edition of the *Journal of Applied Philosophy*. These preoccupations are reflected daily and weekly in the business press. They can be found out by telephoning the press offices of business organizations, and by writing to companies and business people. They can be found out by consulting regulatory bodies and trade unions and pressure groups that campaign for and against business, by talking to people in commercial and employment law, and consumer organizations. They can be found out by making friends with people in business in the most applied sections of business schools. In my experience they are rarely found out by talking to fellow business ethicists. And I cannot imagine how they can be discovered *a priori*, in the armchair.

III

I now turn to the special difficulties involved in writing business ethics for a British business audience. Here some remarks from Stark will help me to bring out a contrast between the position on this side of the Atlantic and the position on his side. He has just made the complaint already quoted, about the ethicists occupying a too rarefied moral atmosphere, about their worrying too much about capitalism in the abstract and so on. Then he adds, 'Such trends are all the more disappointing in contrast to the success that ethicists in other professions—medicine, law and government—have had in providing real and welcome assistance to their practitioners' (Stark 1993: 38). Towards the end of his piece he says that business is a profession like government, with a tradition of moral criticism coming from 'non-practitioners'. He continues, 'Medicine and law provide an instructive contrast. Because these fields are more traditional professions, their greatest moral analysts have tended to be practitioners like Hippocrates or Oliver Wendell Holmes' (ibid.: 44).

Although business may not be all that long established as a profession, a profession is what Stark thinks it is, and so it is fitting that it has its professional ethics, just as other professions do. Again, business schools are professional schools, like law schools and medical schools, and so it is fitting that they should give ethics training, just as other professional schools do. These ways of thinking are not at home in Britain. As the Chartered Manager Initiative of the late 1980s showed, management is seen, if as a profession at all, then a profession on the model of surveying or accounting, rather than law or medicine; and management training is undertaken in a variety of ways, many based outside universities. A very large number of business people in the UK have no academic training of any kind, and the claim of professional status has resonances in the UK that would be unintelligible in Canada or the USA. The idea that a business school curriculum is incomplete without ethics courses, or that business cannot be a self-respecting profession without its own professional ethics, or that it is a profession at all: these ideas seem contestable in the UK in ways they would not be in North America. Nevertheless, much management education in the UK is modelled on North American management education, and the fact that business ethics is a recognized subject over there does create a presumption in favour of its legitimacy over here.

For better or worse, business ethics is being taught in an increasing number of business schools, and not only the idea, but the teaching materials too, are imported from the USA. These materials are often found hard going in Britain. For apart from seeming to be out of tune with business and enforcing a rigorist morality—the things Stark complains of—they also appear, from this side of the Atlantic, to be enforcing an American view of business and an American view of society and of morals. They therefore suffer from a double alienness—the alienness of the ivory tower and the alienness of American social assumptions. A good example of an ethical issue where this alienness is magnified is that of preferential hiring of minorities or of women. Outside Northern Ireland, it is illegal in Britain to hire one rather than another of two equally qualified job applicants because one is a woman, and it is illegal to earmark a post for a woman in advance even if everyone agrees that women are underrepresented in that sort of job. And this is to say nothing of the illegality of the practice—not unknown in the USA—of overlooking the worse qualifications of some applicants on the ground that as women or members of a minority they did not have equal access to good qualifications. In the UK this would strike many people as a violation of equal opportunities rather than an instance of it.

We have before us, then, a triple challenge to a philosopher writing business ethics for a British audience. The first is to make business ethics seem relevant to business, since there is no natural niche for it as an ethics for a recognized profession of business. The second is to make it accessible to those who may have no academic training; and the third is to fit it into a British moral and political tradition. Now that Britain is in the European Union, there is probably an additional obligation: to connect British moral and political values with those of Western Europe. These are difficult challenges to meet, but they would be even more demanding if it were not for a home-grown business ethics tradition in the UK and Western Europe, and if it were not for regulatory and business institutions that already promote business ethics in UK commerce. Perhaps the first thing a philosophical writer of business ethics has to do once he or she has left the armchair is to find out about these institutions and gear his or her writing to the examples of indigenous good practice that they suggest.

Foremost among these institutions are actual businesses with a tradition of ethical practice. In the UK these tend to be family businesses, often run by people with strong religious or quasi-socialistic convictions. Examples include the confectioners Cadbury and Rowntree, the shoemakers Clarks, the manufacturing companies Lever Bros, Pilkingtons, and Scott Bader, the retailers John Lewis, and the security firm Securicor. Littlewoods is another large, well-established family business with a philanthropic tradition, especially in Liverpool. Then there are a range of retailers, including Marks and Spencers and Kingfisher, which are not exactly family businesses, and other enterprises which are harder still to classify, such as Body Shop, businesses run by the cooperative movement, and the retailing arms of charities. There are companies which sponsor big charitable foundations, like Wellcome, and, until recently, Barings. There are business organizations with ethical concerns, such as Business in the Community, and its offshoots, Business in the Environment and the Per Cent Club. Finally, there are the ethical investment arms of the big finance houses.

Writing about these institutions helps to overcome many—but, as we shall see, not all—the problems of writing business ethics for a British audience. First, they are real, live institutions from British business. The companies among them are typically household names, profit-making, long-established, in short, commercially credible. Next, unlike other household names—McDonald's, IBM, Ford— they are home-grown. Finally, descriptions of their practice—in employment, in hiring, in dealings with consumers, competitors, and suppliers—are not likely to appear to come from an ivory tower, even when the descriptions are provided by academic philosophers and combined with criticism. The only drawback of dwelling on these companies is that one can give the impression that ethical practice is *only* in order when business is big and well established. This is a false impression, and it is reinforced when one turns from individual companies with ethical concerns to UK business organizations with ethical concerns. The organizations seem to be made up of 'top' companies, as if ethics were only their prerogative. A broader perspective is sometimes given by the ethical consumer or ethical investment movements, but even they tend to give the impression that business ethics is always ethics for big business.

To counteract this bias without retreating from the real world, it helps to investigate the commercial constraints on smaller businesses, and the ethical problems these constraints give rise to. A relatively well-known problem, and one which is high on the agenda of organizations such as the UK Federation of Small Businesses as the subject of future legislation, is that of late payment of debt. Often the late payers of debts to small companies are big companies which are valued customers of a given small business, and which exploit that status. Competition between small businesses is another area where ethical issues arise. For example, to what extent is it legitimate for established small businesses in a given market in a given locality to try to price a newcomer out of the market (Sorell and Hendry 1994: 155ff)? Then there are a large number of ethical issues which arise from the ways in which small businesses are subject to exploitation by consumers. There are restaurants which accept bookings from people who never turn up to take their meals, builders whose ideas for renovations are stolen by their customers, shops that are asked to take back goods that are not faulty but that for some questionable reason no longer suit the buyer (Sorell and Hendry 1994: ch. 3)—and so on.

Legislation is another rich source of real-world issues in business ethics, and a source, what is more, that helps one to meet the challenge of writing from a Western European perspective, since the legislation reflects the commitment in Western Europe to a 'social market' as against the purer capitalism of the USA. Thus, UK laws or EU directives covering redundancy, working hours, employee consultation, a minimum wage, and so on, are facts of life for many business people, and sometimes facts of life business people think are unjustified. In fact, they are open to various justifications and criticisms from the perspective of different moral theories. Utilitarianism sometimes turns out to assist free market criticisms of social protection legislation for employees; social contract theory can be used both for and against social protection; Kantianism can be used to support employee consultation as well as equal pay legislation.

Other moral issues that belong to the real world and arise more naturally within a European context than an American one are to do with the justifications for various kinds of subsidy in communities or regions which depend on a particular industry, the justification for various kinds of incentive to companies to start up business; the justification for company rescues by the state: in short, the ethics of state support for business (Sorell and Hendry 1994: ch. 7). These issues are at home in Europe, because state involvement in business life is both more widespread and more widely accepted as legitimate than in the USA. And they are only some of the issues in the ethics of relations between the private and public sector. Further questions that arise in this area include: is it right for public services—such as a health service or public transport or prisons or a postal service—to be put on a for-profit basis or sold outright to the private sector? Is it justifiable for state assets in the form of state-owned commercial businesses to be sold off to finance reductions in the public sector borrowing requirement, or to replace income to the state lost through tax cuts? The issues are also timely, since privatization measures are thought capable of solving some of the problems of the transition in Eastern Europe to capitalism, and yet are believed by some people to have been overused in the UK, where they were to some extent pioneered.

IV

Let me now conclude by considering some objections that might be made to my approach. I shall consider three. The first can be put by asking whether it is really for people outside business to orchestrate the discussion of, for example, socially responsible business, if there are individuals or business organizations who want to do this for themselves or for the broader business community. A few European businesses at least are interested in bringing their own approach to values and ethics to a broader audience. Benetton once wanted to start some sort of institute that would make more systematic the thought-provoking and shocking attitudes towards social issues sometimes pursued through their advertising. And Body Shop has started a new Academy of Business which will offer direct, and through established business schools, courses that reflect what they call 'new paradigm' business. I served on a panel advising Body Shop on course design, and I was struck by both the possibilities and limitations of having business ethics teaching reappropriated by a business with a history of energetic campaigning and a strong, though not undisputed, socially responsible image. On the positive side, there is no question that business people getting their MBAs are willing to hear from charismatic figures such as Anita Roddick, or Ben and Jerry, or Benetton representatives, about the way they think socially responsible business and business success go together. On the other hand, it is probably not so easy for them to see how the values of rather unusual businesses can be adopted by very much larger, longer-established, and conventional firms. Then there is the point that while the vision and energy inspire interest, and while the procedures followed at Body Shop for environmental auditing can be imitated, the systematically teachable material provided by a single company may turn out to be limited. Again, though the vision delivered by Anita Roddick in person may be infectious, it may not be so easy to articulate and make transferable until put in other people's—teachers'—hands. Here is where academics appear to be required even for furthering an approach to business that is in many ways anti-business school and anti-academic. And *philosophically* trained academics may be necessary if teaching is to rise above the level of gut moral reaction to systematic theory.

Consider now a second objection to my approach. My way of meeting the challenges of writing business ethics for a British business audience emphasizes institutions. The institutions are drawn from the real world, and they are chosen for their importance to business people, but they are institutions all the same, and, according to some writers, a business ethics geared to these threatens to become a branch of policy studies—of interest to government commissions and top management, perhaps, but not necessarily to people lower down in the organization or student-takers of business ethics from business schools. Robert C. Solomon (1993) has urged an Aristotelian reorientation of business ethics so that the audience missed by policy studies is addressed more effectively. The hallmarks of the Aristotelian approach are its emphasis on the choices confronting individuals rather than organizations, and the difficulties of reconciling personal values with values pursued in the role of manager. The Aristotelian approach enables business ethics to engage with values that people promote in their personal lives and that have some relation to values sometimes promoted in writings about inspirational business culture. I can see that this approach has its uses, but it is not excluded by my own, since the companies that have been important in determining the ethical tradition of the UK have often been set on their course by particular individuals whose example cannot be reduced to moral principles. Keith Erskine of Securicor is an example; so is Spedan Lewis of the John Lewis partnership; so is Ernest Bader of Scott Bader. Gearing one's writing to these exemplary individuals not only gives a concern with personal values a real-life focus; it is also considerably less abstract than talking about community, personal integrity, judgement, and personal excellence in general. Another advantage of the approach is that it enables one to acknowledge and make something of the relation between family business and ethical business, a topic that is crying out to be written about.

The approach I outline does not exclude an Aristotelian angle or a personal rather than an organizational audience. It may, however, be open to a third objection: namely, that by trying to meet business people on their own ground it evades the big questions—about the morality of the free market and consumerism—that are morally prior to the questions of how business practice may be made more benign or more virtuous within a capitalist framework. These questions may be hard to deal with outside the context of grand theories, but there may be strong moral arguments for confronting them all the same. It may be morally complacent to be led by the agenda of business people, and to take one's conception of good practice from actual business. Well perhaps. Once again, however, I do not see how my approach excludes a discussion of the grand questions in business ethics. Indeed, I recognize a generalist approach to business ethics, which fastens on to the typical and everyday features of business, and an essentialist approach, which takes some feature common to all business activity—such as the pursuit of profit—and argues about the morality of business on the basis of the morality of that common feature. The essentialist approach is made for the big questions. What I am not so sure about is who the audience for an essentialist theory is supposed to be, and whether the upshot of discussing the big questions is supposed to be practical or not. I think that philosophy is not just about giving people reason to believe things, such as particular answers to deep questions, but also about giving people reasons for action, and thoughts that move people to action are often shallow by philosophical standards, and closer to reality as experienced than philosophy usually is.

It is another question whether the ideal medium for the identification and transmission of reasons for action is philosophical writing, even philosophical writing about the real world. I have been trying to meet challenges to business ethics as if they were challenges for philosophical writing, and I do not believe that the only source for business ethics is writing, let alone philosophical writing. What I think is that philosophy is one source, that it is particularly good at giving general reasons for action, and good at organizing these reasons, and that both the generality and organization are useful to arguments about what ought and ought not to be done in business and with business. The taste for codes of practice in business as the vehicles for business ethics is itself a gesture in the direction of philosophy; it is a gesture in the direction of philosophy which philosophy can significantly improve upon.

REFERENCES

Fullinwider, R. K. (1975), 'War and Innocence', *Philosophy and Public Affairs*, 5: 90–7.

Glover, J. (1977), *Causing Death and Saving Lives* (Harmondsworth: Penguin).

Harris, J. (1985), *The Value of Life* (London: Routledge and Kegan Paul).

Singer, P. (1986) (ed.), *Applied Ethics* (Oxford: Oxford University Press).

Solomon, R. C. (1993), 'Corporate Roles, Personal Virtues: An Aristotelian Approach to Business Ethics', in Winkler and Coombs (1993): 201–21.

Sorell, T., and Hendry, J. (1994), *Business Ethics* (Oxford: Butterworth-Heinemann).

Stark, A. (1993), 'What's the Matter with Business Ethics?', *Harvard Business Review,* May–June: 38–48.

Sternberg, E. (1994), *Just Business: Business Ethics in Action* (London: Little, Brown and Company).

Thomson, J. J. (1971), 'A Defense of Abortion', *Philosophy and Public Affairs*, 1: 37–56.

Winkler, E. R., and Coombs, J. R. (1993) (eds), *Applied Ethics: A Reader* (Oxford: Blackwell).

7

Research in Real Worlds: The Empirical Contribution to Business Ethics

CHRISTOPHER COWTON

BUSINESS ethics is now firmly established as an academic field of study, with its own journals, institutions, and debates. While much of the growth in scholarly activity has been recent, with a dramatic increase over the past decade or so, the field has a considerably longer pedigree (De George 1987). For a long and indefinite period prior to 1960, De George suggests, the ethical analysis of business was primarily theological and religious, to which was subsequently added a strong philosophical contribution. More recently, the 'sustained and cumulative' normative contribution (Robertson 1993) of the philosophers and theologians has been augmented by the introduction of various social scientific perspectives, most often from social psychology and organization theory (Victor and Stephens 1994), which bring with them an orientation towards empirical research.

While the philosophers and theologians have, to a greater or lesser extent, had real or realistic examples in mind when conducting their analyses, Nicholson (1994: 593) suggests that 'we have reached a point where to move beyond instructive story-telling and philosophical insights we require more soundly based knowledge of the forces which shape the acting out of ethical issues in organizations'. The prospect of such knowledge is offered by empirical research, which connotes something systematic and disciplined in terms of the acquisition of an understanding of the way the world works. In particular it tends to imply the use of scientific method which opens 'vistas not accessible by other modes of inquiry' in business ethics, according to Frederick (1992*b*: 245).

But are the 'vistas' anticipated by Frederick actually being opened, and what are the prospects for the future? In this chapter I wish to examine the contribution of empirical social science research to business ethics, looking first at its potential, and second, at some

of the problems that are deemed to beset its conduct. In the third
section of the chapter, the reasons for some of the particular aspira-
tions for, and worrying about, empirical research will be traced to the
pressures that are experienced in 'leading' business schools. The
implications for the future of business ethics as a coherent and useful
field of academic study will then be discussed.

THE POTENTIAL CONTRIBUTION OF EMPIRICAL RESEARCH

Empirical research in business ethics is concerned with what is
happening in what is often referred to as the 'real world'—of
business, management, and organizations more generally. Such a
project clearly entails the question of the relationship between the
way the world is—the understanding that empirical research offers—
and how, according to one ethical analysis or another, it ought to be.

Is and Ought

The relationship between what is the case and what ought to be
the case is described by Hudson (1969*a*: 11), in a book devoted to the
issue, as the 'central problem in moral philosophy'. Hume's Law, so
called—namely that it is logically impossible to derive an 'ought'
from an 'is'—is, to anyone with a philosophical background, an
obvious starting point for discussing the relationship between
empirical research and normative ethical analysis. While there is
considerable debate about the correct interpretation of David
Hume's is–ought passage (Hume 1739–40/1978: bk. 3, pt. 1, sect. 1),
the logical gap implied by the Law would appear to place a strong
prima facie limitation on the role of empirical research.

A logical gap is, of course, logically unbridgeable. But the insertion
of further premisses into the argument can bridge the gap, for example
a Panglossian adherence to functionalism in believing that what *is*
works for the best. More significantly, though, there is far more to
the relationship between *is* and *ought* than 'mere' logic. Hudson
(1969*a*: 12) notes that, even if Hume's Law is accepted, the question
nevertheless remains: 'how are moral judgements and statements of
fact *related* to one another'. As he observes, whenever people discuss
what they choose to regard as a moral issue, it will be found that they
use *is* and *ought* in very close conjunction. The two words may do

very different work, but that does not prevent them working closely together in ethical argument and debate.

The question of the link between *is* and *ought* has surfaced in a very general way in the business ethics literature. Weaver and Trevino (1994) suggest that the relationship between normative philosophical and social scientific empirical approaches can range from 'parallelism', where the two remain distinct and separate, to 'theoretical integration' or 'hybridization', in which the two projects are substantially interwoven. Their preferred approach, 'symbiosis', lies somewhere in between, providing greater relevance and legitimacy for both normative and empirical enquiry without requiring that the accepted theoretical frameworks and methodologies of either approach be altered or rejected. Having rejected the possibility of integration because of what he calls Hume's Guillotine, Donaldson (1994) similarly expresses support for the symbiotic approach. It certainly seems a reasonable ambition for the field as it develops.

Symbiosis implies mutual dependence, but it does not necessarily entail equality of the parties involved. I view business ethics as a normative field of enquiry to which empirical research might make a valuable, but ultimately subsidiary, contribution. In the following section I discuss the nature of that contribution (rather than examine the symbiotic relationship as a whole) by examining some ways in which empirical research might help in the effort to pose good questions and provide good answers, and hence promote the normative analysis of ethics in business.

Questions and Answers

According to Joanne Ciulla:

One of the first things you hear upon entering a business school is references to something called the 'real world' . . . which dictates what you can and can't do. . . . Because of this reverence for the 'real world,' the most damning indictment of business ethics is that it's not practical. (Ciulla 1991: 213–14)

Since normative statements are underpinned by empirical understandings, a moral philosopher, like anyone else who attempts to make sense of the social world, needs to be something of a social analyst—'To ignore the descriptive aspects of this process is to risk unreal philosophy' (Victor and Stephens 1994: 145). Many philosophers are good at this, and while empirical research might be one input to the development of such an understanding, it is not strictly necessary. Much good applied philosophy is informed by everyday contacts and experience and by the popular media. However, there are risks owing to the unsystematic nature of such information, and it is possible that empirical research can provide greater assurance regarding the practicality of business ethics.

One way of improving the practicality of business ethics is to ensure that attention is paid to relevant questions; it is very easy to focus on 'non-issues' when the academic agenda is developed in isolation. An obvious way is to 'poll' managers on what they consider the ethical problems of business to be. At one level this could be viewed as simply sensible market research activity on the part of academics. An example is to be found in the work of Waters et al. (1986) who conducted open-ended interviews with thirty-two managers based on the question, 'What ethical questions come up or have come up in the course of your work life?' However, since some problems are problems *of* managers and business, rather than *for* managers, and lest business ethics be accused of a managerial bias, it would also be worth asking representatives of stakeholders other than management, for example blue-collar workers or part-time employees.

The aim of such research would be not only to identify problems, but also to prioritize them. It might be thought that business people and others directly involved in the world of affairs are not necessarily good at such exercises, especially where a longer-term perspective is required, but that is a reason not for ignoring them, merely for treating their replies with circumspection as well as respect.

But the empirical contribution to the development of the business ethics agenda can go further than polling or other, more indirect methods of learning about opinions and attitudes. The identification and prioritization of many issues, whether by business ethicists, managers, or others, will often imply a certain view of the world which can be tested by social scientists. For example, if small businesses claim that large firms are paying unethically late, is there evidence that they actually do pay late, that they pay later than other businesses, or that they are taking longer to pay than they used to? These and similar questions might be answered by new research, but it is worth remembering that there will often be answers or indications already in existence, empirical research having been previously conducted on the topic without its being consciously located in business ethics. While this research might not provide all the answers in the form required, at least it is available and hence timely. Thus the contribution of empirical research *to* business ethics need not depend exclusively on empirical research conducted explicitly *in* or *for* business ethics.

Beyond questions or issues there lie, one hopes, answers, solutions, or whatever. It has been suggested that the normative theories that give rise to such answers can be tested by means of empirical research. Although they don't rely on empirical data in the same way as positive or descriptive theories, they do make explicit or implicit assumptions about empirical relations. This is especially so in the case of consequentialist approaches, which Fritzsche and Becker (1984) suggest are likely to be more acceptable than deontological approaches in the context of business because of business people's orientation towards outcomes. One role for empirical researchers would be to test whether the consequences that feature in existing consequentialist arguments are indeed likely. Again, though, it might not be necessary to conduct empirical research especially for the purpose; Greenberg and Bies (1992), for example, 'test' philosophical ethics against various empirical findings in the field of organizational justice—and find it wanting.

In addition to *testing*, Weaver and Trevino (1994) suggest that empirical enquiry may be used to guide the *application* of specific moral theories. One contribution is to identify and publicize certain practices which seem to solve a particular ethical dilemma. Put in more philosophical terms, following Hume's Law, *is* might not imply *ought*. Nevertheless, *is* suggests *can*; and *can* allows the possibility of *ought*, as the corollary of the 'ought implies can' principle usually associated with J. L. Austin. For example, many stockbrokers and other financial advisers used to claim that to manage a share portfolio according to ethical principles was impossible or, at the very least, financially foolhardy. Empirical research has shown that not only is ethical investment possible, it doesn't necessarily involve the investor in major financial sacrifice (Luther and Matatko 1994). In answer to the general question of whether doing good and doing well conflict, so often raised in the context of business ethics, is there evidence of companies or individuals going the extra mile, beyond law and common duty, and still surviving or even thriving in the competitive market-place or corporate jungle? A role for empirical research, though not an exclusive one, is to show how some people have solved ethical problems or dilemmas, how they have succeeded in exercising 'moral imagination' (Ciulla 1991).

But there are dangers in taking too great an interest in the way the world currently is, particularly if the constraints and difficulties are emphasized. While this might legitimately provide reassuring 'excuses' (*ought* implies *can* again), too much practically informed, descriptive content might rob business ethics of its cutting edge. This is a concern voiced be De George (1991), who argues that the 'descriptive approach' serves only 'conventional morality'. While that may not always be a problem—'conventional morality' is not necessarily wrong—there is a need too for a fully critical strand to work in business ethics. The job of business ethicists is not simply to justify current business practice; but then again, it is not to be naïvely overcritical. Criticizing convention has to be done carefully, not just for political reasons but because of the risk that academics have misunderstood. This is not to say, though, that the academic contribution is of value only if it changes things. As Lewis (1969: 1) comments in his study of convention:

[W]hen a good philosopher challenges a platitude, it usually turns out that the platitude was essentially right; but the philosopher has noticed trouble that one who did not think twice could not have met. In the end the challenge is answered and the platitude survives, more often than not. But the philosopher has done adherents of the platitude a service: he has made them think twice.

In conclusion, even if one accepts that an *ought* cannot be logically derived from an *is*, an understanding of the world as it is makes an essential contribution to normative ethical analysis. It is of benefit not only in the conduct of the analysis—the choice of question, etc.—but also in communication, by the use of real or realistic examples. Empirical research is not necessary for this, but it can be useful, and it can make a particularly important and persuasive contribution when yielding relevant evidence. While, as suggested earlier, and perhaps insufficiently appreciated in the business ethics literature, much empirical research of relevance already exists in other fields, it will nevertheless be the case that some will be, and will need to be, conducted with business ethics in mind. It is to questions regarding the conduct of such research that I will now turn.

THE CONDUCT OF EMPIRICAL RESEARCH

For empirical research to fulfil its potential for making a distinctive contribution to the development of business ethics requires that the work be of the appropriate quality. While empirical research may be a relatively recent feature of business ethics, its growth has already prompted a number of reviews which have taken stock of, advised on, and expressed concern about its conduct. The main 'worries' voiced in the literature will be reviewed in two sections: first, those that arise from the particular challenges entailed in researching ethical issues; and second, those that relate more generally to the quality of research carried out to date in business ethics.

Dealing with Delicate Issues

There are many ways of pursuing empirical research, but in an oft-cited review of the contents of ninety-four empirical papers in business ethics, Randall and Gibson (1990) found that most of them (81 per cent) relied on questionnaire surveys using either direct question format or hypothetical scenarios. Questionnaires have continued to be popular.

The use of questionnaire surveys in social research always raises a number of significant technical problems, some of which are likely to be exacerbated as a result of the nature of business ethics research: 'Virtually every empirical inquiry of issues relevant to applied business ethics involves the asking of questions that are sensitive, embarrassing, threatening, stigmatizing, or incriminating' (Dalton and Metzger 1992: 207). It thus may be particularly difficult in business ethics to gather good data on attitudes or behaviour. Two types of problem can occur.

First, many potential subjects might decline to take part in the research. A high response rate might be hard to achieve in business ethics, placing in jeopardy the generalizability of the results. The lower the response rate, the more likely is non-response bias to be present. Standard ways of testing for non-response bias have been developed by survey researchers. For example, using data either available at the time the sample was chosen or gathered through some form of follow-up research, non-respondents can be investigated to determine whether they display characteristics significantly different from those of respondents. Another possibility is to compare early and late respondents. If they are not significantly different, it is generally inferred that non-response bias is not present.

Detecting non-response bias is not the same as eradicating it. Moreover, the tests for detecting it are not entirely satisfactory. But what is notable about many studies in business ethics is that the issue is not even mentioned. Randall and Gibson (1990) discovered thirty-four studies reporting a response rate of less than 60 per cent, but only one of them made any attempt to assess the possibility of bias. It is not clear why this was the case. Were researchers unaware of the tests? If not, did they not wish to conduct them? Or did they conduct them but then fail to report the results?

The second type of problem relates to the subjects who do respond. Can their responses be relied upon? In particular, are their responses not likely to be subject to social desirability response bias, which Randall and Fernandes (1991: 805) define as 'the tendency of individuals to deny socially undesirable traits and behaviors and to admit to socially desirable ones'? This is not a problem unique to business ethics, but it 'may pose an even greater threat to the validity of findings in ethics research than in more traditional organizational behavior research topics' (ibid.). There are ways, however, of encouraging respondents to answer questions candidly.

One common method of encouraging candour, as well as an actual response, is for the researcher to promise that replies will be treated in strict confidence. The problem with this, though, is that some prospective respondents might fear that the confidence will be breached, whether inadvertently, deliberately, or as a result of external pressure. The researcher might go further and promise anonymity. This might be of some help, but it might not be as effective as supposed. Rightly or wrongly, the researcher might not be trusted. There might be a 'credibility gap' (Dalton and Metzger 1992).

In a more sophisticated attempt to overcome apprehension on the part of subjects, randomized response techniques (RRTs) have been developed. The aim is to allow the researcher to learn about the frequency of a particular attitude or behaviour, while ensuring that there is no way that a given respondent can be identified with that response (ibid.). One technique is the unrelated question approach. This involves the researcher asking two questions, one for the research and one totally innocuous, and not knowing which question it is that the subject has answered. For example, subjects might be asked to answer 'yes' if the coin they have been asked to toss has landed heads up or if they have falsified expense claims. An answer in the affirmative does not necessarily indicate that an individual has fiddled expenses, but the excess of 'yes' answers over 'no' allows the researcher to estimate the incidence of the practice.

Of course, this might not totally eliminate the 'credibility gap' that undermines the conventional promises of confidentiality or anonymity. 'That RRT techniques are rational guarantors of confidentiality is unassailable' (ibid.: 216), but it does not necessarily follow that a subject will not harbour a sneaking suspicion that, by some means or other, the researcher or some other party will be able to link them to some misdemeanour or unethical behaviour. Dalton and Metzger suggest that one way to allay such a fear is for the researcher to demonstrate how the technique works by answering very sensitive questions in front of the subjects. They therefore prefer interview or public meeting protocols over the written survey. While this direct contact might be the ideal, it does not seem unreasonable to believe that RRTs, if clearly and simply explained, will at least reduce the nervousness of subjects regarding the anonymity of their replies even in the case of postal surveys.

However, although 'business ethics would appear to present a textbook setting for the effective use of RRTs' (ibid.: 214), they have been used less than they have been discussed. (A rare example is Dalton et al. 1996.) As in the case of failing to report tests for non-response bias, this would appear to be a case of business ethics researchers failing to use the tools that are available to them.

To be fair, it is worth acknowledging that, while RRTs should reduce the tendency of nervous respondents and those with 'a propensity for impression management' (Fernandes and Randall 1992: 186) to veer towards 'socially desirable' responses, they do not address the problems of subjects who have an *unconscious* tendency to view themselves in a favourable light or individuals who tell researchers what they think they want to hear.

However, as in the case of non-response bias, in addition to techniques aimed at *reducing* it, there are methods for *detecting* socially desirable response bias. So-called 'overclaiming scales' can be constructed by including special questions in the questionnaire. For example, subjects might be asked how familiar they are with a particular brand of product—which does not exist. Responses to core questions can then be dealt with in the light of the subject's overclaiming score. Such overclaiming could even be regarded as an interesting phenomenon in its own right. Again, though, there is little evidence of the use of overclaiming scales in business ethics surveys.

Questions about Quality

The discussion in the previous section suggests that researchers are failing to take advantage of the full range of techniques available for coping with the particular difficulties likely to be present in business ethics survey research. Moreover, the general impression given by other reviewers of empirical research in business ethics is that it is of relatively poor quality when compared with similar research carried out in business schools and social science faculties.

A major concern is the place of theory. Randall and Gibson (1990) criticize empirical business ethics articles for their 'distinct absence of theory' and their failure to develop testable hypotheses. Robertson (1993) similarly recommends a stronger base in theory, be it normative or empirical. Perhaps this concern is beginning to be addressed; Trevino (1992: 121) believes that a shift is already apparent with researchers 'moving beyond descriptive surveys of managers' attitudes and beliefs . . . to develop theory-based approaches'. But it is not just a question of starting with theory. Robertson, who regards the contribution to theory as the major deficit of current empirical research, is keen that results should feed back into theory-building.

Reviewers are also worried about the manner in which the research is carried out, although there is a prior, significant problem of many papers failing to discuss their research methodology adequately. To the extent that methodology is visible, a number of general shortcomings have been identified. Randall and Gibson (1990) want researchers to decrease their reliance on 'convenience' samples (though student samples are rarer than might be expected) and to increase the use of random samples. They suggest that researchers take positive steps to improve response rates, which they consider to be low. Randall and Gibson are also critical of the questionnaires themselves: 'the questions and scenarios used in survey research are typically too vague and lack realism, while the close-ended questions force responses into pre-defined categories' (p. 466). And they would like business ethics researchers to develop reliable and valid research 'instruments' and to make more use of multivariate statistics.

Weber (1992) makes similar criticisms in his review of twenty-six scenario-based studies: little consistent theoretical foundation, lack of testable hypotheses, and unsophisticated statistics, amounting to a 'general lack of rigor'. He concedes that such limitations 'are generally symptomatic of a new, emerging field', but concludes that 'they should be addressed and resolved' (p. 153).

Robertson (1993) also echoes many of Randall and Gibson's concerns, but goes beyond purely methodological issues to make some recommendations regarding the *content* of research. For example, she would like to see more longitudinal studies and more research on 'marketplace ethics', 'workplace ethics' having been more prominent to date. And she desires that more attention be paid to behaviour and less to attitudes. The worry that even candidly stated attitudes might bear little resemblance to actual behaviour has been voiced elsewhere in the business ethics literature (Gatewood and Carroll 1991), but attitudes, intentions, and ethical reasoning have been the focus of many direct question and scenario-based surveys (Weber 1992), and Ford and Richardson (1994) describe empirical studies of ethical decision-making as distressingly small in number and weak in design. Frederick (1992*a*) is surely right, therefore, to question how secure our empirically derived knowledge is of the role that values and ethics play as business practitioners make decisions.

Like much of the work on which they are commenting, reviewers such as Randall and Gibson, and Robertson represent a particular research tradition. Randall and Gibson base their review on Babbie's (1986) conception of empirical research, referring with approval to the positivistic deductive approach. While Robertson does not make clear the basis on which her recommendations were made, the overall impression given is that she is sympathetic to that research tradition, particularly as she cites Randall and Gibson on a number of occasions with apparent approval.

However, some commentators are sceptical of the value of the recommendations discussed earlier, believing that other research traditions offer greater potential for understanding behaviour. Thus, in his introduction to a special issue of the *Business Ethics Quarterly* devoted to consideration of empirical methodologies, Frederick (1992*a*: 92) contends that to correct only the more technical shortcomings of research methods would risk leaving the empirical study of business ethics 'in the shadow of positivism'. Brady and Hatch (1992: 312) take a similar position in viewing the 'dogma' of the empirical research tradition predominant in business ethics as 'highly questionable'. Yet while researchers such as Liedtka (1992) and Phillips (1991, 1992) have brought some alternative perspectives into the business ethics literature, as yet the number of empirical studies that have taken such sentiments to heart is limited. Positivistic research and concerns remain dominant. The reason for this, and its implications, are discussed in the following section.

THE PURSUIT OF ACADEMIC RESPECTABILITY

Any emerging or relatively immature field of study, particularly when inter- or multidisciplinary, tends to have problems gaining academic respect and credibility. Business ethics is no exception. De George (1987: 203), himself a philosopher and a long-established contributor to the business ethics literature, comments that many philosophers 'looked askance' at their colleagues who turned to this 'suspect area'. To gain respect, those writing in business ethics 'must measure up to the standards of their disciplinary peers' (ibid.: 207).

This applies not only to those writing in a philosophical tradition, but also to those who align themselves with social science. Surveys of the teaching of business ethics in the USA, which is still where the major quantity of academic activity takes place, show that many courses are now delivered within the business school itself, rather than provided as a service activity by a department of philosophy or religious studies. Members of faculty specializing in business ethics within the business school will be judged for tenure and promotion, in terms of their research, according to the established criteria of the business school. Unfortunately, there is still substantial resistance to business ethics within most schools of business, and the critics are often not only vocal but also, according to Murphy (1996), the most 'productive and respected' faculty members whose reputations tend to be based upon publishing in the most prestigious academic journals.

Prestigious journals are, in the main, heavily positivistic in their orientation. Seeking to mimic the natural sciences (or at least a perception of them), the social sciences have, particularly in the USA, undergone a process of 'scientification' (Scott 1984: 141). So-called 'leading' business schools have been caught up in this process since the 1970s, seeking to emulate their disciplinary roots and so establish their academic credentials. Mulligan (1987: 593) notes that, while both of C. P. Snow's 'two cultures' should be represented in business education, in recent decades business research has 'moved progressively in the direction of science'. Invoking a strong adherence to the fact/value distinction—and tending to accept some form of Hume's Law—there has been an increasing intolerance of primarily normative analyses (Brady and Hatch 1992). Trevino (1992) is, accordingly, concerned that in such an environment the study of business ethics is vulnerable to the charge that it is 'unscientific' because of its association with philosophy and religious studies, a charge which amounts to anathema in influential business school research circles.

This is not the place to amplify or criticize the dominant view of social science in North American business schools, although its popularity and power might surprise some philosophers. As Norman Bowie points out, hardly any philosophers subscribe to logical positivism in its original form, yet in naïve form it is chiefly held by business faculty and social scientists—'possibly to help separate themselves from their origins and to buttress their claims to scientific status for their disciplines or to avoid having to make normative judgments at all' (Bowie 1991: 23). Victor and Stephens (1994: 145) were quoted earlier in this chapter to the effect that there is a risk of 'unreal philosophy' if the world as it is is ignored. They go on to say that to ignore the normative is to 'risk amoral social science'. But that is exactly what North American business school faculty, and many other social scientists, seem intent on doing.

Yet, argues Bowie (1991: 31), 'none of the business disciplines nor the discipline of economics that underlies so many other business disciplines have achieved the status of sciences the way natural sciences have'. He further suggests that a task of business ethics might be to bring a halt to what he terms this 'economic imperialism'. The humanities roots of business ethics could be used to open up for scrutiny the ends of business as well as the means, revealing that economics and business have an ethical dimension. Bowie surely has a point, but the problem is that business ethics, as already explained, does not find itself in a position of strength within the business school. If an academic challenge to the current orthodoxy is to be mounted successfully, it is more likely to be from sources closer to the dominant disciplines; Etzioni's work on economics is an obvious example (Etzioni 1988). Perhaps business ethicists will be able to align themselves with any such challengers, but for younger researchers who, possessing the right tools at a time when business ethics is becoming established and 'catching up', it would be understandable if they were to seek to emulate respected and powerful colleagues. And with the more positivistic tradition likely to hold sway for the foreseeable future, such research will at least make a contribution in aiding the academic standing of the field, if it matches up to espoused standards of rigour. In other words, if empirical research of the type discussed in the previous section is going to be done, it should be done well, where 'well' is more likely to be defined in terms of methodological technicalities than the substance of results. Fleming (1990: 21) anticipates that empirical researchers will indeed 'utilize methods of greater sophistication and complexity', thus enhancing the business school credentials of business ethics. The previous section of this chapter demonstrates that they are at least being talked about.

While it may take some time for academic debate to overturn the current orthodoxy, pressures for change also emanate from outside the business school, with research coming under increasing public scrutiny. Although empirical research might be thought to be absolutely grounded in the 'real' world beloved of managers, the charge of 'irrelevance' has been forcefully levelled at many of the leading institutions. While some of this criticism is simplistic, failing to recognize the subtle but powerful ways in which social science research influences practical affairs, it is nevertheless the case that the impression of relevance having been sacrificed in favour of rigour remains. Business school academics are no more immune than philosophers and theologians, it would seem, from accusations of working in an 'ivory tower'. If such criticism is maintained it is possible that what is valued in the business school research environment will change, with less of a premium on methodological purity in the pursuit of academic respectability, and more of an emphasis on usefulness and relevance, broadly conceived. However, whether the game is really changing remains to be seen, and in the meantime business ethics research conducted in business schools will be expected to conform to common standards of acceptability. If it is going to be done, empirical work of the conventional variety should be done 'well'. There is certainly no advantage, whether in terms of the substance of the findings or the academic standing of the field, in doing it poorly. The worries and advice of the reviewers, discussed in the previous section, should not be ignored.

However, there remains one danger; that the strengthening of ties to social science disciplines is likely to hinder the development of business ethics as an interdisciplinary field (Kahn 1990), thus exacerbating the somewhat fragmented condition that has been of concern to De George (1987: 208) and other leading business ethics scholars (Fleming 1990). As Trevino and Weaver (1994) point out, the socialization and training processes of academics from philosophical and management backgrounds are so different that they might not think of themselves as colleagues and peers, instead referring back to their disciplinary base and, in the case of management academics, perhaps managers too. The gap between the 'two powerful streams' of business ethics research might become considerably greater than the 'respectful distance' that Donaldson and Dunfee (1994: 253) perceive.

In conclusion, the worrying about the progress of empirical research in business ethics, reviewed in the previous section, can be understood as reflecting the conventions and pressures of the context in which it is conducted. Remedying the present shortcomings is important for the academic standing of business ethics within business schools, but whether such improvements will deliver much more in the way of benefits has to be open to question; first, because it is not clear that empirical research in other areas of business has been as useful as might have been hoped, and second, because of the pressures towards fragmentation that will be intensified within the business ethics community itself.

Perhaps this is unduly pessimistic, and it is not meant to imply that empirical research will yield nothing of value. Rather, the aim has been to put the worrying in context, sound some cautionary notes about what empirical research, as it tends to be conceived by the majority, has to offer, and to point out the difficulties of the context in which business ethics academics who are not philosophers have to work. Whether that context will become more benign towards, and more tolerant of, different research traditions, because of either academic trends or external influences, remains to be seen, but it seems unlikely that business ethics can lead the way. The most it can do is to be ready to take advantage of any opportunities that might arise.

CONCLUSION: PAST IMPERFECT, FUTURE TENSE?

Empirical research has something to offer to business ethics, and it is increasingly being carried out. It is also being widely discussed and commented upon. This chapter has reviewed many of the major themes discernible in those discussions and, standing back, put them in the context of the general 'empirical social science' project of business schools. In doing so, certain technical matters relating to the conduct of research, rather than details of content, have been highlighted. This mirrors most existing reviews, which tend to be concerned with the 'how' rather than the 'what' of empirical research. Of course, the two are not unrelated, and there are signs that some business ethics scholars are beginning to take notice of non-positivistic research traditions—different 'hows'—which offer the prospect of yielding insights inaccessible to previously employed research traditions or paradigms, however well designed or ingeniously conducted.

Yet whatever the research tradition invoked, and the skill with which it is carried out, there must be limits to the contribution that empirical research can make to the study of good or right behaviour in business. Unlike the many other fields of management to which social scientists have made a contribution, it will be more difficult in business ethics to neglect the explicitly normative dimension, not least because of its title. For this reason, and with a sustained and related contribution from philosophers and theologians, there is some hope that business ethics will not come to be dominated by empirical research, thus enabling it to be in a position to address fundamental and important issues about business and management. Business ethics, currently viewed by both its supporters and detractors as peripheral to the central concerns of the business school, might conceivably find itself, in the fullness of time, making a valuable contribution to the construction of a much-needed philosophy of management (Hendry 1991). At present there are few, if any, claimants to the 'high ground' of management studies.

The difficulty will be in holding business ethics together. Full integration of the social scientific and philosophical strands is, as suggested earlier, a non-starter, but the increase in scale of activity (permitting specialized conferences, networks, journals, etc.) and the desire to relate to a primary academic discipline or intellectual tradition will intensify the forces towards schism, putting even a reasonable 'symbiosis' at risk. Thus while the 'real world' of business poses both an opportunity and a challenge to academics interested in business ethics, there is a danger that the very real world in which they carry out their research and pursue their careers will prove to be the dominant influence, leading to fragmented scholarship inadequately grounded in its practical field of reference. The principal solution to this problem lies, I would suggest, beyond the reach of most business ethicists and in the agenda with which business schools enter upon the next century.

REFERENCES

Babbie, E. (1986), *The Practice of Social Research*, 4th edn (Belmont, CA: Wadsworth).

Bowie, N. E. (1991), 'Business Ethics as a Discipline: The Search for Legitimacy', in Freeman (1991): 17–41.

Brady, F. N. and Hatch, M. J. (1992), 'General Causal Models in Business Ethics: An Essay on Colliding Research Traditions', *Journal of Business Ethics*, 11: 307–15.

Ciulla, J. B. (1991), 'Business Ethics as Moral Imagination', in Freeman (1991): 212–20.

Dalton, D. R. and Metzger, M. B. (1992), 'Towards Candor, Cooperation, and Privacy in Applied Business Ethics Research: The Randomized Response Technique (RRT)', *Business Ethics Quarterly*, 2: 207–21.

——, Wimbush, J. C., and Daily, C. M. (1996), 'Candor, Privacy, and "Legal Immunity" in Business Ethics Research: An Empirical Assessment of the Randomized Response Technique (RRT)', *Business Ethics Quarterly*, 6: 87–99.

De George, R. T. (1987), 'The Status of Business Ethics: Past and Future', *Journal of Business Ethics*, 6: 201–11.

—— (1991), 'Will Success Spoil Business Ethics?', in Freeman (1991): 42–56.

Donaldson, T. (1994), 'When Integration Fails: The Logic of Prescription and Description in Business Ethics', *Business Ethics Quarterly*, 4: 157–69.

—— and Dunfee, T. W. (1994), 'Toward a Unified Conception of Business Ethics: Integrative Social Contracts Theory', *Academy of Management Review*, 19: 252–84.

Etzioni, A. (1988), *The Moral Dimension: Towards a New Economics* (New York: Free Press).

Fernandes, M. F. and Randall, D. M. (1992), 'The Nature of the Social Desirability Response Effects in Ethics Research', *Business Ethics Quarterly*, 2: 183–205.

Fleming, J. (1990), 'A Survey and Critique of Business Ethics Research, 1986', in Frederick and Preston (1990): 1–23.

Ford, R. C. and Richardson, W. D. (1994), 'Ethical Decision Making: A Review of the Empirical Literature', *Journal of Business Ethics*, 13: 207–21.

Frederick, W. C. (1992a), 'The Empirical Quest for Normative Meaning: Introduction and Overview', *Business Ethics Quarterly*, 2: 91–8.

—— (1992b), 'Whither Method? And Why?', *Business Ethics Quarterly*, 2: 245–6.

Frederick, W. C. and Preston, L. E. (1990) (eds), *Business Ethics: Research Issues and Empirical Studies* (Greenwich, CT: JAI Press).

Freeman, R. E. (1991) (ed.), *Business Ethics: The State of the Art* (New York: Oxford University Press).

Fritzsche, D. J. and Becker, H. (1984), 'Linking Management Behavior to Ethical Philosophy—An Empirical Investigation', *Academy of Management Journal*, 27: 166–75.

Gatewood, R. D. and Carroll, A. B. (1991), 'Assessment of Ethical Performance of Organization Members: A Conceptual Framework', *Academy of Management Review*, 16: 667–90.

Greenberg, J. and Bies, R. J. (1992), 'Establishing the Role of Empirical Studies of Organizational Justice in Philosophical Inquiries into Business Ethics', *Journal of Business Ethics*, 11: 433–44.

Hendry, J. (1991), 'We Need a Philosophy of Management', *British Academy of Management Newsletter*, September: 16.

Hudson, W. D. (1969a), 'Editor's Introduction: The "is–ought" problem', in Hudson (1969b): 11–31.

—— (1969b) (ed.), *The Is–Ought Question* (London: Macmillan).

Hume, D. (1739–40/1978), *A Treatise of Human Nature*, ed. L. A. Selby-Bigge, rev. P. H. Nidditch, 2nd edn (Oxford: Clarendon Press).

Kahn, W. A. (1990), 'Toward an Agenda for Business Ethics Research', *Academy of Management Review*, 15: 311–28.

Lewis, D. (1969), *Convention: A Philosophical Study* (Oxford: Basil Blackwell).

Liedtka, J. M. (1992), 'Exploring Ethical Issues Using Personal Interviews', *Business Ethics Quarterly*, 2: 161–81.

Luther, R. G. and Matatko, J. (1994), 'The Performance of Ethical Unit Trusts: Choosing an Appropriate Benchmark', *British Accounting Review*, 26: 77–89.

Mulligan, T. M. (1987), 'The Two Cultures in Business Education', *Academy of Management Review*, 12: 593–9.

Murphy, P. E. (1996), 'Business Ethics: A Mature Product', *Business Ethics Quarterly*, 4: 383–9.

Nicholson, N. (1994), 'Ethics in Organizations: A Framework for Theory and Research', *Journal of Business Ethics*, 13: 581–96.

Phillips, N. (1991), 'The Sociology of Knowledge: Toward an Existential View of Business Ethics', *Journal of Business Ethics*, 10: 787–95.

—— (1992), 'Understanding Ethics in Practice: An Ethnomethodological Approach to the Study of Business Ethics', *Business Ethics Quarterly*, 2: 233–44.

Randall, D. M. and Fernandes, M. F. (1991), 'The Social Desirability Response Bias in Ethics Research', *Journal of Business Ethics*, 10: 805–17.

—— and Gibson, A. M. (1990), 'Methodology in Business Ethics Research: A Review and Critical Assessment', *Journal of Business Ethics*, 9: 457–71.

Robertson, D. C. (1993), 'Empiricism in Business Ethics: Suggested Research Directions', *Journal of Business Ethics*, 12: 585–99.

Scott, P. (1984), *The Crisis of the University* (Beckenham: Croom Helm).

Trevino, L. K. (1992), 'Experimental Approaches to Studying Ethical-Unethical Behavior in Organizations', *Business Ethics Quarterly*, 2: 121–36.

—— and Weaver, G. R. (1994), 'Business ETHICS/BUSINESS Ethics: One Field or Two?', *Business Ethics Quarterly*, 4: 113–28.

Victor, B. and Stephens, C. U. (1994), 'Business Ethics: A Synthesis of Normative Philosophy and Empirical Social Science', *Business Ethics Quarterly*, 4: 145–55.

Waters, J., Bird, F., and Chant, P. F. (1986), 'Everyday Moral Issues Experienced by Managers', *Journal of Business Ethics*, 5: 373–84.

Weaver, G. R. and Trevino, L. K. (1994), 'Normative and Empirical Business Ethics: Separation, Marriage of Convenience, or Marriage of Necessity?', *Business Ethics Quarterly*, 4: 129–43.

Weber, J. (1992), 'Scenarios in Business Ethics Research: Review, Critical Assessment, and Recommendations', *Business Ethics Quarterly*, 2: 137–59.

8

Commercial Ethics: A Victorian Perspective on the Practice of Theory

JANE GARNETT

LIKE so many revivalists, students and advocates of modern business ethics have been highly selective in their points of reference and have largely eschewed consideration of historical precedents. Preoccupation with the establishment of business ethics as an element of the curriculum in universities and management schools has perhaps contributed to the implicit assumption that coherent thinking on the subject did not exist before it was 'professionalized'. In the *Journal of Business Ethics*, for example, which was established in 1982 to examine business activity from a moral point of view, there has been almost no historical discussion and relatively little reference to Christian teaching. Moreover, because more attention has been paid at an academic level to business ethics in the USA, there has been a more limited perspective on the development of debate in Britain. Whilst there is a vast literature on the history of economic thought and specifically on the origin and development of classical political economy, its emphasis has been on theoretical shifts, and it has been less concerned with the problems created by the attempts to correlate economic and other (social and moral) codes *in practice*. Much recent debate has been concentrated upon establishing whether or not Adam Smith did validate market principles and the pursuit of self-interest, and, if so, in what sense. The appropriate interpretative emphasis is clearly relevant for modern economists in their search for philosophical mentors. But it has less pertinence for consideration of the development of arguments about applied economic ethics in the intervening period. An understanding of the ways in which such arguments were constructed could prove highly illuminating in the formation of questions for current debate.

Here Victorian business communities' perceptions of the epistemological claims of political economy and estimations of the cultural hegemony of its language and ways of thinking are central. Which sorts of theoretical perspective were felt to be most fundamental to the practical conduct of economic life? What were seen to be the dangers of the cultural predominance of certain types of theoretical language? In a period in which religious principles and institutions were still of fundamental significance, did the claims of political economy complement or compete with those of Christian ethics? A range of rhetorical and ideological structures was in operation. Failure to engage with aspects of the contemporary *debate* about the practical impact of different forms of rhetoric has led to a tendency to fix on particular positions as if they were normative, or on oppositions as if they were straightforwardly black and white.

Perspectives on the Victorian business world have been coloured both by the views of nineteenth-century cultural critics—Coleridge, Carlyle, Arnold, Ruskin, Dickens, Eliot—and by those of early twentieth-century social critics such as R. H. Tawney. In *The Acquisitive Society* (1921/1982), Tawney painted a vivid and rhetorically compelling picture of the gospel of economic success—an axiom which was predicated on a sharp separation of the sphere of Christianity from that of economic expediency. In his view this separation had been sanctified by nineteenth-century practice, and no moral limitations were recognized to the pursuit of individual self-interest. It was a separation made all the easier by the religious predominance of an excessively narrow, individualistic Protestantism (Tawney 1982: 17–30, 88–9, 176–84). It has too readily been assumed that the values of the Victorian business world were indeed shaped either by utilitarian principles *tout court*, or by an unproblematic internalization of 'Christian political economy'. From T. R. Malthus and William Paley to evangelical popularizers of Malthus such as Thomas Chalmers and J. B. Sumner, natural theology and classical economic theory had been susceptible of identification with each other ([Chalmers] 1844–5: 10; [Poulett Scrope] 1832: 39–69; Soloway 1969; Waterman 1983: 231–43 and 1991). A Congregationalist in 1845 proclaimed: 'Economical truth is not less divine than astronomical truth. The laws which govern the phenomena of production and exchange are as truly laws of God, as those which govern the phenomena of day and night' (*British Quarterly Review* 1845: 560). God's laws and the laws of political economy could be held to go hand in hand, and Christianity could thus provide legitimation for a particular view of economics—and vice versa. In fact, it was precisely against such a characterization—or, more particularly, the *effects* of belief in such a characterization—that an energetic mid-nineteenth-century debate on economic ethics took its stance.

John Stuart Mill's essay on the definition of political economy (1844/1967; first written *c.* 1830) was itself an attempt to delineate more precisely the proper scope of the science, in reaction to those who, in his view, had confounded science and art—and had treated political economy *both* as an explication of economic laws *and* as a set of precepts for the achievement of a broader social end. He presented political economy as working with the model of man solely as a being who desires to possess wealth. Without the use of such a model, no explanatory hypotheses could be constructed, because the real world was too complex and uncertain. Mill distinguished between causes, each of which was the particular province of its respective science (e.g. political economy in respect of economic causation, strictly defined), and effects, which might result from an unpredictable concatenation of causes, each of which could only be analysed in isolation. The definition of a man and of human nature used as a working assumption by political economists was an abstract one, and the conclusions drawn from it constituted abstract rather than concrete truth. Crucially, however, Mill conceded that 'such is the nature of the human understanding, that the very fact of attending with intensity to one part of a thing, has a tendency to withdraw the attention from the other parts' (Mill 1967: 332). He acknowledged that no matter what precautions were taken, the human mind would still have a tendency to become the slave of its own hypotheses, ultimately mistaking these for laws of nature. As Alfred Marshall was later to argue, Mill was nevertheless led in his methodological writing to exaggerate the scope for the deductive method in economics (although by the time he wrote his *Principles of Political Economy*, published in 1848, his practice was significantly less extreme than his profession), and to underestimate the full range of motives affecting economic decisions (Marshall 1961: 771–2, 783). Certainly, Mill's work did not significantly modify the *popular* stereotype of orthodox *laissez-faire* political economy in the mid-nineteenth century.

In organizations like the National Association for the Promotion of Social Science, in which businessmen, lawyers, politicians, and religious and social theorists gathered from the 1850s to debate matters of practical economic and social interest, those who most strongly advocated the wider dissemination of the principles of political economy revealed—wittingly or unwittingly—the strength of such popular views of it. W. B. Hodgson, lecturer and education-alist and a regular contributor at annual meetings, spoke at a committee on labour and capital set up in 1868. He deplored the popular misconceptions of political economy—the belief that it was a purely abstract science—and the ways in which the language of great and unrelenting laws obscured the necessary operation at every point of human motive, will, and character—'the keystone in the arch which bridges over the interval between economic cause and effect'. He stressed the need to form and train such character by a proper education in economic science which indicated the intimate and practical relationship between moral and material progress. Some of the works which he commended for such purposes were, however, open to criticism for their unproblematic conflation of religious and economic criteria (Hodgson 1870*b*: 7–9, 26–31; 1870*a*: 49; 1859: 552–6). In a later part of the discussion, the chairman, Lord Houghton, commented that people were wrong to suppose that political economy was a *theory*. Rather, he urged that it was an *explanation* of the laws of society—a position which underscored the conceptual problems to which Hodgson had drawn attention (Hodgson 1870*c*: 84–5).

Recognition both of such problems and of Mill's pivotal status led John Ruskin to use him as the target of his polemical essays published in serial form in 1860, then as *Unto this Last* in 1862. An 1894 survey of London libraries showed this to be the best-read work of 'the most popular author who deals with political economy and sociology' (cited in Jay and Jay 1986: 137). Ruskin famously compared Mill's definition of the science of political economy to a science of gymnastics which assumed that men had no skeletons:

It might be shown, on that supposition, that it would be advantageous to roll the students up into pellets, flatten them into cakes, or stretch them into cables; and that when these results were effected, the re-insertion of the skeleton would be attended with various inconveniences to their constitution. The reasoning might be admirable, the conclusions true, and the science deficient only in applicability. (Ruskin 1903–12: xvii, 26)

Although Ruskin travestied some aspects of political economy, his focus on the corrupting effect of the analytical language was not an isolated one in the mid-century. By the end of the century it was to dovetail with significant modifications within the discipline of classical political economy itself, of which Marshall is one exemplar. Ruskin was also not alone in seeing that the distinction which Mill adopted between the laws and conditions of the production of wealth, which he held to partake of the nature of physical truths, and the distribution of wealth, which he allowed to be a matter for human institution (Mill 1965: ii, 199), was dangerous, because people could cease to look at the subject as a totality. This in turn could give rise to even greater potential problems of moral compartmentalization.

Ruskin both drew on and set out to confront Victorian Protestantism—especially Protestantism in the evangelical form in which he had been brought up. Evangelical Protestantism was held by its critics both to be coterminous with the business community and to exemplify the moral double standards of that world. The assumption of an intimate relationship between Britain's industrial and commercial success and the nation's Protestantism was a commonplace, although the inferences to be drawn from this were increasingly contested (see, e.g., H. Hughes 1852; Arnold 1869; de Laveleye 1875). The smugness of an ever more stridently proclaimed Protestant ethic was challenged not just by Catholics and radicals critical of the social consequences of capitalism (see, e.g., Cobbett 1824–6; Gilley 1971: 64–89), but also by evangelicals confronting the practical working through of Protestant ethics within business communities. The Wesleyan Robert Spence Hardy cast himself in the role of Ezekiel in urging his country to beware, 'for if there is iniquity in thy traffic, the same calamity shall overtake thee [sc. as the ruin of Tyre], though now thou callest thyself, in thine arrogance, The ruler of the waves' (Hardy 1858: 192). The evangelical Anglican Hugh Stowell, rector of Salford, who clearly saw Britain's commercial status and her Protestantism as implicitly linked, saw even more sharply the danger of using each side of the assumption to prop up the other, without really thinking through the implications. There were many reasons, in practice as well as in theory, why the two should not fit together so neatly, and he stressed that it was essential to get down to the particular case, and show precisely where individually held principle could meet practical circumstances. At the same time he gave this a positively Protestant note of inspiration: 'For a man to dare to do justly at whatever risk or cost, requires an amount of heroism which would bear no unfavourable comparison with the intrepidity of the

Christian hero who fell at Sebastopol, or the Christian martyr burned at Smithfield' (Stowell 1858: 95).

Evangelical clergy and ministers who were strongly represented in industrial and commercial areas (and often had first-hand experience of commerce themselves) recognized the acute problems which the rapid development of the economy in the mid-nineteenth century was creating. The economy in the 1850s and 1860s was expanding, but was susceptible to considerable fluctuations. Bankruptcy was an ever-present threat. Although there were notorious large-scale collapses, insecurity was particularly felt by small and medium-sized businesses in sectors such as grocery and drapery (Evans 1969; J. R. T. Hughes 1960; Lester 1995). Evangelical churches and organizations such as the Young Men's Christian Association (YMCA)—which attracted large numbers of clerks, warehousemen, and traders—in the major urban commercial centres catered especially for this middle- and lower-middle-class constituency—a class comprising employers and those who might become employers, a group with a certain independence or aspiration to independence (Binfield 1973).

Competitive pressures were posing severe dilemmas for those who wished to maintain their Christian integrity. Moreover, the business world and the capitalist system as a whole were held to depend for their very continuance on certain basic ethical assumptions and conventions of trust which were themselves in large part religious in origin. How could such conventions be maintained, and to what extent could they be supplemented or replaced by formal regulatory codes? At a time when a profession such as accountancy was only beginning to become established and when commercial law was relatively undeveloped, the response of the evangelical communities was particularly significant. They argued for the establishment of a more sophisticated set of ethical criteria by which to judge behaviour in the business world. A high degree of consensus concerning the ethical basis of business activity was held to be vital to the promotion of initiative and to the sustaining of commercial confidence. Regulatory legislation did not necessarily seem the answer. It was widely recognized by proponents of law reform that bad law—such as bankruptcy legislation which failed to distinguish effectively between misfortune and fraud—and inadequate or impossibly cumbersome legal structures, could themselves encourage commercial immorality (Hawes 1858: 91–3). But it was also recognized that, to be effective, legal reforms had to go hand in hand with the reinforcement of a framework of trust: 'Without honour, commerce must stop at every step to prepare her writings; and suspicion, like a heavy armour, would impede the march of enterprise' (Freedley 1853: 34; cf. Bourdieu 1977: 16–17). At the same time the point was underlined that only by a conviction of the importance of individual personality could moral energy be generated. As the web of economic interdependence grew more complex it was all too easy to lose sight of this, and to blame economic dislocations on impersonal forces (whether human or divine). This acceptance of personal responsibility and conviction of its importance was not intrinsic. It had to be argued through, and made inspiring to the individual engaged in the commercial world.

Such a process required the self-conscious cultivation of a collective ethos—a culture within which common values could be assumed as well as a common moral commitment to engage actively with the problems presented by modern economic life. The evangelical churches had both the visibility in commercial areas and the institutional framework to provide the impetus. Sermons, books, and tracts proliferated. Lectures were given in civic halls—especially to audiences of young men, including members of the YMCA, under whose auspices a hugely popular series of lectures was given at Exeter Hall in London from 1848 to 1868. By 1855 eight volumes of the lectures had been published and an aggregate of 58,000 sold. Many of these lectures focused on issues of economic ethics, and the most prominent individuals in the national debate were represented. In these discussions the concerns were with the revitalization of evangelicalism no less than the morals of the commercial world. The rhetoric which they developed assailed interrelated anxieties and complacencies. It was very easy to believe that just because one was a Christian one necessarily had a nobler sense of moral duty. But a Christian might not have thought sufficiently about moral distinctions in the particular sphere in which he operated. It was not enough to do right; it was necessary to take pains to discover what, in each sphere of individual action, the right was (Dale 1867*b*: 10–37; 1880*a*: 95–6, 98–101).

A central element in the burgeoning Protestant evangelical literature was that of biography—the identification of heroes suitable for modern inspiration, who could illuminate in practical detail the dilemmas which manufacturers and merchants confronted. That there was a need for such a genre was widely argued. As a leading article in a trade journal commented: 'We have too readily accepted the novelist's unreal "Gradgrind" as a fair picture of a successful manufacturer and employer' (*Warehousemen and Drapers' Trade Journal* 1872: 257). The period saw a huge upsurge of self-help and success literature, much of which took its cue from Samuel Smiles's *Self-Help* (first given as lectures in the 1840s and published in 1859) and Thomas Carlyle's lectures *On Heroes, Heroism and the Heroic in History* (1841). Although Smiles was not sanguine about a straight-forward correlation between hard work and success and certainly did not present an apologia for free market principles, he did not explore the potential ambiguities in his version of the Protestant ethic (the ease with which the virtue of thrift could become the vice of avarice, for example) in the way in which evangelical commentators were concerned to do. Carlyle's discussion of such diverse heroes as Mohammed, Cromwell, Napoleon, and Rousseau did not present any clear-cut moral lessons for the ordinary person. This lack was all the more keenly felt at a time when a series of widely publicized commercial crises exposed famous and apparently respectable people as swindlers. The accepted criteria of reliability and respectability seemed to have become unstable, and the relationship between different aspects of a man's life to have become blurred, so that, for example, philanthropy could seem to be offered in compensation for commercial misdeeds. Leopold Redpath, notorious defrauder of the Great Northern Railway, presented the image (and the reality) of a sincere philanthropist in his private life (*Baptist Magazine* 1856: 690–1; Evans 1968: 434–5).

Hence the perceived need for an exemplary literature which would provide models for the formation of an integrated moral identity. Eighteenth- and earlier nineteenth-century biographies of businessmen-saints had tended to point out merely that involve-ment in commercial life need not *impair* men's spiritual state; they seldom made out a carefully sustained and positive case for the spiritual potential of a constructive involvement in trade: 'they have dropped business as a leaden thing, a dead weight, that would sink the book; and so you float away with a fragrant cargo of philanthropy and public life'. Thus commented the Wesleyan Methodist William Arthur (1852: 27) in *The Successful Merchant*, a life of the grocer and commodity merchant Samuel Budgett. This book had sold more than 84,000 copies by the end of the century, and was translated into Welsh, Dutch, French, and German. Arthur transformed the secular self-help success model within a Christian framework; he described the particular areas of temptation in commercial life—questions of adulteration, speculation, the offering of loss-leaders to attract custom. He neither glossed over his subject's lapses in these areas, nor treated these faults as only occurring in his unregenerate days, but emphasized that these were continuous challenges even for the truly Christian merchant. Arthur developed a rhetoric which elevated to a heroic level the moral struggle required to follow the right path, yet still engaged with the reader by depicting it in everyday, realistic terms, and encouraging the conclusion that such difficulties were not only normal but also potentially capable of confrontation.

Analogies were made between the moral struggle of the Christian in his workplace and those of the soldier in military combat. Such a rhetorical device could reinforce the 'manly virtue' required of the successful businessman and also elevate the business world as a sphere of honour in which chivalric qualities were to be looked for. The use of such language in conscious opposition to the language of 'cold, selfish calculation' was fundamental to this purpose (Arthur 1851: 335; 1852: 20). Viewed in a historical perspective, religious men had found it easier to be heroic in times of obvious adversity, 'in the martyr ages'. It was more difficult to see the need in an age 'professedly on good terms with Christ' (Birrell 1865: 84). Real heroism lay in trying to clarify personal motivation, in continuous, scrupulous attention to the concealed selfishness which lay behind many an apparently splendid achievement. Professed Christians often failed to relate broad ethical precepts to particular circumstances. Moralists emphasized that it could not be an excuse then to say that they were forced into wrongdoing only under the extreme pressure of a moment. 'What man would dream of raising money in dishonest ways who was not in difficulties? It is only when the difficulties come that the test of honesty assumes this form' (Dale 1880*b*: 113–14, 116–17). The Methodist Benjamin Gregory discussed how commercial selfishness took different forms in different periods—the commercial crime of usury was a totally different thing from the current system of legitimate banking business. He defined the essence of 'usury' in its pejorative sense as being the same in all ages: the cruel or heartless use of capital. He gave a modern example, that of a man finding out which particular manufacturers were in pressing need of money, buying at reduced prices, and thus crippling fellow tradesmen who had the backing of much smaller capital (Gregory 1871: 226).

Although it was the duty of a good businessman to make a profit, this could not justify knowingly bringing about the downfall of others. Nor would such behaviour benefit the commercial world at large. In a text setting out the collective moral and religious responsibilities of public companies with reference to detailed scriptural exegesis, J. W. Gilbart urged that public companies should endeavour to promote each other's interest, and that banking and insurance companies should be 'pitiful', being as accommodating as possible when honest clients were in trouble (Gilbart 1849: ii, 687–8). Here the emphasis was on *duty*—both to the individual conscience and to a wider commercial culture—rather than on *rights* to individual gain. The prominent Birmingham Congregationalist R. W. Dale developed this theme: he vehemently rejected what he termed the 'old and vulgar distinction' between a profession (in which a man put duty before his own interests) and a trade (in which the right to pursue self-interest was paramount). This distinction was one reason why professions had been regarded as honourable and trades as sordid. If the distinction were accepted, the scorn with which people in trade had once been regarded would be deserved. But no *intelligent* Christian trader or manufacturer who had grasped the proper relationship of the law of Christ to the secular order would let his life be governed by such a narrow outlook. It was crucial that such an outlook should be vigorously challenged by the clear substitution of one language for another—the language of duty for the language of rights (Dale 1867*a*: 4–5; 1884: 12–15; cf. Ruskin 1903–12: xvii, 40–2).

Dale also used the analogy with the code of military honour, which required that a captain in the army put his men's safety before his own, and urged this ethic on industrial and commercial employers. This was pertinent to the spheres both of production and of exchange. Responsibility to employees included rewarding talent, maintaining high standards of workmanship and service, as well as providing good working conditions and terms of employment. One writer on the moral identity of banking companies even extended the principle of promoting public good to the need to express concern about smoking cigars in public places to the annoyance of others (Gilbart 1849: 693n.). 'No large charitable contributions can make up for lack of charity in your own business' (Braden 1876: 105–13; cf. Dale 1877: 256–61; Dale 1890: 5–6); nor, on the other hand, could the need for reinvestment to create employment—itself commended by economic theory—be held to preclude the setting aside of resources for compassionate giving and for philanthropic activity in the community at large (Arthur 1855; Freedley 1853: 207; Ross 1853: 332–3; Garnett 1987). Accounts of exemplary Christian businessmen stressed that consistency of behaviour in and out of the workplace and integrity of dealing would earn the respect and loyalty of the workforce. Such loyalty would itself conduce to the healthy running of the enterprise. Such respect would extend also to the wider Christian community of which the professedly Christian businessman acted as a representative (Kirkman 1886). In this way the integrative potential of evangelical commitment could be fully realized.

The fact that companies could be formed with limited liability after 1855 extended the ramifications of duty and the perceived need for intelligent reflection. Evangelicals welcomed the new opportunities for small investors, although they warned about the need for caution (see, e.g., *Record* 1855; 1864; 1866*a* and *b*). R. W. Dale emphasized that people who invested in highly speculative schemes about which they knew nothing showed a lack of sense as culpable as more direct dishonesty (Dale 1867*b*: 18). Again, the remedy lay in establishing a systematic set of principles within which to operate, and against which repeatedly and regularly to test one's actions. It was important to publicize the limitations on the power of shareholders, so that neither could the company be referred to as a conveniently abstract entity, nor could those with real responsibility shelter behind the monolithic notion of duty to a shareholding public which was solely interested in the dividends. Even if this were true, it could not justify proprietors operating on the narrow criterion of profit at any price (Gilbart 1849: ii, 674, 676, 679). In some cases shareholders' votes did count—for example on the question of the opening of the Crystal Palace on Sundays (*Record* 1858). Several manufacturers converted their companies to limited liability in the 1870s and 1880s, with the express aim of bringing their employees into part-ownership and increasing their interest in the firm (*In Memoriam John Rylands* 1889: 30; Jenkins 1984–6: 262–5). But ultimate control still rested with the proprietors, who needed constantly to be reminded of their responsibility and power of choice. In fact, until the last quarter of the nineteenth century well over 90 per cent of British firms remained family-based partnerships

(Jeremy 1988: 6), so that many issues which were to arise from the relationship between owners and managers, managers and share-holders were still in the future. But the emphasis on the need for clarity about the ramifications of responsibility would not cease to be pertinent, even though the circles within which it was to operate would grow ever wider.

The relationship between private and public misdemeanours and obligations—which was generally felt to be inadequately addressed by the law—was one around which all aspects of this debate turned. In England many commercial frauds in the mid-nineteenth century (including abuse of trade marks) were regarded as civil injuries rather than crimes—as private wrongs rather than public offences (Ryland 1860: 229–36). Both lawyers and moralists argued that this could not be satisfactory, since the impact of such frauds could not be localized, and since they had a debilitating effect on commercial ethics. In this context, as in others under discussion, the issue was one of the moral impact of such conceptual categorization. There were those who advocated codification: 'Law in the present day seems to consist of precedents and cases entirely, *instead of first principles*' (*Business Life* 1861: 129–34). But this idea too was open to challenge on the grounds that it could imply a misleading tidiness. The issue was also debated in relation to the perceived status of *laissez-faire* principles (see, e.g., Atiyah 1979). Moralists saw the need for a sharper focus on the fostering of active trust and on distinguishing more precisely between fair and unfair competition. As one evangelical commentator put it: 'A man may be able to say "I have committed neither theft nor fraud", and yet he may have been a reckless debtor, an unfaithful servant, an inattentive agent, an extravagant partner, or a negligent consignee' (Hinton 1851: 270).

One important area of concern was that of adulteration, which continued to be a serious problem insufficiently curbed by legislation. A witness before the Parliamentary Select Committee set up in 1855 to investigate the problem, himself a solicitor and chairman of the Local Board of Health, asserted: 'I think the public are sufficiently protected by competition. Competition does not enable the public to know that an article is adulterated; neither do I think it necessary that it should. I think it is sufficient for the public if they get the article at the cheapest price' (*Adulteration* 1855: 220). The legislation of 1860 which implemented the recommendations of this Committee was limited in its scope and penalties, and failed adequately to cover relations between wholesalers and retailers (Hayman 1863; Rees 1910: ii, 186; H. S. Brown 1863: 142). Most telling was the distinction made in the report between pecuniary frauds and injuries to public health, by which only the strictly dangerous adulterations were unequivocally condemned (*Parliamentary Papers 1856*: viii (379), I, iv). Moralists were quick to denounce the implications of this position. They pleaded that it was not good enough to put forward the principle of *caveat emptor*: too much was at stake—the honest trader, the whole trading community, the reputation of the entire nation as a trading nation (*Record* 1856; for J. A. Froude's passionate invective on this theme, see Clarkson 1871).

In trying to establish ground rules in relation to competition, the responsibility of both sides in a transaction to take proper precautions was underlined. It was recognized that customers could be culpable in demanding ever greater cheapness (a practice apparently sanctioned by economic orthodoxy), and thereby driving tradesmen into illegitimate practices. But this could also be used by fraudulent traders as an excuse. Greater emphasis was placed on the need for tradesmen to work together to exert a reasonable and positive influence on the tone of commercial life. Some particularly blatant abuses of position were condemned, when the tradesman was clearly much more experienced than the customer: one Oxford student was said to have been visited during his first week by fifty tradesmen— wine-merchants, tailors, bootmakers, cigar-sellers—all offering credit without enquiring into his personal circumstances (*Record* 1848; Elliott 1845: 11).

The question of time-scale was critical in assessing risk and in discussing competitive practice. The Methodist Benjamin Gregory defined crises in terms of overtrading: of expending capital faster than it could be recouped, sinking money even in useful and valuable projects which were almost certain to be profitable *in the long run*, faster than it could find its level (Gregory 1871: 322). Here one might be dealing not with fraud, but potentially with carelessness. A critic of Mill's *On Liberty* commented that he was prepared to accept that the presence of perfectly free competition was *ultimately* the best guarantee of excellence; but people were so apt to be carried away by abstract ideas of this that they lost sight of the qualifications contained in the word 'ultimately'. Economic theorists were particularly inclined to disregard time altogether, forgetting that life was often too short for fraud to be properly exposed (Williams 1870: 76).

The practical remedy lay in proper accounting procedures, regularity in stock-taking, the ability to estimate average income and commitments over several years, and then to be able accurately to assess risk. These principles had an interlocking religious and economic significance. Again, legal procedures relating to bankruptcy, and the public response to large-scale commercial failures seemed unhelpful. Attention was typically focused on the immediate circumstances, rather than on the moral conduct of the business over the longer term and the rules of credit applied (Arnot 1851: 17; Boardman 1853: 187; Kemp 1858: 11). The tensions between different perceptions of responsibility were made manifest by the behaviour of those facing impending crisis. The evangelical Anglican newspaper, the *Record*, discussed the case of Davidson and Gordon, which was before the Bankruptcy Court in 1859. Charges had been levelled against David Chapman, one of the acting partners of Overend, Gurney, and Co., which had discounted bills of Davidson and Gordon on a massive scale. One of the principal points at issue was that Chapman had not publicly revealed and denounced fraud as soon as it was detected; he had kept quiet for eight months so as to try to preserve the credit of the firm. The *Record* was particularly critical of Overend, Gurney, and Co.'s policy of giving enormous credit to a firm which was so young and one of whose principals had recently been bankrupt. If it had been more on its guard against the possibility of overtrading, it would have investigated the young firm more carefully and would not have ended up bolstering what were effectively gamblers (*Record* 1859; cf. *Christian Observer* 1858: 82).

A firm which was to fail in connection with the celebrated collapse of Overend, Gurney, and Co. itself in 1866 was that of Sir Morton Peto, large-scale Baptist building contractor and MP. A good employer, he was unusual in preferring to employ directly and not to subcontract, in order to keep a tight control of the work and working conditions of his men. However, this meant that he needed more capital, and for his contract in connection with the building of the London, Chatham, and Dover railway, his company was dependent on Overend, Gurney, and Co. for some of its funding. In arranging finance, Peto effectively took control of the railway itself as well as his own business. But he took on too much liability, which he could not cover; his own contract with the railway company gave insufficient attention to the problem of externalities—of the effects on third parties. This lack of obligatory definition was felt to be a great weakness in contract law and indeed in classical economic theory (*Record* 1866*b*). In his responses to the committee of inquiry instituted by members of his chapel to investigate his bankruptcy, Peto made it clear that he was dissatisfied with his own explanation of the relationship between the directors and the contractors. He was aware that he had failed to be sufficiently vigilant, or to make himself fully aware of what lack of vigilance in this context would entail.

The investigation of Peto in 1866–7 by members of Bloomsbury Chapel—which he himself had built in 1848 and of which he was the most prominent member—was one example of nonconformist disciplinary practice at work (Bowers and Bowers 1984: 210–20). Nonconformist churches had specific conditions of membership, and instituted committees of investigation if members seemed to have transgressed the rules. The most frequently investigated cases were those of dishonesty, insolvency, adultery, drunkenness, and non-attendance. Someone who became bankrupt was automatically investigated. This was a very practical way in which such religious communities could demonstrate their concern with the commercial probity of their members. The exercise of this sort of discipline was not intended to be simply punitive, although those found guilty of serious offences could be expelled. It was also meant to be a means of helping people who were faced with difficult problems. If the committee felt that sympathy was merited, the chapel would offer support to people in carrying out the morally approved course of action. The very fact that people thought it worthwhile to submit to investigation is itself a sign of a degree of consensus about the value of such disciplinary activities. In forty years of records of Carr's Lane Chapel in Birmingham, where R. W. Dale was minister, there is only one case noted of someone refusing to come before the committee (Carr's Lane II: 93–4). The reinforcement of this moral framework of course helped to maintain the usefulness of church membership as a public index of moral and business respectability (cf. Weber 1922–3: i, 207–36). At the same time such respectability was not easily won: there were no special privileges for those of higher social standing. The case of Peto is a telling one: his status was such that all the temptations might have been to side-step the issue. Yet he was investigated, and, whilst specific accusations of dishonesty were dismissed, the committee did criticize him for taking on too much liability: 'we cannot forget that something more than conventional morality is demanded from the followers of Christ . . . not to assume positions in which the duties are inconsistent one with the other and to avoid the appearance of evil'. At Carr's Lane in 1865 three noted members of the chapel were investigated in connection with the suspension of the Penny Bank. Two resigned, having given explanations of their conduct. The third, who had himself been on the annual discipline committee for 1865, was dismissed from fellowship, having admitted that, as early as 1859, he had suspected the Bank to be in difficulties (Carr's Lane II: 219–53 [1865]).

These inquiries were also intended to serve an exemplary function. The detailed setting out of a case was intended to act as a stimulus to self-examination on the part of other members of the chapel, and also to nip rumour in the bud in close-knit communities where the fact of a member's bankruptcy would in any case be known. In reaching a verdict, the way in which the business had been conducted over a period was more important than the immediate fact of exposure. The case of a Quaker shoemaker who had drifted towards insolvency in 1856, having started business with insufficient capital, prompted the committee to advise their fellows to keep clear and correct accounts and carefully to inspect the state of their affairs once a year (Hardshaw East Monthly Meeting 1856: 279–82). At Carr's Lane in 1867, the investigation of Philip Levin's bankruptcy revealed that his books had been very carefully kept. The problem lay in his receipts being so small that his business could not be made to pay. Thus his failure could not be held to reflect on his moral character (Carr's Lane II: 65–7 [1867]). In some cases ignorance was felt to be blameworthy (Carr's Lane II: 78–9 [1872]; 39 [1862]). In others, men were expelled for having been bankrupt more than once, without having improved the way in which they conducted their business (Carr's Lane II: 69–70 [1869]). Sometimes the chapel meeting could be used as a forum for arbitration between two members, and could thus facilitate business relations and serve as a sanction for good practice (see, e.g., Birmingham East (Methodist) Circuit 1853; Cannon Street Baptist Church (Birmingham) 1829–53). A crucial point about all these procedures was their close accord with the ethical teaching which was being offered in the pulpit, on the platform, and in the periodical literature. At Bloomsbury Chapel Peto's minister William Brock was a noted contributor to the debate on commercial morality (see especially Brock 1856), as was R. W. Dale at Carr's Lane. Thomas Binney, Congregationalist minister of King's Weigh House, London, and author of the best-selling *Is it Possible to Make the Best of Both Worlds?*, published in 1853 and aimed at young people entering commercial life, took enormous pains over those in his chapel suffering business difficulties (King's Weigh House MS 209: July–September 1852; 29 September 1854). In all these cases the practice of theory was very precisely realized.

Such a fully integrated ethic was only available to members of these particular communities. But the public demonstration of such practice had a wider impact. The ethical debates which have been discussed in this paper acquired a central position in Victorian life. Naturally, all Victorian businessmen did not conform to such prescriptive ideals, but what is significant is the sorts of emphasis which were placed, and the positions and ways of thinking which were commended. As the century progressed some of these concerns began to be taken up into new theoretical or legal frameworks. But at the same time a new wave of revivalists such as the late nineteenth-century Christian Socialists, out of which tradition Tawney came, felt the need to reiterate some of the fundamental principles in what they presented as a novel ethical initiative. Questions of appropriate guides to practice in commercial life were no less complex, and continued to challenge ethical reflection. There have been cycles of action and reaction in the development of theoretical perspectives in economics, and recent work has argued how necessary it is again to confront the implications of models predicated on a narrow concept of self-interest (see, e.g., Sen 1987; 1993). The relationship between the respective languages (and claims to ideological hegemony) of economic theory, law, and morality is still a contested one. The aspects of the Victorian debate touched on here reveal a keen appreciation of the equal dangers of glibly conflating one language with another and of regarding them as operating in wholly distinct spheres. Human personality could not be so understood, and the psychological context of economic behaviour was infinitely more complicated. Such considerations are as pertinent now as they were then to an understanding of the interrelationship between norms and practice in an ethical economy.

REFERENCES

Adulteration of Food, Drink and Drugs, being the Evidence taken by the Parliamentary Committee (1855) (London: David Bryce).

Arnold, M. (1869), *Culture and Anarchy: an Essay in Political and Social Criticism* (London: Smith, Elder).

Arnot, W. (1851), *The Race for Riches and Some of the Pits into which the Runners Fall: Six Lectures, applying the Word of God to the Traffic of Men* (London and Edinburgh: Johnstone and Hunter).

Arthur, W. (1851), 'Heroes', in *Lectures delivered before the Y.M.C.A in Exeter Hall 1850–51* (London: James Nisbet; Hamilton, Adams): 287–338.

—— (1852), *The Successful Merchant: Sketches of the Life of Mr. Samuel Budgett late of Kingswood Hill* (London: Hamilton, Adams).

—— (1855), *The Duty of Giving Away a Stated Proportion of Our Income* (London: James Nisbet).

Atiyah, P. S. (1979), *The Rise and Fall of Freedom of Contract* (Oxford: Clarendon Press).

Baptist Magazine, 44 (1856).

Binfield, J. C. G. (1973), *George Williams and the Y.M.C.A., A Study in Victorian Social Attitudes* (London: Heinemann).

Binney, T. (1853), *Is it Possible to Make the Best of Both Worlds?* (London: J. Nisbet).

Birmingham East (Methodist) Circuit, Local Preachers Meetings 1851–67, Belmont Row Class Room, 9 and 17 June 1853 (Birmingham Central Library).

Birrell, C. M. (1865), 'The Influence of the Present Times on Personal Religion', *Papers Read before the Baptist Union of Great Britain and Ireland at its autumnal session in Cannon Street Chapel, and Wycliffe Church, Birmingham, October 12th and 13th 1864* (London: Henry James Tresidder): 79–88.

Boardman, H. A. (1853), *The Bible in the Counting House: a Course of Lectures to Merchants* (London: Trubner).

Bourdieu, P. (1977), *Outline of a Theory of Practice*, trans. by R. Nice (Cambridge: Cambridge University Press).

Bowers, B. and Bowers, F. (1984), 'Bloomsbury Chapel and Mercantile Morality', *Baptist Quarterly*, 30: 210–20.

Braden, W. (1876), *Our Social Relationships and Life in London* (London: J. Clarke).

British Quarterly Review (1845).

Brock, W. (1856), 'Mercantile Morality', in *Lectures delivered before the Y.M.C.A. in Exeter Hall 1855–56* (London: James Nisbet; Hamilton, Adams): 411–57.

Brown, H. S. (1863), 'Defaulters', in *Lectures delivered before the Y.M.C.A. in Exeter Hall 1862–63* (London: James Nisbet; Hamilton, Adams).

Business Life. The Experiences of a London Tradesman, with Practical Advice and

Directions for Avoiding many of the Evils connected with our Present Commercial System and State of Society (1861) (London: Houlston and Wright).

Cannon Street Baptist Church (Birmingham), Deacons' Minutes (1829–53).

Carlyle, T. (1841), *On Heroes, Heroism and the Heroic in History* (London: James Fraser).

Carr's Lane Discipline Committee II (July 1859–July 1894) (Birmingham Central Library).

[Chalmers, T.] (1844–5), 'The Political Economy of the Bible', *North British Review* 2: 1–52.

Christian Observer, 58 (1858).

Clarkson, S. (1871), *J. A. Froude and the Right Hon. J. Bright. The Censor Censured in Correspondence with Mr Froude* (Manchester: Tubbs and Brook).

Cobbett, W. (1824–6), *A History of the Protestant 'Reformation' in England and Ireland* (London: Charles Clement).

Dale, R.W. (1867*a*), 'Preliminary', in *Week-Day Sermons* (London: Alexander Strahan): 1–9.

—— (1867*b*), 'The Use of the Understanding in Keeping God's Law', in *Week-Day Sermons* (London: Alexander Strahan): 10–37.

—— (1877), 'Pastoral Preaching', in *Nine Lectures on Preaching Delivered at Yale* (London: Hodder and Stoughton): 221–62.

—— (1880*a*), 'The Education of the Conscience', in *The Evangelical Revival and other Sermons* (London: Hodder and Stoughton): 85–103.

—— (1880*b*), 'The Necessity of Doing the Will of God', in *The Evangelical Revival and other Sermons* (London: Hodder and Stoughton): 104–24.

—— (1884), 'Everyday Business a Divine Calling', in *Laws of Christ for Common Life* (London: Hodder and Stoughton): 1–15.

—— (1890), *The Duties of Church Members* (London: James Clarke).

Elliott, J. H. (1845), *Credit the Life of Commerce* (London: Madden and Malcolm).

Evans, D. M. (1968 edn), *Facts, Failures and Frauds; Revelations, Financial, Mercantile, Criminal* (1859; repr. New York and Newton Abbot: David and Charles).

—— (1969 edn), *The History of the Commerical Crisis 1857–8 and the Stock Exchange Panic of 1859* (1859; repr. New York and Newton Abbot: David and Charles).

Freedley, E. (1853), *Money: How to Get, Save, Spend, Give, Lend and Bequeath it, being a Practical Treatise on Business, with an Inquiry into the Chances of Success and Causes of Failure* (London: Partridge and Oakey).

Garnett, J. (1987), '"Gold and the Gospel": Systematic Beneficence in mid-nineteenth-century England', in *Studies in Church History*, 24, ed. Sheils, W. J. and Wood, D.: 347–58.

Gilbart, J. W. (1849), 'The Moral and Religious Duties of Banking Companies' (1846), in *A Practical Treatise on Banking*, 5th edn, 2 vols (London: Longman, Brown, Green and Longmans), ii: 665–728.

Gilley, S. (1971), 'Heretic London, Holy Poverty and the Irish Poor 1830–70', *Downside Review*, 89: 64–89.

Gregory, B. (1871), *The Thorough Business Man. Memoirs of Walter Powell, Merchant, Melbourne and London* (London: Strahan).

Hardshaw East Monthly Meeting Minutes, Manchester Central Library M 85 2/1/5, minutes 7 and 15, 1856, 279–82.

Hardy, R. S. (1858), *Commerce and Christianity. Memorials of Jones Sugden of Oakworth House.*

Hawes, W. (1858), 'On the Effect of Commercial Legislation upon Commercial Morality', in *Transactions of the National Association for the Promotion of Social Science for 1857*: 91–3.

Hayman, J. (1863), *An Appeal to Tradesmen, relating to Sundry Abuses deeply affecting their Interests* (London: J. Briscoe).

Hinton, J. (1851), 'On the Elements Supplied by the Holy Scriptures for the Formation of an Industrial Character, Individual and National', in *The Useful Arts*, ed. Martin, S. (London: James Nisbet; Hamilton, Adams): 256–300.

Hodgson, W. B. (1859), 'The Educational Aspect and Necessity of Economic Science', in *Transactions of the National Association for the Promotion of Social Science for 1858*: 552–6.

—— (1870a), *On the Importance of the Study of Economic Science as a Branch of Education for all Classes* (1854; 3rd edn 1870; London: Trubner).

—— (1870b), 'The Scope of Economic Science', *Lectures on Economic Science. Delivered under the Auspices of the Committee on Labour and Capital appointed by the National Association for the Promotion of Social Science*: 1–32.

—— (1870c), 'Competition', *Lectures on Economic Science.* 59–85.

Hughes, H. (1852), 'Protestantism the Basis of National Prosperity', in *Six Lectures on Protestantism* (London).

Hughes, J. R. T. (1960), *Fluctuations in Trade, Industry and Finance* (Oxford: Clarendon Press).

In Memoriam John Rylands (1889) (Manchester: printed for private circulation).

Jay, E. and Jay, R. (1986) (eds), *Critics of Capitalism: Victorian Reactions to Political Economy* (Cambridge: Cambridge University Press).

Jenkins, D. (1984–6), 'Sir Henry Mitchell (1824–98)', in *Dictionary of Business Biography*, ed. Jeremy, D. J. and Shaw, C. (London: Butterworth).

Jeremy, D. (1988), *Business and Religion in Britain* (Aldershot: Gower).

Kemp, H. W. (1858), *The Same Rule for the Merchant and the Private Man* (London: Whittaker).

King's Weigh House MS 209, Deacons' Minutes (1852–71), (Dr Williams Library, London).

Kirkman, W. (1886), *T. C. Hincksman of Lytham (1799–1883)* (London: T. Woolmer).

Laveleye, E. de (1875), *Protestantism and Catholicism in their Bearing upon the Liberty and Prosperity of Nations: a Study of Social Economy* (London).

Lester, V. M. (1995), *Victorian Insolvency. Bankruptcy, Imprisonment for Debt, and Company Winding-up in Nineteenth-Century England* (Oxford: Clarendon Press).

Marshall, A. (1961 edn), *Principles of Economics* (1890) (London: Macmillan).

Mill, J. S. (1967 edn), 'On the Definition of Political Economy', in *Essays on Economics and Society, Collected Works of J. S. Mill*, ed. Priestley, F. E. L. and Robson, J. M. (Toronto: University of Toronto Press; London: Routledge and Kegan Paul), iv: 309–39.

—— (1965 edn), *Principles of Political Economy with some of their Applications to Social Philosophy, Collected Works of J. S. Mill*, ed. Priestley, F. E. L. and Robson, J. M. (Toronto: University of Toronto Press; London: Routledge and Kegan Paul), ii.

Parliamentary Papers 1856.

Record (1848): 6 Jan., no. 2125.

—— (1855): 10 Aug., no. 2964.

—— (1856): 25 Aug. 1856, no. 3127.

—— (1858): 10 Nov., no. 3473.

—— (1859): 10 Jan., no. 3499.

—— (1864): 19 Feb., no. 4301.

—— (1866*a*): 30 May, no. 4657.

—— (1866*b*): 17 Oct., no. 4717.

Rees, J. A. (1910), *The Grocery Trade, its History and Romance*, 2 vols (London: Duckworth).

Ross, J. (1853), 'The Christian Weekly Offering', *Gold and the Gospel: the Ulster Prize Essays on the Scriptural Duty of Giving in Proportion to Means and Income* (London: James Nisbet).

Ruskin, J. (1903–12 edn), 'Unto this Last', in *Works of John Ruskin*, ed. Cook, E.T. and Wedderburn, A. W. W., 39 vols (London: George Allen), xvii: 17–114.

Ryland, A. (1860), 'The Fraudulent Imitation of Trade Marks', in *Transactions of the National Association for the Promotion of Social Science for 1859*: 229–36.

[Scrope, G. P.] (1832), 'Dr Chalmers on Political Economy', *Quarterly Review*, 48: 39–69.

Sen, A. (1987), *On Ethics and Economics* (Oxford: Basil Blackwell).

Sen, A. (1993), *Moral Codes and Economic Success* (London: Development Economics Research Programme, Suntory-Toyota International Centre for Economics and Related Disciplines, London School of Economics).

Smiles, S. (1859), *Self-Help* (London: John Murray).

Soloway, R. (1969), *Prelates and People: Ecclesiastical Social Thought in England 1783–1852* (London: Routledge and Kegan Paul and Toronto: University of Toronto Press).

Stowell, H. (1854), *A Model for Men of Business. Lectures on the Character of Nehemiah* (London).

—— (1858), 'The Christian Man in the Business of Life', in *Christianity in the Business of Life* (London: John F. Shaw), 69–102.

Tawney, R. H. (1982 edn), *The Acquisitive Society* (Brighton: Harvester Press).
Warehousemen and Draper's Trade Journal (1872), 1.
Waterman, A. M. C. (1983), 'The Ideological Alliance of Political Economy and
   Christian Theology 1798–1833', *Journal of Ecclesiastical History*, 34: 231–43.
—— (1991), *Revolution, Economics and Religion: Christian Political Economy
   1798–1833* (Cambridge: Cambridge University Press).
Weber, M. (1922–3), 'Die Protestantischen Sekten und der Geist des Kapitalismus',
   Gesammelte Aufsaetze zur Religionssoziologie (Tübingen), i: 207–36.
Williams, R. (1870), 'Laissez-Faire', *Fraser's Magazine*, n.s. 1: 72–83.

9

The Potential for a Universal Business Ethics

S. N. WOODWARD

1. CONTEXT, COMMON HUMANITY, AND CORE VALUES

THIS chapter takes as its departure point an article by Donaldson in the *Harvard Business Review* which advocates three core values, based on three principles, for application in the relationship between US corporations and other cultures (Donaldson 1996). Such a relationship requires awareness of context, and is predicated on acknowledgement of common humanity. In the first section of this chapter, I shall examine these notions of context and common humanity. However, such principles tend to be denied within corporations themselves, through the dynamics of personal agenda, of organization, and of hierarchy in contemporary economic and civil societies. The remainder of the chapter will consider the nature of these dynamics, suggesting that the tendency is as old as civilization, but emerges starkly and damagingly in corporations through their control over resources and people, enabled by the technologies of progress, where through cultural evolution 'we have created a world for which we are not biologically made' (Eibl-Eibesfeldt 1989: 718).

Donaldson sees the practical challenge as 'to help managers distinguish between practices that are merely different, and those that are wrong.' To this end he proposes three principles: respect for core human values ('the absolute moral threshold for all business activities'); respect for local traditions (practical acknowledgement and accommodation of cultural difference); and the belief that context matters when deciding what is right and what is wrong. These principles in turn translate into three core values which 'should' help frame minimum standards for all companies, 'if only as a starting point':

(1) respect for human dignity: individuals must not treat others simply as tools, must recognize 'a person's value as a human

being', as part of the principle of reciprocity, the Golden Rule, not to do to others what they do not want done to themselves;

(2) respect for basic rights; including the right to good health and the right to economic advancement and an improved standard of living;

(3) good citizenship: 'members of a community must work together to support and improve the institutions on which the community depends'.

Donaldson's is a sensible and helpful contribution for corporate managers concerned about the problems of dealing ethically with alien cultures. His examples cite Third World and non-Western cultures, but I would include European, Canadian, and American, since cultural differences obtain within and between cultures. For his principles, if adopted and sensitively understood, should significantly help US corporate managers in dealing with other cultures and coping with the ethical dilemmas which emerge from acknowledgement of cultural differences, and the challenges presented in living in and dealing with alien cultures. Let me now briefly explore some of the underpinnings of the importance of context and the evidence for core human values.

The first way in which context matters in business ethics is in *understanding* how ethics works—or can work—within organizations. Donaldson emphasizes the importance of context in dealing with other cultures, citing the case of Japan where gift-giving is a normal aspect of business relations in contrast to the USA, where this might be classified as bribery. Acknowledgement of this enables the outsider to make judgements on the appropriateness and value of such gifts (rather like understanding the manners, rituals, and courtesies—learning the values and behaving accordingly). It should be added that the tendency for gift-giving to shade into influence and bribery is of current concern in Japanese society.

However, context matters equally in many within-cultural dilemmas. The killing of a fellow human being may range from murder to justifiable homicide to battlefield heroism: here the moral nature (and ascription) of the act is based on its justification in terms of motive and context. Larmore (1987: ix) criticizes Kantianism and utilitarianism for 'seeking a fully explicit decision procedure for settling moral questions. As a result, they have missed the central role of moral judgement, or the faculty of insight into how general rules are to be applied to particular situations.' The need for such interpretative contextual judgement is embodied in the tradition of case law, an example which should be sufficient to make an *a fortiori* case for moral judgements (and some legal systems include moral judgement in their calculus—Geertz 1993: ch. 8). Lucas (1993) likewise, in exploring the nature of responsibility ('why did you do that?'), sufficiently demonstrates the critical importance of context in justification of behaviour.

What then is the general context of purposive business organizations? A sense of purpose is integral to human activity, and myths of purpose, from the practical to the existential, provide meaning, as well as legitimization of the social order. In purposive organizations Gowler and Legge (1983: 229) identify three kinds of myth which are constructed to maintain order:

[T]he management-as-hierarchy theme expresses meanings about social order, whilst the management-as-accountability theme expresses meanings about the moral order. And it is the management-as-achievement theme that cements the social and moral orders into a rational 'natural' order, where any other state of affairs would be seen to result in anarchy and despair.

However, these myths of management (as hierarchy, accountability, and achievement) generate dynamic practical problems. First, they may be inconsistent, one with another (as when bureaucratic rules and procedures take precedence over achievement). Second, the implications of a particular myth may be violated by behaviour (as when a superior takes credit for a subordinate's achievement—Donaldson comments that 'in some parts of the Far East, stealing credit from a subordinate is nearly an unpardonable sin'). Third, modern corporations, as a result of size, geographical dispersion, functional and other specialization and status differentiation, tend to generate multiple internal cultures, each with their own differing versions of these generic myths: this in turn leads to breakdown in internal communication, territorial disputes, competition for power and resources, and so on, to the stuff of organizational politics, and a corresponding need for order and for management as authority. Contemporary fashions for culture change, leadership, re-engineering, quality programmes, and mission statements constitute attempts to counteract this tendency, thereby attesting to its prevalence. They are practical attempts to assert the primacy of a myth of achievement over hierarchy and accountability. Fourth, stemming from size, hierarchy, and the nature of power and authority in hierarchical systems, senior managers tend to be relatively ill-informed, partly because their prior experiences frame their cognitive processing ('top managers tend to misperceive what is happening even more than many of their subordinates'—Starbuck 1985: 365); partly because information has to be filtered and framed by subordinates, who have an interest in playing down the unwelcome and emphasizing the welcome (Dixon 1988: 254).

For the practice of ethics in business, the dynamic, political, negotiated nature of the organization's internal myth-making and justifications forces more general non-instrumental values (such as Donaldson's core human values) into the background: where they are asserted and internalized by corporate fiat, they are likely to be seen as constraints upon primary achievement purposes (profits, sales, other less public goals, and the behaviours which generate these), and so always under pressure of compromise, with appropriate justification, when they conflict with core achievement and other myths.

That cultures differ, radically and in most categories of behavioural and cognitive description, is a commonplace of anthropology, attested by a large corpus of ethnography. These differences apply at the deepest levels of belief, perception, and attitude. Leach (1982: 51), for instance, states that 'the fundamental characteristic of human culture is its endless diversity. It is not a chaotic diversity, but it is not a predestined diversity either.' Leach goes further, however, in arguing that there are no grounds for deriving 'fundamental values that cross cultures' (Donaldson's phrase) from the biological fact of common humanity. He sees the search for a common basis of ethics as deriving from 'the dialectic between the fact of the unity of man as a biological species and the fact of the disunity of man as a social being' (p. 58). What are the implications of this for a purported universal ethics such as Donaldson's?

The first point to note is that wherever humans meet, the meeting evokes potential for relationship on the basis of common humanity (a form of discourse ethics), with moral force, as well as potential for conflict and destruction. The unity of man as a biological species (and as part of the natural world) provides the basis for common morality, for common humanity generates common patterns in behaviour across human groups and bases for relationship, even though these are cognitively and culturally mediated with evidently endless and significant variety. But this is not inconsistent with the assertion that no universalistic *propositions* about morality can be derived from empirical evidence across cultures and time. However, there is ample evidence that across cultures and time the notion of common humanity has been seen as a basis for morality, and that this position has biological roots. It is this potential which is the underpinning of Donaldson's core human values.

In ethology, psychology, and aspects of neuroscience we see a picture of humans as a species adapted for living in small individualized communities, with corresponding emotional, psychological, and neurological dispositions, confronted by a quite different natural and social environment. Universal phylogenetic tendencies ('common humanity') are mediated through a great variety of cultural mechanisms. The potential for affiliative/aversive tendencies is universal, culturally mediated from birth, and incorporated into psychological disposition. For instance, there appears to be a universal (phylogenetic) norm against killing others: this holds despite the potential for psychologically damaged individuals or societies to lack or modify this inhibition—cases which for Leach would empirically refute a universalistic proposition. In war a cultural norm is superimposed upon a biological one. But, according to Eibl-Eibesfeldt (1989: 711):

only upon a superficial examination would one come to the viewpoint of cultural relativism. . . . True, infanticide is considered to be a crime in our society, while it is necessary in some tribal societies. At this level there are cultural differences, but we have shown that no society is known where mothers kill their own children lightheartedly.

In short, humans inherit innate inhibitions, mediated psychologically by early childhood experience, and dependent also on neurophysiological integrity, over which are laid cultural norms and the capacity for reasoning (and rationalization). In Eibl-Eibesfeldt's words (pp. 717–18):

Man behaves morally out of emotional engagement, custom, and, finally, out of thoughtful consideration. We can distinguish general virtues, such as self-control, and the more specific virtues such as those belonging to the agonal system (heroic virtues) and those belonging to the affiliative system serving bonding.

. . . The danger of maladaptive behaviour derives from man's inclination to one-sided exaggeration of virtues . . . into vices.

How, then, *do* people behave morally in business organizations, in 'the real world of business decision-making'? And what are the implications for a universal ethical principle, such as Donaldson's?

2. ETHICS IN ORGANIZATIONS

Formal organizations of all kinds have great potential to isolate the personal from the formal, internal functioning from external: 'the enduring genius of the organizational form is that it allows individuals to retain bewilderingly diverse private motives and meanings for action as long as they adhere publicly to agreed-upon rules' (Jackall 1988: 6). This is particularly notable in cultures where individualism is valued and can lead to a tendency for employees in a public role to limit their commitment and energy in their employment—a form of psychic withdrawal, which both limits moral concern about the employment situation, and leaves the field free to those whose personal ambition centres on the organization's power structure (Pym 1980). Jackall (1988: 6) observes that 'bureaucratic work causes people to bracket, while at work, the moralities they might hold outside the workplace or that they might adhere to privately, and to follow instead the prevailing morality of their particular organizational situation', and, quoting a former vice-president of a large US firm, 'what is right in the corporation is what the guy above wants from you. That's what morality is in the corporation.'

This separation of moral spheres is exacerbated by two factors. First, because organizations are purposive (contrasted with natural/communal), their decisions, behaviour, and procedures tend to be moulded by and legitimized in terms of instrumental criteria, so that considerations of external morality and legality tend to be marginalized rather than central, often seen as a matter of external public relations or of legal tactics and calculation—a constraint to be managed. Second, both because of their *raison d'être* (formal) and because of size, they tend to be relatively depersonalized (with bureaucracy as the extreme stereotype). So they necessarily employ strategies of distancing, dehumanizing, and formalization, which can generate a form of moral agnosia.

If this constitutes a general tendency, two unfortunate consequences follow. First, those with a strong personal sense of morality
either do not join, or leave; or where they attempt to assert it, *qua*
morality and divorced from political context, they are isolated, or
ignored, or subjected to a graded scale of group pressure, regulating
aggression, victimization, and persecution—as in many reported
cases of whistle-blowing. Second, while there are levels and arenas
in organizations where competence in skills, technique, and brain
(separately or in combination) is recognized and valued, yet such
competence does not typically translate into recognition by promotion, except with the addition of the mysterious and magical
ingredient, management. But 'management' is rooted fundamentally
in power and politics (Woodward 1991). And the exercise of power
attracts its fair share of neurotics, authoritarians, and psychopaths
(see section 3), a dynamic recognized by Plato's advocacy of the
reluctant ruler. Indeed Kets de Vries and Miller (1984) suggest that
whole organizations tend to reflect the neuroses of their constituent
influential managers—whether paranoid, compulsive, depressive, or
whatever. But these observations relate to tendencies, not universals,
for organizations have all the potential for variety, complexity, and
unexpected outcomes which one would expect from living systems.

However, such tendencies are biased, in modern corporations,
towards a particular pole, if the agenda relates to the personal quest
for power control and privilege, with the interests of stakeholders
(customers, investors, employees, community, etc.) as constraints on
those ends. So Jackall's conclusion, based on extensive interviews in
a small sample of US companies, rings true:

Corporate managers who become imbued with this ethos pragmatically take
their world as they find it and try to make that world work according to its
own institutional logic. They pursue their own careers and good fortune as
best they can within the rules of their world. As it happens, given their pivotal
institutional role in our epoch, they help create and re-create, as one unintended
consequence of their personal striving, a society where morality becomes
indistinguishable from the quest for one's own survival and advantage. (1988:
204)

Jackall's work was US-based, but his observations would apply in
cultures where organizations serve as means to individual ambition,
where individuals advance their careers by switching employment

(public job adverts provide a simple index), as opposed to cultures where individuals identify long-term with a single organization, and are personally committed to its fortunes, as in Ouchi's (1981) description of Japanese corporate families as 'clans'. However, 'clan' organizations, though less dependent on formal control, are likely to have stronger internal codes relating to purpose, function, behaviour, and loyalty, which may or may not be consonant with private or general external notions of moral behaviour. Indeed, the Mafia, with their code of *omertà*, constitutes an extreme example.

With such an internal dynamic the ideology of economics and finance, grounded in a rhetoric of mutual struggle, of social Darwinism abstracted from Darwin's insights, provides a supportive legitimizing rhetoric to separate the internal from the extra-organizational (the construction of meaning) which has been widely and uncritically adopted in business schools (Woodward 1991; Punch 1996). If, then, organizations tend to adopt the characteristics of a power hierarchy, they will tend also, through a variety of mechanisms, to neutralize their members' capacity for moral judgement and consonant action.

The corporation is so general in contemporary societies that it seems unrealistic to draw attention to its moral tendencies. But Punch (1996: 1), in a survey of corporate misconduct, comments:

In terms of everyday social interaction . . . we all engage in a measure of concealment and impression management. The difference lies in the control over powerful resources that managers enjoy and the potentially deleterious consequences of their misconduct in the corporations they run. This must raise our acute concern because some companies have killed, maimed, gassed, poisoned, and blown up people, while others have robbed us.

Punch's examples are based on public scandals from the USA, UK, Italy, and the Netherlands (often with wider ramifications), and he acknowledges 'reputable firms with exemplary reputations'. But in generic terms he argues that 'the corporation, and the business environment, are potentially criminogenic' (p. 4); that 'managers emerge as something of amoral chameleons, buffered by moral ambiguity and organizational uncertainty' (p. 5); that 'organizations are labyrinths of deceit. They create pressures, dilemmas, contradictions, and tensions that induce lies, deception, double-think, moral ambiguity, conspiracies, and devious role-playing' (p. 215), yet 'what hardly occurs to most businessmen, however, is that what they are doing is illegal, unethical, or criminal' (p. 245). In short, his public cases of delinquency are an extreme of a tendency. One should add that similar observations could be adduced from politics, history, and literature through the ages. Corporations enact a dynamic as old as civilization.

If Jackall and Punch (and earlier, Dalton 1959) are right in their diagnoses, then it would seem that US (and generally Western) corporations should consider the beam in their own eyes first. To Japanese eyes, at least until recently, the Western tradition of hiring and firing workers, and of managers pursuing careers across firms, seems distinctly alien, unethical, and short term. Donaldson's respect for human dignity and the right to economic advancement is widely denied by employment practices at lower levels of organization; the right to good health is threatened by stresses imposed at many levels, in both public and private institutions and by work practices in plants; and firms close plants in communities for economic reasons— transferring work across national boundaries in pursuit of lower labour costs. In terms of respect for 'core human values', 'the absolute moral threshold for all business activities' seems routinely and generally crossed. Korten (1995) provides a detailed analysis of the external consequences of corporations' practices for human values.

Yet Donaldson's principles, rooted in the universal affiliative system, would probably be acknowledged as appropriate, proper, and desirable by most corporate managers, whose firm's conduct blatantly (to outsiders) violates them. Why should this be? How might one account for this inconsistency?

3. THE DIVIDED INDIVIDUAL

Etymologically, 'individual' means 'cannot be divided', and the notion of the whole, responsible, rational, choosing, independent individual is central to much Western moral philosophy, sociology, economics, and politics. But, according to Geertz (1993: 59):

the Western conception of the person as a bounded, unique, more or less integrated motivational and cognitive universe, a dynamic centre of awareness, emotion, judgement, and action organized into a distinctive whole and set contrastively both against other such wholes and against its social and natural background is . . . a rather peculiar idea within the context of the world's cultures.

It is also a rather peculiar idea in behavioural terms, for no individual is divorced from the social context of upbringing, education, family, group, class, and so on. This context matters, for not only do current reference groups constitute the social domain of adult behaviour, but early upbringing lays down the template, the personality, of the adult. Most psychologists, whatever their espoused intellectual tradition, acknowledge the critical importance of early nurture, a perspective supported by evidence on neurological/physiological development at this critical stage of learning and socialization. Deep behavioural programmes are laid in early childhood relating to sense of identity, self-esteem, conscience, and acceptable modes of satisfying physiological drives, which are carried through into later life. Most of our behaviour, including modes of perceiving, reasoning, judging, and relating, is programmed (not determined).

The implications of the divided, possibly damaged, repressed self for practical ethics are profound, if it cannot be assumed that individuals are responsible, rational, amenable to argument—whole. For moral suasion then is not separate, not just a matter of reason and calculation, but part of the game, the dialogue of influence, as much a part of materialism, of the Third Reich, and of colonial enterprise as of any other society. The mechanisms of morality as influence are visible in all social interaction, but particularly evident, and particularly damaging, in what Dixon (1988: 136–7), echoing Punch's observations on corporate behaviour, terms 'traditional child rearing practices—poisonous pedagogy':

[T]hrough corporal punishment, threats of divine retribution, threatened and actual withdrawal of love, odious comparisons between the child who is 'bad' and some other paragon, real or fictitious, who is 'good'; by trickery, ridicule, humiliation, lies and deception—all under the mantle of that adult hypocrisy 'It's for your own good'—children of all ages have been systematically manipulated, crushed and frustrated. And for some of them their lives were permanently spoilt—in the course of time they become transformed into a more or less conscious hatred towards a variety of often quite undeserving individuals and groups.

This is in contrast, but consistent with, Bettelheim's (1991: 310) account of the message of stories such as Snow White and Cinderella, which deal with a 'generational conflict as old as man', but 'also tell that where this conflict exists, it is due only to the self-centredness of the parent and his lack of sensitivity to the child's legitimate needs.' Where the message, and the parent–child relationship, take root, 'the child will grow up to bring peace and happiness to even those who are so grievously afflicted that they seem like beasts . . . he will be at peace with himself and the world.' Dixon's strictures relate particularly to the traditional practices of Victorian/post-Victorian nurture, which can be transmitted through generations, but our contemporary economy is characterized by broken families, tends financially to reward parents for neglecting children, and provides a diet of television as infant placebo, with psychological consequences likely to be no less damaging.

Among the many outcomes of such recurring practices are what Dixon (1988: 138–9)—with apology and justification for the Freudian terminology—terms 'authoritarianism' and 'psychopathology'. The authoritarian personality, not an uncommon syndrome, is particularly impervious to moral suasion:

[N]ot only are such people rigid, dogmatic, closed-minded and therefore incompetent at handling complex situations, but they also retain from their childhood almost inexhaustible reserves of hostility which they are eager to discharge. . . . Such people are 'always right'. They always 'know best'. What they do to other people is 'always justified'. Even as the world might, largely through their own doing, come crashing about their ears they would manage to remain protected from guilt and shame by an impenetrable shield of self-righteous indignation. Part of their plight is that the shield precludes anything approaching a meaningful rapport with their fellow men.

And just as there is no shortage of authoritarian personalities nestling in institutionalized hierarchies, there is:

unfortunately no shortage of psychopaths—strangers to shame, unrestrained by guilt, living by their wits and sometimes ruthlessly aggressive. They may lie and cheat their way through life. If sufficiently clever, sufficiently attractive (until one knows them better) and sufficiently aggressive, they may acquire enormous wealth or power and end up as dictators, presidents, or chairmen of huge multi-national companies. (ibid.: 53)

It may be disturbing, irrational, to suggest that our world is peopled by psychologically maladjusted souls. For we have doctors, law courts, and police to inhibit, certify, and neutralize the insane, the dangerous, the abnormal. But it is Dixon's thesis that the conventionally normal (us) can acquire power or be placed in situations where our responses (and neuroses) can be personally and generally lethal, for our technologies have outrun our ability to control ourselves and their effects. To take a simple instance, highways and cars serve not just for transport, but as arenas for competitive, sometimes lethal, display extending even to 'road rage': even our platonic guardians, the traffic police, occasion accidents and innocent deaths while playing cops and robbers. Nor are experts, professions, or institutions immune (cf. Foucault's (1991) comparison of traditions of incarceration and education). In the caring medical profession Sacks (1995: 58) comments on the 'huge scandal' of the postwar explosion of 'psychosurgery' (an invention of the Portuguese neurologist Moriz, awarded a Nobel Prize in 1951): 'the ease of doing psychosurgery as an office procedure, with an ice pick, aroused not consternation and horror, as it should have, but emulation . . . between 1966 and 1990 I saw dozens of these pathetic lobotomized patients—damaged, some psychically dead, murdered, by their cure.' Twenty thousand such operations had been conducted in the USA by 1951.

One of the more traumatic events of the twentieth century was the Holocaust. Yet Fromm (1974: 573), after a careful retrospective diagnosis of Hitler's character and behaviour, concludes:

[C]ertainly, had Hitler been a defendant in a court of justice, even in a most impartial one, a plea of insanity would have had no chance. Yet although in conventional terms, Hitler was not a psychotic man, in dynamic, interpersonal terms he was a very sick man . . . much more often the intensely destructive person will show a front of kindliness; courtesy; love of family, of children, of animals; he will speak of his ideals and good intentions. . . . Hence, as long as one believes that the evil man wears horns, one will not discover an evil man. . . . There are probably hundreds of Hitlers among us who would come forth if their historical hour arrived.

A similar message, of warning and of hope, emerges from the writings of concentration camp survivors (e.g. Bettelheim 1960; Levi 1989; Frankl 1964). For these camps were extreme microcosms of organizational control, and, consistent with the theme of endless variety, not all victims were virtuous, nor guards vicious. Frankl, an Auschwitz survivor, mentions that the SS commander of his satellite camp paid considerable sums from his own pocket to purchase medicines for the inmates, and was saved, on liberation by the

Americans, by the intercession of three young Hungarian Jews, whereas 'the senior camp warden, a prisoner himself, was harder than any of the SS guards. He beat the other prisoners at the slightest opportunity, while the camp commander, to my knowledge, never once lifted his hand against any of us.' Levi's account (1987: 163 ff.) of Chaim Rumkowski, the Nazi-appointed Jewish President of the Lodz ghetto, underlines the point.

So the notion of the normal individual as always rational, fair-minded, responsible, and reasonable, is supported neither by historical nor by psychological evidence, nor by comparative ethnography, especially in those repressed areas which touch him or her most deeply, or on occasions or in situations which are threatening. For there is a common tendency, observable starkly in military, civil, political, and industrial disasters, in Dixon's words (1988: 65), 'to shut out, deny, repel, suppress, misinterpret or ignore those realities of a situation which, were they consciously experienced, would endanger peace of mind'. The history of academic argument and disputes (supposedly the *locus classicus* of reason), however formally polite the publication or debate, both within and between disciplines, should be sufficient to convince the sceptical academic.

This is not to belittle reason or evidence, but rather to point to the fact that rationality and appeals to facts may have emotional roots which ignore reason and evidence (let alone moral principles), in business, in religion, in science, in academic disputes, and everyday life. And in organizations the context exacerbates this tendency if, as Dixon (1994: 307) suggests:

[T]hose personality characteristics which take people to the top and establish them as all-powerful decision-makers tend to include the very nastiest of human traits—extremes of egocentricity, insincerity, dishonesty, corruptability, cynicism, and on occasions ruthless murderous hostility towards anyone who threatens their position. Even worse, if that is possible, than the traits which take them to the top are those which they acquire upon arrival—pomposity, paranoia, and megalomaniac delusions of grandeur.

4. VALUES, EMPATHY, AND AFFILIATION

If 'respect for core human values' constitutes 'the absolute moral threshold' for all business activities (and *a fortiori* for social interaction), how can this be maintained in mass anonymous societies, in cities full of strangers, in corporations with employees in the thousands, customers in the hundreds of thousands? For such respect is rooted in the affiliative system, with loyalty graded according to closeness, where attachment, sympathy, and trust grow over time, and with rituals of sharing and giving needed constantly to reinforce the bond (Eibl-Eibesfeldt 1989: ch. 4). The natural tendency is for individuals in organizations to form groups with multiple categorizations of 'other' within the organization (based on department, location, status, skill, and so on), and outside the organization (customers, suppliers, government regulators, etc.). Add the need for control (often to an authoritarian extreme), the pressure for results, and personal ambitions and political agenda, and it is not surprising that within organizations 'respect for human dignity and basic rights' tends to be violated (or, if maintained, requires a strong degree of contextual interpretation), with a tendency to generate scenarios of the kind portrayed by Jackall and Punch. *A fortiori*, external stakeholders, unless possessed of relevant countervailing power, are likely to be seen as 'other', subjected to similar treatment—and competitors, customers, and suppliers are often themselves seeking to gain advantage, both within and without the law.

Yet this is the real world, of markets, choice, and competition, in which individuals, at home and work, conduct their daily business, enacting patterns of behaviour, of 'passions, jealousies, friendliness and active curiosity' common across the world.

The social mechanism by which order and relationship is maintained is, through roles relating to the social situation, widely understood and enacted (and the source of much comic writing)—as customer, patient, citizen, employee, motorist, and so on, with both law and custom framing the relationships and roles. However, the tendency of role relationships is to depersonalize, even in face-to-face interaction—thus Sacks (1986: x) writes of the conventional medical case history:

[T]here is no 'subject' in a narrow case history: modern case histories allude to the subject in a cursory phrase which could as well apply to a rat as a human being. The patient's essential being is very relevant in the higher reaches of neurology, and in psychology; for here the patient's personhood is essentially involved, and the study of disease and identity cannot be disjoined.

However, in much manufacturing and service the supplier has little contact or knowledge of the consumer, let alone his or her identity, with market research acting as surrogate. For such is the nature of economies of scale in mass societies. Branding, whether by product, store, or corporation, constitutes an expensive attempt to establish relationship and reputation. So distancing and depersonalization is a necessary concomitant feature of our contemporary 'real world'. But herein lies the moral danger if 'people are much more inclined to behave ruthlessly towards those they do not know' (Eibl-Eibesfeldt 1989: 719). So, accepting the depersonalized character of much contemporary society, what guides might there be (consistent with Donaldson's values)?

First, at a personal level, in relationships, in modes of thinking and discovery, one can choose between an affiliative or aversive approach—between relating or distancing. One illustration of the former, and its potential, is that of Sacks (1986; 1991), and is typically visible in good teachers, nurses, service employees, and managers. Formally, this constitutes a general form of discourse ethic, based on mutual respect (Habermas 1990). Yet the tendency for many managers has been to rely on coded information, rather than the evidence of their senses, a tendency counteracted by the phrase 'management by walking about'. For distancing isolates one not only from information, but from relevant relations. As Pym (1991: 304) puts it, discussing education:

[T]his approach stresses separation, physical distance and impersonal control. *The pattern of movement is away* and it is the only way the bureaucrat in us knows. This strategy has much in common with the philosophy of 'mutual struggle' which thrives off and sustains human anxiety and fear.

The other strategy looks very much like Kropotkin's 'mutual aid' and emphasises *patterns of movement toward and with* in the way we organise our affairs . . . where we attend to: connections, physical proximity, commonalities, conversation as keeping company with . . . Moving towards and with has the long term effect or reducing anxieties too.

This distinction is general in the social sciences—phenomenological/objectivist; cognitive/behavioural; emic/etic; experience-near/experience-distant (Geertz 1993: 56). The strategy of inclusion, of relating, of building on commonalities, of getting close, tends to deepen understanding and reveal commonalties when cultures meet. It is necessarily contextual, and, subject to personal agenda, tends towards respect for local traditions and human dignity, and lies at the core of the methodology of ethnography.

For given that living systems (including human) are characterized by variety, disorder, redundancy, messiness, and lack of fit, a relational strategy of moving closer, of involving, rather than distancing, enables both understanding and moral engagement. Fromm (1990: 485) uses the term biophilia (love of life, contrasted with necrophilia) in this context, but with more generic and emotional import:

[B]iophilia is the passionate love of life and all that is alive: it is the wish to further growth, whether in a person, plant, an idea or a social group. The biophilous person prefers to construct rather than retain . . . to be more rather than have more. He is capable of wondering . . . prefers to see something new rather than find confirmation of the old . . . loves the adventure of living more than certainty . . . sees the whole rather than only the parts, structures rather than summations . . . wants to mould by love, reason and example; not by force, by cutting things apart, by the bureaucratic manner of administering people as if they were things . . . evil is all that stifles life, narrows it down, cuts it into pieces.

Not a bad precept for the teacher and the parent; but organizations, through specialization, division, and hierarchy, produce tendencies towards the latter stereotype.

How then might such tendencies be counteracted? First, at the personal level, the agenda of relating was advocated above. But this depends on personality, which in turn is influenced by upbringing (see section 3). Second, by deliberate attempts within organizations to assert values, as advocated by Donaldson, with programmes aimed at communicating and internalizing the appropriate behaviours. In these, the example and behaviour of the influential is as important as mission statements, training programmes, and other such managerial devices, for the assertion of moral values is subject to all the well-known problems of managing culture change— and these devices are usually legitimized in terms of instrumental ends (rapid technological change, competition, globalization, and so on, threatening corporate survival). My guess is that a 'value change' programme would be legitimized in terms of a myth of achievement, rather than because such values constitute 'the absolute moral threshold' and in a world of competition, performance, and pressure, codified values are always likely to be shaded and interpreted in context.

The third line, if one acknowledges 'the seductive power and potent influence of organizational life in general, and corporate existence in particular, on "good" people' (Punch 1996: 247), is to look for external regulation, by law, policing, and public exposure—a course explored by Punch in the context of business crime. But regulation and law is an expensive and complex business, and subject to manipulation and influence, along the lines of the 1996 libel case concerning the *Guardian* newspaper (Leigh and Vulliamy 1997). Punch (1996: 272) sees the central issues as

[V]isibility, accountability, responsibility, openness, trust and morality . . . can a new managerial 'revolution' liberate executives from the moral and emotional stranglehold of the institution on their identities and consciences? In terms of regulation this also means more than the snapshot of routine control but deep penetration to the shadow, where the covert action is. This requires a determination and sophistication that equals that of bent business.

In a world of international competition and comparative advantage, regulation and policing can lead to comparative disadvantage, where competitors are not so constrained. So where the dominant ends are economic rather than communal, moral criteria *per se* are always likely to be under threat.

So what way forward is there, if one acknowledges the tendency in organization and in depersonalized market transactions to bracket private moralities and 'to shut out, deny, repel, misinterpret or ignore those realities of a situation which, were they consciously experienced, would endanger peace of mind' (Dixon 1994), and the universal tendency to care less about the distant (remote local wars, famines, exploitation, disease)? First, to acknowledge that within corporations, within industries, standards of conduct systematically vary (cf. Mars 1982) and then concentrate on influencing internal standards, along the lines of Donaldson's project, or on influencing external regulation, as discussed by Punch. Both these approaches are essentially top-down, within-system strategies. The second alternative is more bottom-up, based on the communal, cooperative, convivial, and relational (Pym 1980; 1991), and visible in a plethora of contemporary self-help initiatives among the young and the idealistic. The latter acknowledges that we 'have created a world for which we are not biologically made' (Eibl-Eibesfeldt 1989: 718), and attempts to rebuild one more consonant with our biology and common humanity.

REFERENCES

Bettelheim, B. (1960), *The Informed Heart* (Glencoe, IL: Free Press).
—— (1991), *The Uses of Enchantment: The Meaning and Importance of Fairy Tales* (Harmondsworth: Penguin).
Dalton, M. (1959), *Men Who Manage: Fusions of Feeling and Theory in Administration* (New York: John Wiley).
Dixon, N. (1988), *Our Own Worst Enemy* (London: Futura).
—— (1994), 'Disastrous Decisions', *The Psychologist*, 7: 303–7.
Donaldson, T. (1996), 'Values in Tension: Ethics Away from Home', *Harvard Business Review*, September–October: 48–62.
Earl, M. J. (1983) (ed.), *Perspectives on Management: An Interdisciplinary Analysis* (Oxford: Oxford University Press).
Eibl-Eibesfeldt, I. (1989), *Human Ethology* (New York: Aldine de Gruyter).
Foucault, M. (1991), *Discipline and Punish: The Birth of the Prison*, trans. by A. Sheridan (Harmondsworth: Penguin).
Frankl, V. E. (1964), *Man's Search for Meaning: An Introduction to Logotherapy*, 2nd edn, trans. I. Lasch (London: Hodder and Houghton).
Fromm, E. (1990), *The Anatomy of Human Destructiveness* (Harmondsworth: Penguin).
Geertz, C. (1993), *Local Knowledge* (London: Fontana).
Gowler, D. and Legge, K. (1983), 'The Meaning of Management and the Management of Meaning', in Earl (1983): 197–233.
Habermas, J. (1990), *Moral Consciousness and Communicative Action*, trans. C. Lenhardt and S. W. Nicholsen (Cambridge: Polity).
Jackall, R. (1988), *Moral Mazes* (New York: Oxford University Press).
Kets de Vries, M. and Miller, D. (1984), *The Neurotic Organization* (San Francisco: Jossey-Bass).
Korten, D. C. (1995), *When Corporations Rule the World* (London: Earthscan).
Larmore, C. E. (1987), *Patterns of Moral Complexity* (Cambridge: Cambridge University Press).
Leach, E. (1982), *Social Anthropology* (Glasgow: Fontana).
Leigh, D. and Vulliamy, E. (1997), *Sleaze: The Corruption of Parliament* (London: Fourth Estate).
Levi, P. (1987), *Moments of Reprieve*, trans. by R. Feldman (London: Abacus).
—— (1989), *The Drowned and the Saved*, trans. R. Rosenthal (London: Michael Joseph).
Lucas, J. R. (1993), *Responsibility* (Oxford: Clarendon).
Mars, G. (1982), *Cheats at Work: An Anthropology of Workplace Crime* (London: Allen and Unwin).
Ouchi, W. (1981), *Theory Z: How American Business Can Meet the Japanese Challenge* (Reading, MA: Addison-Wesley).
Pennings, J. M. and Associates (1985) (eds), *Organizational Strategy and Change* (San Francisco: Jossey Bass).

Punch, M. (1996), *Dirty Business: Exploring Corporate Misconduct* (London: Sage).

Pym, D. (1980), 'Towards the Dual Economy and Emancipation from Employment', *Futures*, 12: 223–37.

—— (1991), 'The Axe, The Chainsaw and Education', *The Raven*, 4: 324–32.

Sacks, O. (1986), *The Man Who Mistook His Wife For a Hat* (London: Picador).

—— (1991), *Seeing Voices: A Journey into the World of the Deaf* (London: Picador).

—— (1995), *An Anthropologist on Mars: Seven Paradoxical Tales* (London: Picador).

Starbuck, W. H. (1985), 'Acting First and Thinking Later: Theory Versus Reality in Strategic Change', in Pennings (1985): 336–72.

Woodward, N. (1991), 'Management as a Cultural Artefact', *Gestion 2000*, 2: 49–66.

10

Education and Business

RICHARD PRING

1. INTRODUCTION

THE relation between the worlds of education and of business is complex and needs to be examined very carefully. The relationship is particularly problematic when there is the attempt to make education more relevant to business, or to see how those who work in industry and commerce might help to improve our schools. Furthermore, the problem is partly ethical. That is, the problem of relating the one world to the other lies in deeper, and often unacknowledged, questions about what makes life worth living, about the values which ought to guide people, about the kinds of relationship which bind people together for different purposes—indeed, about the very language through which business and educational activities might be described and evaluated.

It was not ever so. Until comparatively recently, the two worlds seemed far apart. That of education was concerned with learning those things, and developing those qualities, which helped one become an educated person. And such a person, though at home perhaps in the University Library, might have no interest in, or skills relevant to, the world of business. Indeed, in England, it was typical of the great 'public' schools of the nineteenth century, of many of the private schools of the twentieth century, and of the universities created in the 1960s and 1970s that they should be distant from the locations of commerce and of industry. Schools and universities should, as Oakeshott argued, be more like monasteries, free from the distractions and bustle of working life: 'In short, "School" is "monastic" in respect of being a place apart where excellencies may be heard because the din of worldly laxities and partialities is silenced or abated' (Oakeshott 1972: 69). An age of 'romance'—in which one explores ideas, enjoys poetry, engages in the arts and humanities—should precede the age of 'usefulness'.

Much, however, has happened to change this view which brings to the fore the relationship of education and business. First, there is a widespread concern in late twentieth-century Britain, which is paralleled elsewhere, that, as a country, we are falling behind others in economic competitiveness, and this is blamed partly upon our schools and universities. Hence, our schools and universities need to change both what is taught and how it is taught so that students may be better prepared for the world of work.

Second, education is expensive. It costs the taxpayer far too much. Public education is too much of a strain upon public funds. Therefore, there is a need to privatize much of education and training, and to put it in the hands of business so that it can receive private funding.

Third, much education and training is thought to be poorly managed. Resources, expensive and increasingly in short supply, so we are told, need to be more carefully targeted and 'audited'. Hence, the world of education is thought to benefit from being managed like a business. Indeed, it is seen as a business.

One can see, therefore, that in three ways—education as a preparation for business, education as financed by business, and education as managed like a business—there is a shifting relation between the worlds of education and business, such that the former has taken on features which would have been quite foreign only a short time ago.

In this paper, I wish to illustrate each of these different sorts of relation, to show how they are in danger of undermining a particular idea of liberal education. And yet that liberal view itself needs to be examined critically. This I shall do. It may be the case that there is something illiberal and narrow in a view of education which ignores or disdains the economic and commercial context in which it takes place.

In pursuing this argument, I shall:

(1) remind the reader of what is signified by 'education', especially within a particular liberal tradition;
(2) rehearse the criticism of that tradition by those who wish, in various ways, to link the world of education with that of business;
(3) indicate how this change of emphasis is reflected in the changing control and language of education—and in a morally impoverished concept of education;

(4) suggest how the liberal tradition and that of economic and social relevance might be reconciled.

2. CONCEPT OF 'EDUCATION'

We talk about an educational system—namely, the institutions and the organized activities through which learning is systematically encouraged and promoted. In that sense 'education' is a morally neutral term. We can talk, in this sense, of the Spartan or the Nazi educational system, whilst disapproving of the understandings and qualities systematically learnt within it.

Nonetheless, such a system would be distinguished from one which is concerned exclusively with specialized training, and, viewed from the inside of the system, it would have picked out those skills, kinds of knowledge, qualities, attitudes, etc. which the organizers of the system (for example, the state or the religious order) thought worthwhile. Indeed, viewed from the position of the participant, an educational system would have selected certain kinds of learning to be of greater value than others.

Put in another way, any educational system has built into it an idea of success or failure, of coming up to standard or of failing to do so. Those who succeed and who come up to standard would be seen as educated persons. The idea of an educated person contains a particular view of what knowledge, qualities, and skills are valuable and transform the person into someone better. 'Education' presupposes a particular view of what is worth learning, of what qualities are worth acquiring.

Let us take this analysis a little further. 'Education' would seem to be an evaluative concept—it picks out those activities which lead to the kind of learning which is valued. The 'educated person' is one who has acquired those qualities, etc. which within a particular culture have come to be thought worthwhile—and no doubt these change as cultures vary and as different virtues are highlighted at different times and in different places. 'Enterprise' is a recently arrived 'virtue', and many would nowadays put 'enterprise' and 'entrepreneurship' amongst the qualities which an educated person should have acquired. But others would not agree, and the disagreement is essentially a moral one concerning the sort of person (and the sort of society) which we seek to produce through an educational system.

The liberal tradition of education which we have inherited emphasizes those qualities of mind—the capacity to know and understand—through which individuals are empowered to think for themselves, to examine critically the ideas through which they have come to perceive the world, to recognize misrepresentations and distorted accounts of that world, to explore further ways of seeing things. Indeed, as Oakeshott argues, we live in a world of ideas (the concepts and beliefs and the understandings through which experience is sieved and made sense of), those ideas are the product of a conversation which has transpired between the generations, and education is the introduction of the next generation to that conversation—whereby they are able to listen to, to come to understand, and possibly to add to, the voices of poetry and of literature, of science and of history, of philosophy and of morality.

We might summarize such a view of liberal education as those activities through which young people are initiated into what is considered to be worthwhile understandings, such understandings giving the learner a broad cognitive perspective as befits a person who is to make sense of the complex world he or she inhabits (see Peters 1965: chs. 1 and 5).

This view of liberal education, which has so captivated the system of education that we have inherited, is, of course, clearly reflected in Newman's *Idea of a University*: 'liberal education, viewed in itself, is simply the cultivation of the intellect, as such, and its object is nothing more or less than intellectual excellence' (1852: 121). Furthermore, it permeated the critique of prevailing practices in the American schools and universities which was offered by Bloom (1987) in his *Closing of the American Mind*. It persists in the recent Victor Cook lectures given by Lord Quinton (1992) and by Professor O'Hear (1992). They emphasize 'the importance of traditional learning' (see O'Hear 1987), namely, the study of those subjects of the curriculum through which are transmitted the kinds of knowledge, understanding, judgement, sensitivities, and appreciations which we have come to value in the educated person. Through such subjects, appropriately engaged with, the young learner becomes acquainted with 'the best that has been thought and said', thereby being transformed as a person—that is, in those qualities and forms of judgement which affect one most profoundly as a person. To that extent, education is essentially a moral enterprise, and the difficult and complex arguments concerning what is worth learning (what is the best that has been thought and said in literature, what historical knowledge is required of a person from this or that cultural tradition, what religious and moral concepts are indispensable to a distinctively human life, what aesthetic sensitivities and appreciations are to be encouraged) take us into the realm of ethics.

I want briefly to summarize this idea of liberal education. First, its primary aim is to develop the intellect. Second, that development of the intellect requires the acquisition of the different forms of know-ledge and experience through which one comes to understand the physical world in which one is located, the social and economic world in which one acts, the moral world through which one forms relation-ships with others or through which one is inspired by ideals, and the aesthetic world through which one finds delight and pleasure in physical things. Third, the point or the value of being apprenticed to such intellectual, aesthetic, and moral traditions requires little further justification than reference to their intrinsic value—'this is what it is to live a distinctively human life'. Fourth, such acquisition of worthwhile learning is a demanding task; many fail through lack of motivation or indeed lack of capacity, and remain trapped in their ignorance or moral blindness; and thus it requires teachers who will mediate the best in that world of ideas to the often unwilling learner. Finally, the task of education—its control and its direction—must be in the hands of the educational experts, those who, by dint of their own learning, are 'authorities' within the different kinds of know-ledge and understanding.

We have inherited such a view of education, a system of teaching, dominated by 'the authorities' within the universities, in which different subjects, which encapsulate the key ideas through which we believe experience should be organized and understood, are transmitted to the next generation. Such control has traditionally been exercised through examinations, and more recently in Britain through a national curriculum which prescribes what should be taught and in what order—which prescribes, in other words, a twenty-first-century British view of the 'educated person'.

3. CRITICISM OF THE LIBERAL IDEAL—THE WORLD OF WORK

There has been, however, in the late twentieth century, growing criticism of this liberal ideal. One kind of criticism has been that such an emphasis upon intellectual excellence for its own sake too easily ignores the economic relevance of what is learnt. And that is important. First, the quality of life for each individual requires the capacity to be economically successful; the pursuit of intellectual and aesthetic excellence generally speaking requires a certain amount of economic well-being. Second, the fortunes of each individual depend upon the good of the community as a whole, and that 'good', in turn, requires the abolition of poverty, a degree of prosperity, a buoyant employment market, and so on. The idea of an educated person cannot be divorced from the economic and social context in which that person is to live a fully human life. The qualities and understandings required for a full life are different in a feudal society from those required within a capitalist or post-capitalist society. The technological revolution brought about by information technology requires different kinds of understanding if persons are to understand and to behave intelligently in the world in which they find themselves.

Of course, there may not be an opposition between intellectual excellence, as an aim of education, and economic relevance. As John Stuart Mill argued in his inaugural address in 1867:

[Although the object of universities] is not to make skilful lawyers, or physicians, or engineers, but capable and cultivated human beings, [nonetheless] men are men before they are lawyers and if you make them capable and sensible men, they will make themselves capable and sensible lawyers—what professional men should carry away with them from an University is not professional knowledge, but that which should direct the use of their professional knowledge, and bring the light of general culture to illuminate the technicalities of a special pursuit.

For Mill, the truly educated person was well prepared intellectually and morally to engage in the more economically and professionally relevant occupations to be pursued after the university. The best preparation lay in the formation of the intellect and of moral sensitivity, not in vocationally relevant skills and knowledge.

Such a view, however, is now not so widely shared. Greater vocational relevance, and more explicit links with the world of industry and commerce are called for from different quarters— from government (see in Britain, for example, DE and DES 1985*a* and 1985*b*; DES 1991; and DE 1994), from employers (see, for example, CBI 1989 and 1993), and from students and their parents. Indeed, ever since the establishment in Britain of the Manpower

Services Commission (MSC) in 1974, there has been a government-inspired attempt to transform education into a more economically relevant, business-related system.

Prime Minister Callaghan's Ruskin College speech in 1976 set out the agenda. In schools, the launch of the Technical and Vocational Education Initiative (TVEI) in 1982 backed that agenda, over a decade or so, with over one billion pounds sterling. Enterprise and entrepreneurship became key words in the educational list of qualities to be acquired, and the spirit of TVEI entered universities through the 'Enterprise in Higher Education' initiative of the MSC. Business studies and economics became the fastest growing subjects in schools, colleges, and universities. City Technology Colleges were created in which business would be encouraged to sponsor schools and have their names immortalized in the newly named institutions. There is even a Burger King school in East London—a form of sponsorship imported from the United States. A range of vocational qualifications entered schools, such as the Certificate of Pre-Vocational Education and the General National Vocational Qualification. And many extra activities were promoted and taken up, such as 'Young Enterprise', whereby young people are encouraged to establish small businesses within schools. 'Enterprise Awareness in Teacher Education' enjoyed a brief life. Core skills—skills which were economically relevant—were to be incorporated within syllabuses for public examinations.

This emphasis upon a greater vocational orientation might be contrasted with the liberal ideal outlined above—competence at work rather than intellectual excellence, subject-matter selected from an analysis of what that competence requires rather than from the inherited forms of knowledge, usefulness rather than intrinsic worth as the dominant purpose and value, workplace learning rather than 'a place set apart', and the authority and control in the hands of employers rather than in those of the professional educators.

This contrast is reflected in the changing structure, control, and content of education. TVEI set out the criteria which should govern curriculum initiatives from 14 to 18—links with the business community, economic awareness, technological understanding and skills, knowledge of career routes and possibilities, vocational orientation, basic skills of communication and numeracy. 'Enterprise in Higher Education' encouraged entrepreneurial activities in universities. Employers were encouraged to become governors of schools and people from business and commerce were encouraged to work in schools so that business-related knowledge and skills might be imparted. Business was invited to sponsor schools—a privatization of what previously had been public institutions with local accountability.

But 'the new vocationalism' is not a straightforward or simple matter, as is shown in recent accounts (see Wellington 1993; Coffey 1992). The recently created National Curriculum totally ignored the achievements of TVEI, and reasserted a more traditional under-standing of education. Indeed, the contrast between liberal education and vocational relevance remains, and is becoming institutionalized further in the developments of Curriculum 14–16, as the Dearing Report (1996), recommending a three-track system of qualifications, affects the subsequent structure of education.

My interest here however is more fundamental than that. I wish to show that, in the absence of a much more careful analysis of the liberal tradition of education, the new 'relevance to business' might undermine education as essentially a moral enterprise, causing us to neglect the moral questions which education is centrally concerned with. There is a level at which such a possibility is obvious— namely, where what is taught is conditional upon the sponsorship of business and where there might be commercial interests in pro-moting a certain curriculum content in health education, say, or in environmental studies. But, more deeply and less obviously, the problem arises through the changing control and language of education.

4. CHANGING CONTROL AND LANGUAGE OF EDUCATION

A distinguished historian, Dr Marjorie Reeves, was appointed to the Central Advisory Council for Education (England) in 1947. When she asked the Permanent Secretary to the Ministry of Education what the main function of the members of the Council was, she was told it was 'to be prepared to die at the first ditch as soon as the politicians try to get their hands on education'.

This attitude towards political and central control of education was, in Britain, deeply rooted in the liberal tradition which I have so briefly described and which was suspicious of political control over what people should learn and how they should think. The role of the state was simply to make sure that there were sufficient resources, a sufficient supply of teachers and an adequate legal and organizational framework within which all children might be educated according to their 'age, ability and aptitude'. 'The secret garden of the curriculum' was not the government's concern. The government had no special wisdom which warranted its interference in the content of what should be taught or in the method whereby it might be taught. Education, at every level, was in the hands of the teachers, for they, by reason of their education, participated in that conversation whereof Oakeshott spoke, and, by reason of their experience and training, were able to translate such conversation into the language and mode of representation intelligible to the young learner. Indeed, teaching was essentially a transaction between teacher and learner, as the teacher (mediating inherited understandings and values) engaged with the learner who might value quite different things and who might conceptualize experience in quite different ways. The idea of 'negotiation' belies the authority of the teacher, but certainly the relationship within the liberal ideal is more akin to a negotiation of ideas between thinking and critical people (however immature the learners might be, for the good teacher takes their thinking seriously) than it is to the pursuit of clear and measurable objectives—decided by state or politicians or business executives, irrespective of the perceptions or interests or understandings of the learner.

To be educated was to be admitted to a certain community—a community that, having mastered the arts of conversation about many different matters, sought to develop that conversation further, and, in doing so, introduce a new generation to it. Good history teachers would seek to convey the delights as well as the skills of a mode of understanding which had transformed their views of the world, and which (it was hoped) would transform the view of those in their charge. The science teacher would convey those ideas without which one would not be able to think or speak or act as a physicist, chemist, or biologist. Indeed, as the American psychologist Jerome Bruner (1960) argued, the curriculum of our schools needed the combined effort of both those in the universities at the frontiers of knowledge, who would be able to say what are the key ideas which structure the thinking in this or that intellectual discipline, and those in schools who would have the pedagogical expertise to say how those key ideas might be translated, in an intellectually respectable way, into the mode of representation of the learners themselves.

The control of education, therefore, within the liberal tradition, lay within the community of educators. Such a community might be dominated by the universities. After all, was it not within such places that the logical structure of knowledge was defined and protected? And was it not the job of the schools to benefit from this university-based wisdom in setting the educational objectives for their pupils? Nowhere was there seen to be a role either for government or for business in determining what content should be taught, for neither government nor business had any special insight into the objectives and values of education. Such a tradition is the preserve of the professional educators.

In *Decline of Donnish Dominion*, A. H. Halsey (1995) describes the gradual shift from such a conception of the university community.

[A] new conception—the modern university—is thought of . . . as based on an emerging redefinition of knowledge as product rather than process. A scientific rather than a cultural definition of knowledge emphasizes research more than teaching, intellect more than sensibility. A reconstruction of intellectual life displaces humanism by academicism; technology replaces education. The university is more fissiparous, less integrated, more anxious to respond to external influences, less separate from the mainstream of profane life, and therefore more serviceable as well as more pliant to the power of the state . . . less independent of government and the pressures of industry.

This shift has, of course, taken place gradually and over a long period of time, but the 1990s have seen it hastened, no doubt for the reasons which I outlined above, namely, the desire to control the relevance of learning to economic and social goals as perceived by government, the tendency to control and make accountable that which depends on public funds, and the domination of business models of management which seem incompatible with the more collegiate form of a 'community of educators'. Hence, the anxiety 'to respond to external influences, less separate from the mainstream of profane life, and therefore more serviceable . . . to the power of the state . . . less independent of government and the pressures of industry'.

There are two, interrelated aspects of this lesser 'independence of government and the pressures of industry'. They are, first, the greater control of the content and values of education by those who are not professionally engaged in it, and, second, a changed language of education which reflects and makes possible that control. Consider, for instance, the announcement of an international conference 'Managing Diversity Through ISO 9000':

The Vice-Chancellor of the University of W is proud to host this one day international conference to give colleagues in Higher Education Institutions and other stakeholding organizations a unique opportunity to hear—first hand from people who did the job—why and how the University . . . achieved University-wide registration to BS5750 Part 1 (ISO 9001) 1987 (now named BS EN ISO 9001; 1984). . . . We are not trying to sell you a Quality Management System . . . [but] giving you direct insight into the *process* of developing your own Quality Management System.

The language of such systems is that of goal-setting, of precision of objectives in the light of which those goals might be evaluated (were they reached or not?), the logical separation of those goals from the means of attaining them, of the teacher as someone who 'delivers a curriculum' which is likely to attain those goals, of the learner as a 'client' or 'customer' who may want to purchase those outcomes (to help which, education and training vouchers might be distributed). This is reflected in a report into higher education by Her Majesty's Inspectorate (HMI 1991).

As public interest in management efficiency and institutional effectiveness has increased, there has been a general acknowledgement of the need to use performance indicators to monitor the . . . system . . . some concrete information on the extent to which the benefits expected from educational expenditure are actually secured . . . an approach finding most favour is the classification of performance indicators within an input, output process model.

The 'Quality Management Systems' have imported to education the language of inputs (of which 'student intakes', socio-economically described, are a significant component), of outputs (amongst which test-score outcomes have an important place), and of processes as the intervening variables between inputs and outputs which make the difference. Furthermore, given certain 'performance indicators' whereby the output achievements might be measured, frequent 'audits' of the institutions will show how much 'value-addedness' has been attained through the intervening processes (which on the whole refer to the 'delivery of a curriculum'). And, as money gets tight, so institutions are expected to make 'efficiency gains'—that is, do the same work for less money.

Such language, taken from the world of business and supporting a particular mode of management, gives an air of precision, of measurable and manipulable factors, of clear and limited criteria of educational success. But it is part of a wider network of concepts which reinforces a particular conception of education. The curriculum, as I have indicated, becomes one 'variable', amongst several possible ones, which is 'delivered'—and, indeed, with the emphasis upon measurable goals only contingently related to the learning processes which might or might not lead to those goals, so the 'time-serving' in a particular community of learners is seen as unimportant. The important thing is that one displays the competences or the intended 'outputs'. The 'Quality Management Systems' attach particular importance to the 'management' of the system of learning, including the regular assessment of the quite explicit learning objectives which are usually printed out in long lists.

This language of 'teaching' as the 'delivery of a curriculum', of 'professional judgement' as measurement against preconceived 'performance indicators', of that interaction between teacher and learner as the 'process variable' between 'input and output factors', of 'learning' as measurable behaviour which demonstrates 'value-addedness', is a far cry from the language of 'conversation between the generations of mankind', of learning as striving 'to make sense of' experience, of education as an initiation into a world of ideas, a community of thinkers, and a worthwhile form of life. Educational institutions become different places, different sorts of community, with different aims and criteria of assessment. Teachers, as deliverers of someone else's curriculum, are excluded from the deliberations over what is worthwhile or what is the quality of life to which the young learner should be introduced. For many excellent teachers in both university and school, the humanities are no longer the area of the curriculum in which 'teachers emphasize their common humanity with the students' as they explore together the themes of literature or the events of history or the explorations of philosophers (see Pring 1995).

Furthermore, just as the educational institutions at every level take over the language of management borrowed from business, so do they perceive themselves operating in a 'market', the regulations for which are constantly adapted by those in whose interest the market is intended to operate. The regulations—the national curriculum, the differentiated manner of funding according to government formulae, the process of assessment and public audit, the creation of league tables based on measurable outcomes—provide the framework within which schools and universities compete for custom and money, rather than cooperate in the pursuit of learning, in the interchange of ideas, and in the education of the next generation.

5. EDUCATION AND BUSINESS RECONSIDERED

To educate and to engage in business are two quite different activities. In no way does that mean that the one should not serve the other. But they are different and they should not be confused. There is a danger, mainly through the concern for greater 'relevance' of a major public expenditure, to model educational activities on those of business, but that would be a mistake because it would undermine what is distinctively educational, in particular the moral nature of the educational enterprise.

The aims of education concern 'learning', but not any kind of learning. They are concerned with those sorts of learning which enable the students to become educated persons. That requires an entry into the world of ideas through which, given the state of public knowledge and understanding, all according to their abilities are enabled to appreciate and understand the material, social, and moral worlds which they have to inhabit. Such an initiation requires selection of those understandings, skills, and qualities which are considered to be worth learning. Of course, such judgements of what is worthwhile are disputed—and the disagreements are essentially moral ones about what sort of life is worth living. But the kinds of learning which students are introduced to—those within literature, history, social studies, economics, the sciences—are precisely those which enable the students to enter into that debate—to consider for themselves, in the light of evidence, not just the means to worthwhile goals, but the goals themselves. As Bruner (1966) argued in defence of 'Man: a Course of Study', education poses the three questions: What makes one human? How did one become so? How might one become more so? To be educated is to be able to pursue the central questions of value, but in an informed and intelligent way, knowing, however, that there are no certain and non-controversial answers to such important questions. To that extent, education is an introduction to the conversation between the generations, and like all good conversations, one cannot predict or predetermine the outcome. Good teachers are those who, from whatever their intellectual vantage point, do something to enable the learner to enter into that conversation and to take seriously the search for value.

It is hoped that such an educated person would thereby be, as Mill argued, better equipped to conduct business or to engage in the professions. Such persons would have developed general qualities of intellect which, one suspects, would enable them to be more thoughtful and to see things from a broader perspective. One would hope that the educated person would be more effective in reflecting upon the moral dimension to his or her occupation. The aims of business as such, however, are different, usually concerned with the selling of a product, generally for a profit, for which particular sorts of learning are deemed necessary, not as worthwhile in themselves, but as a means to the purposes of the business. The language of precise objectives, of measurable outcomes, of value-neutral goals set by managers, of performance indicators, of clients, and of value-addedness makes sense within that context.

Of course, the liberally educated person would be expected to have the knowledge, qualities, and attitudes required for intelligent living within such a commercial and business world. Too often, 'education' is contrasted with the useful or with the economically relevant. The educated person, however, should have the theoretical and practical knowledge necessary for making a contribution to such a society rather than being a parasite within it. But also such a person would have the intellectual capacity and the moral sensibility to challenge, where necessary, the values which inhere within it. Any idea of the truly human life—of the life worth living, reflected as much as possible in our institutions and forms of social life—must have a productive economic base. The educated person cannot treat with disdain the practical know-how and theoretical understanding which shape his or her life, for he or she could not exercise self-determination in such a state of ignorance. For that reason, the content of any society's educational programme must be constantly open to revision, constantly keeping up with the relevant commercial and industrial understanding of that society.

But more than that. Each person, in seeking that quality of life which makes it worth living, must be concerned with very practical, personal and economically relevant questions—such as the sort of career and occupation which he or she intends to pursue. As Dewey (1916) so forcefully argued, a liberal education has to be vocational in this broad sense—but too often, disdainful of the world of practical and commercial matters, it has not been:

A vocation means nothing but a direction of life activities as renders them perceptibly significant to a person because of the consequences they accomplish, and also useful to his associates. The opposite of a career is neither leisure nor culture, but aimlessness, capriciousness, the absence of cumulative achievement in experience, on the personal side, and idle play, a parasitic dependence on the others on the social side. Occupation is a concrete term for continuity. (p. 307)

Furthermore, the pursuit of such vocational ends, broadly conceived, should, even in the case of very practical and work-related skills, be educational. Such skills might be acquired critically, with a moral sensibility nurtured through example and questioning, with an aesthetic appreciation developed through sensitive guidance. Indeed, it must surely be the aim of education to get rid of the false dualisms between the liberal and the economically useful, between the intellectually respectable and the practically relevant, between the intrinsically worthwhile and the prudential, for the useful and the relevant can be taught in a manner which develops the intellect and refines the emotions and forms the critical faculties. The same activity can serve both business and educational values. And this is not just a dream. In Britain, it was part of the thinking and initiatives within the curriculum developments of the 1970s and 1980s, sadly neglected and destroyed in the centrally controlled curriculum of the 1990s.

Nonetheless, although the same learning activities can be both educational and serve the economic needs of the society and the individual—although the same learning might be worthwhile in itself and economically useful—such activities and learning are logically open to different sorts of description and evaluation. The same activity can be conceptualized, and thereby evaluated, in different ways. The danger is, as I have argued, that the distinctively educational descriptions and evaluations, which refer to the moral character of education, are being subverted by the very different language borrowed from the worlds of management and business.

REFERENCES

Bloom, A. D. (1987), *The Closing of the American Mind: How Higher Education Has Failed Democracy and Impoverished the Souls of Today's Students* (New York: Simon and Schuster).

Bruner, J. S. (1960), *The Process of Education* (Cambridge, MA: Harvard University Press).

—— (1966), *Towards a Theory of Instruction* (Cambridge, MA: Harvard University Press).

CBI (1989), *Towards a Skills Revolution* (London: Confereration of British Industry).

—— (1993), *A Credit to your Career: Routes for Success* (London: Confederation of British Industry).

Coffey, D. (1992), *Schools and Work* (London: Cassell).

DE and DES (1985*a*), *Education and Training for Young People* (London: HMSO).

—— (1985*b*), *Working Together: Education and Training* (London: HMSO).

DES (1991), *Education and Training for the 21st Century* (London: HMSO).

DE (1994), *Competitiveness: Helping Businesses to Win* (London: HMSO).

Dearing Report (1996), *16–19: Review of Qualifications* (London: SCAA).

Dewey, J. (1916), *Democracy and Education* (New York: Free Press).

Fuller, T. (1972) (ed.), *Michael Oakeshott on Education* (New Haven: Yale University Press).

Haldane, J. (1992) (ed.), *Education, Values and Culture. Victor Cook Memorial Lectures* (St Andrews: Centre for Philosophy and Public Affairs).

Halsey, A. H. (1995), *Decline of Donnish Dominion: The British Academic Professions in the Twentieth Century* (Oxford: Clarendon Press).

HMI (1991), *Higher Education in the Polytechnics and the Colleges* (London: HMSO).

Mill, J. S. (1867), 'Inaugural Lecture at the University of St Andrews', in Cavanagh, F. A. (1931), *James and John Stuart Mill on Education* (Cambridge: Cambridge University Press).

Newman, J. H. (1852), *The Idea of a University* (London: Longman, Green and Co.) (1912 edition).

Oakeshott, M. (1972), 'Education; the Engagement and its Frustration', in Fuller (1972): 63–94.

O'Hear, A. (1987), 'The Importance of Traditional Learning', *British Journal of Educational Studies*, 35: 102–14.

—— (1992), 'Values, Education and Culture', in Haldane (1992): 40–69.

Peters, R. S. (1965), *Ethics and Education* (London: Allen and Unwin).

Pring, R. A. (1995), *Closing the Gap: Liberal Education and Vocational Preparation* (London: Hodder and Stoughton).

Quinton, A. (1992), 'Culture, Education and Values', in Haldane (1992): 11–39.

Wellington, J. J. (1993) (ed.), *The Work Related Curriculum: Challenging the Vocational Imperative* (London: Kogan Page).

11

Teaching Ethics to Managers: Contemporary Problems and a Traditional Solution

J. THOMAS WHETSTONE

THIS chapter has two parts. The first identifies the major problem with business ethics to be an increasing fragmentation between academics and business practitioners. This points to the need for a clearer understanding of the practical role of business ethics teaching in helping people to improve their workplace behaviour. Teaching is not succeeding in this, based upon the all-too-frequent assessment that the field of business ethics is irrelevant or at most only of public relations value in the 'real world' of business. Specific deficiencies with much of current teaching include an over-emphasis on cognitive analysis of individual acts, a preoccupation with difficult dilemmas, and the message that often no correct solution exists. The most comprehensive of several proposed solutions is to promote the development of personal moral character of ethical actors as well as their cognitive decision-making techniques. This would include teaching virtues to those people, primarily adults, preparing for and already engaged in business practice. This proposed solution not only addresses the current teaching deficiencies, but also serves to focus business ethics research, teaching, and practice on the improvement of behaviour.

The second part proceeds to practical implementation. It discusses ways that qualities of virtue might be deliberately developed, in particular through re-emphasizing the practice of personal mentoring in the workplace.

1. PROBLEMS WITH TEACHING BUSINESS ETHICS

Business ethics is now taught in some form at most business schools in North America and at many in Europe. Nevertheless, some still perceive it as resting outside the circle of academic respectability. A particular complaint in the UK and Europe is a lack of culturally appropriate (i.e. non-US) case materials (Dunfee and Cowton 1993). But even American colleges and universities are not moving fast enough to build ethics into their graduate or undergraduate business curricula. Although many agree that ethics is crucial, very few institutions, fewer than 10 per cent, actually *require* that their business graduates take a *separate course* in business ethics. There are many reasons for this low figure. The difficulty of finding room in the curriculum is one common reason. Some programmes have integrated ethics into existing courses, which is a start—but not the whole answer (Hoffman and Fedo 1994: 148).

On the corporate front, some executives use ethics and hire ethicists primarily to dress up their images, or to draft ethics codes that support their current strategies—instead of seriously trying to enhance the ethical culture of their organizations (Sorell and Hendry 1994). Business ethics consultants 'are rarely asked to do much more than run a few sporadic training programmes in ethics' (Hoffman and Fedo 1994).

The Problem of Fragmentation

Thus, in spite of its growth as an academic field, all is not well with business ethics. The most noticeable problem is the breakdown in communication between those academics who research and teach business ethics and the men and women who practise business. There is fragmentation within the research community as well—between normative theorists and positive empiricists (Robertson 1993*b*; also COWTON).

Arguing that moral behaviour is the product of training rather than reflection, Levin (1989) proclaims that ethics courses are 'useless', 'pointless exercises' that fail to deal with real-life issues. Solomon (1994) observes that there is a suspicious gap between the practical aims and personal virtues promoted by business ethics advocates and the often abstract and dialectical contents of the courses that business ethicists teach. French (1994) declares that most contemporary ethics bores students because its favoured theories have abstracted the individual actor almost off the stage of meaningful moral decision-making. Although some communication difficulties are to be expected in any developing field, the extent and persistence of miscommunication associated with business ethics suggest a lack of consensus as to what business ethics is and what its role should be. Indeed, the question hovering behind almost every debate in this field is, 'What is business ethics?' (Olson 1995: 371).

The fragmentation of business ethics became a topic for public debate after Stark (1993) boldly charged that the work of many academics is largely irrelevant for most managers, not because they are hostile to the idea of business ethics, but because it has failed to provide much concrete help. Managers would welcome help in identifying ethical courses of action in difficult situations (e.g., choosing between two 'right' options) and in navigating those courses where the right course is clearly known, but where real-world competitive and institutional pressures lead even well-intentioned managers astray. Indeed, the traditional purpose of teaching someone courage is to make them courageous—not to allow them to define it and defend it in debate.

The business ethics establishment in the United States reacted quickly to Stark's article. At short notice a panel was convened at the August 1993 Society for Business Ethics meeting in Atlanta. This group basically agreed to condemn it, and several letters from prominent business ethicists, including Duska (1993), and Werhane (1993) criticized the article. Although much of Stark's analysis has failed to withstand critical attack, Monast (1994) observed that intelligent and altruistic practitioners seem to agree with its thrust that business ethics research and teaching is not proving helpful to business practitioners.

The Persistence of the Problem

The differing views as to what business ethics is and should be is not surprising since it is a burgeoning field at the intersection of several disciplines. Moreover, the identity problem is not a new phenomenon; over a decade ago Phillip Lewis (1985) wrote 'Defining "Business Ethics": Like Nailing Jello to the Wall', reporting on his survey of definitions used in textbooks, articles, and surveys. Documenting, although perhaps inadvertently, the persistence of the identity problem is Randall and Gibson's (1990) finding that most studies of ethical decision-making fail to offer a clear definition of ethical conduct.

What Business Ethics Should Teach

What is the role of business ethics? In particular, what should business ethics teach? Until recently a British or American ethicist generally adopted a value-neutral, objective posture, merely describing how people talk about what they ought to do. Gellner observed: 'No one at Oxford would dream of telling undergraduates what they ought to do, the kind of life they ought to lead' (Mehta 1965: 29). But business ethics courses '*can* and *should* improve business behavior, and if they don't, there's not much point to them' (Duska 1991: 336). If ethics does seek to change the ways humans behave, the ethicist is necessarily involved with attempting to change the values and behaviours of humans. Therefore, if it is to answer the question attributed to Socrates, 'How should one live?', ethics must be normative as well as grounded in description.

Teaching is a key link between business ethics research and practice. It communicates research findings to practitioners and to other researchers, and serves as a contact point with practitioners, allowing teachers and researchers to know what the students and practitioners already know, how they behave, and what they desire from ethics. This rather broad role suggests that merely sensitizing practitioners to ethical issues is an insufficient teaching objective. People in business need to focus on the 'how to' rather than the philosophical abstractions.

A Critique of Business Ethics Teaching

This call for practical help can be appreciated more clearly after discussing some deficiencies typical of business ethics teaching aims and approaches. This should strengthen the case for teaching managers not only ethical sensitivity and decision-making skills but also moral character virtues. The primary deficiency is the over-emphasis typically placed on the cognitive and rational, to the exclusion of the emotional, volitional, and spiritual aspects of human nature. The moral sense is mistakenly considered to be comprehended in the intellect. Other deficiencies include an enthralment with cases, especially the hardest dilemmas, and the misdirected lesson that there often is no correct solution to an ethical problem.

An Over-emphasis on Cognitive Rationality Ultimately, academic thought can influence the practice of people in the world only if it makes acceptable (i.e. valued-grounded) normative recommendations. A cognitive approach is generally recommended by business ethicists for doing this. Freeman (1991) says that the essential function of this discipline is enquiry into the nature of ethical dilemmas in the practice of business. According to De George (1991), instruction in business ethics can sharpen one's awareness of, and sensitivity to, ethical issues. It can provide guidance for resolving ethical problems, and it can give students some ideals to emulate. The primary aim is that students learn to develop sound philosophical arguments, to be critical ethical thinkers, not to become better people who will be motivated to improve the ethical climate in business. According to Duska (1993: 190), 'The function of ethics is not to modify behavior but to analyze and evaluate possible courses of action with the hope that the articulation of those choices might lead to the adoption of an ethical course of action.' However, this does not mean that the teacher is or can remain neutral. He or she is to teach and defend a position (Duska 1991).

Consistent with the rational, cognitive orientation, most ethics textbooks and casebooks are organized either according to the levels of business or by systematically treating business ethics as a rigorous academic discipline that covers an introduction to morality, ethical theory, and theories of justice, the capitalist and socialist economic systems, the corporation as an institution, and the nature of moral issues internal and external to it (Olson 1995). The first organizational approach reinforces individualist assumptions and individual versus society themes. The second reinforces the view of ethics as an elective exercise involving the imposition of philosophical theories onto business, an approach better suited to the academically inclined than to the practising business person. This latter view tends to result in students being 'turned off' ethical analysis, eventually even adopting the 'realistic, real-world' view that ethics questions are best handled by some combination of consultations with the legal department and avoidance of personal responsibility.

The 1993 Wharton programme for teaching business ethics to undergraduates exemplifies the cognitive moral reasoning approach—an 'intellectual' approach that focuses on ethical dilemmas—instead of the traditional approach of teaching specific values in the classroom. It was designed to present a wide variety of ethical issues and to equip students with normative decision tools for analysing ethical decision alternatives (Foglia 1993), not to develop moral character in the students. Its ambitions in terms of behaviour change were limited: 'The intellectual understanding of ethical obligations may not be sufficient to insure ethical behavior, but it is probably at least necessary' (ibid.: 6). This cognitive emphasis is typical of business ethics teaching in North America and the United Kingdom (see Mahoney 1990; Cowton and Dunfee 1995). An alternative that combines discussion of realistic and comprehensive cases with recognition of the importance of mentoring students is suggested by research at Harvard Business School (Piper et al. 1993).

The Enthralment with Cases Cognitive assessment of discrete decision choices is typically stressed through the use of cases. Kennedy and Lawton's (1992) analysis of twelve US business ethics textbooks, most published between 1989 and 1991, reveals that a majority utilize a combination of essays, case-studies, and questions that can be used for class discussion based upon the issues derived from the case examples. Moreover, the American business ethics establishment remains committed to the case method (Werhane 1993).

Nevertheless, there is a deficiency in dialogue between theory and case analysis in contemporary business ethics textbooks. Derry and Green (1989) found that few business ethics textbooks address the problem of what one should do when the advice of a teleological theory conflicts with that of a deontological theory, that is, when the good end conflicts with the right means. Van Luijk (1993: 211) agrees, saying that the major missing ingredient is theory: 'Business ethics today suffers from being taught too early at too large a scale and at too low a level. . . . Students learn to apply two or three basic ethical approaches to every single topic, and that's it.' Dunfee and Donaldson (1995: 175) observe that 'hard cases make bad law' because they see the need for a general theory of business ethics, something beyond merely using collections of cases as ethics textbooks. There is a need for practical wisdom, a way to exercise what the Greeks called *phronesis* (Larmore 1987).

Ciulla (1994) suggests that a revival of casuistry might be a reasonable means for successfully correcting the excesses of overly rigid laws by bridging the gap between abstract principles and particular cases. This is a traditional approach to moral reasoning that proceeds by analogy and differentiation rather than by deductive syllogism (Velasquez 1994). A recent casuistic approach is C. Edward Weber's (1995) stories derived from interviews of executives. These accounts collectively act as an outline and analysis of how particular people apply their ethical principles. But casuistry is not without risk. Indeed, seventeenth-century Jesuits developed casuistry to such an extreme that Pascal claimed this effectively allowed them, when in doubt, to do whatever they wanted to do. Moreover, teaching casuistic theory and method to men of vice can turn them into sophists who can defend their crimes with moralistic arguments. Brenkert (1994) observes that principles are needed as well as case examples if the case-study method is to build on understanding rather than legalisms.

The Lesson that there is No Correct Solution   Teaching using the case-study method tends to focus on the tougher issues, the most interesting problems. But rather than converging on solutions, such an emphasis upon 'quandary ethics' stimulates an atmosphere of argument and counter-argument between two or more positions. Furthermore, the typical practice of restricting case discussions only to the major dilemmas teaches that all important moral questions are controversial, encouraging relativism. If there is no obvious solution to the dilemma used for class discussion, students tend to jump to the conclusion—admittedly without logical justification— that there never is a correct solution. This reinforces the relativistic idea that there is no absolute right or wrong, that ethics itself has no moral foundation. But if that is accepted, there seems to be no basis for ethics as an academic field. At least this is the assessment of an American undergraduate: Why try to behave in an ethical manner at all? Why not just pick the alternative that gives the most profits and do that? If you are going to do something wrong anyway, you might as well be rich and wrong, instead of poor and wrong (Shane 1993).

The Need for Additional Perspectives

Although students need to learn how to identify issues and to develop cognitive skills for analysing decision alternatives, something more is needed from business ethics teaching. Because the deficiencies of teaching business ethics are now recognized to be serious, business ethicists recently have suggested a variety of solutions.

Treating Business as a Humanity   The American business ethics academic establishment denounced Stark's charge that business ethics teaching is considered irrelevant by the average business practitioner. Nevertheless, hearing a ring of truth in the basic claim, some business ethicists have responded with a proposal for positive improvement. Recommended by Bennett (1989), this seeks to broaden and humanize the world-view of the business students by adding a liberal arts perspective to students now trained basically to be technocrats. This approach would require business students to consider the depth and motivational complexity of the people responsible for the success of businesses. The business ethics instructor is to consider what kind of person his or her students might become.

Humanizing business education is the explicit thrust of *Business as a Humanity*, a pioneering collection of essays edited by Donaldson and Freeman (1994). The authors believe ethics can be taught, in part by drawing lessons from the humanities that resuscitate habits of the mind and of the heart, both too often stifled by mere technical training. The basic intent is to add the value-embodying perspectives of history, philosophy, literature, and languages to inform the business student concerning his or her own culture and the cultures of other societies. Walton (1994) argues that the present time is propitious for introducing into management education significant connections with humanistic tradition. Notably, Solomon's (1994) concept of the humanities is from Cicero's concept of *humanitas*, which did not focus only on literacy and education but was also concerned with the cultivation of the virtues and with being a good, 'humane' person.

How can this be done? Business ethicists disagree concerning means and, to some extent, ends; the best answer might include a diversity of approaches. De George (1994) continues to stress the cognitive, although he also opines that teaching moral theory and method to those who seek virtue can help make them morally articulate. Nevertheless, he focuses on how to mould students as critical thinkers rather than on challenging the assumptions, goals, and values that underlie business and business education (Green 1994). Walton (1994) proposes curriculum reform directed towards refining the theories of self, society, and thought, as recommended by the European Foundation for Management Development and the American Assembly of Collegiate Schools of Business. He also suggests concentrating on certain pedagogical themes (e.g. truth, justice) to unify a student's conception of humanity in business. Solomon (1991; 1994) proposes use of literature as an antidote to cure bored students and frustrated practitioners, allowing each student to live vicariously through the difficulties and dilemmas of life. This suggests the value of biographical studies and the expansion of business ethics course materials to include great novels, short stories, and plays.

While support for adding the perspective of the humanities is increasing, it has yet to be widely implemented. Moreover, it is unrealistic to believe that business schools will or can now expand their curricula substantially. There is doubt as to whether business teachers can or even should undertake such an approach for which they are not trained, taking on what is generally considered to be a mission of liberal arts educational institutions. Dunfee (1994) denies that advocates of humanizing business education show that the humanities relate to valid business school objectives. His view is that humanities-oriented training will be adopted if and only if proponents can demonstrate that it would improve decision-making.

But even if implemented, does the change envisioned in *Business as a Humanity* go far enough? While it does suggest a need to study and understand character, it does not commit to its development. Instead, it would retain the cognitive focus of philosophical ethics. Moreover, merely adding humanities courses is insufficient; students need to learn to understand people and their motives, to know how to read and judge character, and to be empathetic (De George 1994). According to De George, it is incorrect to think that ethics merely requires virtuous people instead of a dramatic change in the very nature of business and the way it is structured and practised.

Visionary Leadership Teaching leadership as being necessarily visionary is another proposed solution (De George 1994). An example is the linking of ethics and leadership in the academic programme of the Harvard Business School. Parks (1993: 181) observes:

To step into an MBA classroom to observe ninety talented students between the ages of twenty-four and thirty-two is to become immediately aware that it is not difficult to teach ethics—understood as philosophical ethical systems theory—to bright young minds. Yet as important as that is, if we are concerned with the teaching of ethics understood as the practice of accountability to a profession vital to the common good, the underlying and more profound challenge before all professional schools is located in the question, how do we foster the formation of leadership characterized, in part, by practise of moral courage?

She wants to understand how her students perceive their world and their roles within it. This is the time of formation of an adult's life dream—dependent upon imaginations of the future that are available in their environment. Therefore, the hypothesis is that if the students are introduced into complexity and ambiguity, their moral imagination can be strengthened and enlarged. However, the substantive content of this approach is rather subjective and unclear; a more objective approach is still needed.

Solberg et al. (1995: 71) offer an organized programme for training future business leaders, one whereby schools of business can deliver experiential ethical education 'in which students can "live ethics" instead of merely learn ethics'. The aim is to 'cultivate the discovery process needed to truly produce greater integrity in a new generation of business leaders' (ibid.). Their specific programme recommendations include student-created and faculty-created codes of ethics, emphasis on ethical theory within existing course(s), applications of ethics approaches in functional area capstone courses, in which the students choose the business and a particular dilemma for analysis, class discussion and case-studies of moral dilemmas supplemented with works of thought-provoking fiction, and community service experience. Although the stated aim of this approach is 'to allow students to discover and refine their own values rather than simply learning ethical theories from an ethical point of view', the focus is still on cognitive analysis of moral dilemmas. Furthermore, although it has been designed to improve the teaching of business ethics that its authors describe as 'indiscriminate, unorganized, and undisciplined' (ibid.), it pragmatically addresses the effects of the problem rather than the need to mould student character.

Adding a Character Perspective   A holistic view of moral education is that there are three interrelated, though non-sequential, phases: first, conscience, moving from consciousness-raising to the critical appraisal of one's values; second, decision-making, applying imagination and reasoning skills to moral decisions; and third, character, acting with responsibility based on moral identity and virtue (Holmes 1991). A complete effort for teaching business ethics should address all three.

Classroom approaches for the first two phases are well developed. Group discussion can serve to enhance the awareness of the moral implications of business practices. Moreover, techniques for sound analytical reasoning can be learned and applied to well-developed and thoroughly documented cases—the major corporate dilemmas and also more mundane situations. Practice, including the use of role-playing, can enhance sensitivity and develop competence and confidence in ethical reasoning. However, as previously noted, there are substantial disadvantages associated with over-reliance on case-studies and an abstract principle-based ethics approach.

The Need for an Ethic of Virtues   If ethics education is also to be concerned with forming and developing values and thus with actually changing behaviours, then a programme limited to cognitive consciousness-raising and decision-making, but excluding character development, renders too narrow the objectives of research and teaching of the applied discipline of business ethics (see Sommers 1991). This deficiency is understandable given the lingering influence of positivism in the academy, especially among social scientists (see COWTON). Human behaviour is a deep and complex subject; knowing what should be done and actually doing it are not the same. 'Being sharp-witted is perfectly consistent with being immoral' (Kristol 1987). Humorist Will Rogers observed that whereas an uneducated person might steal from a railcar, after receiving an education that person might very well steal the whole railroad. A comprehensive ethic needs to address character development as well as cognitive decision analysis, influencing who people are as well as what they do and how they do it.

Barker's discussion of General Dynamics' efforts to establish an ethics programme illustrates this need. Although the programme succeeded administratively, it failed in human terms, according to a group of employees who rated it a 'whitewash scheme to present a false front' (1993: 172). Because of the finding that a strength of its ethics programme is the sense of integrity of its average employees, the programme audit report concluded that in order for employee treatment to change, employee supervisors must change by developing certain 'common civil virtues' (General Dynamics 1988: 23–4).

The need for having a moral character perspective is addressed by the theory of virtues. By adding a focus on the nature and motivations of the human actor, an ethic of virtues complements the act-oriented philosophical theories based primarily on outcomes or duties. The implicit motivational dynamic for seeking to act in the moral (the right) way towards the proper ends (the good) springs from the actor's virtues. The character of the actor is potentially the wellspring of the act. The actor strives towards some standard of perfection (e.g., the 'good' life, or the ethic revealed by God). A focus on the virtues could thus bring a personal and dynamic emphasis to ethical analysis.

A virtue, as a settled moral disposition, is part of the essence of the human, which includes the cognition, the emotions, and the will (Crabb 1987), in relation to one's valued ends (Holmes 1991). Virtues, enacted in behaviour and conversation, are generally considered beneficial and can be taught by example and learned through experience. An excellent manager is thus a virtuous manager. Character virtues provide the motivation and understanding needed to develop appropriate moral codes and standards of conduct. A virtues perspective highlights those dispositions of character required for managers to follow rules faithfully, though not blindly, with the right amount of flexibility. Indeed, the organization that expects to develop and successfully use a code of ethics and cultivate ethical behavioural habits among its employees needs to understand the moral qualities of its managers—those who will implement the code.

An ethic of virtues addresses the deficiencies characteristic of much business ethics teaching that are discussed above. It enables managers to formulate objectives and policies within the scope of the organization's mission. By its very nature, this perspective extends beyond the cognitive realm of one-off acts and impersonal decision-making, involving all aspects of humanity in relationships that affect decision-making and motivating human agents to behave in the right manner towards good ends. The emphasis is on better decisions and behaviours and their implementation, rather than the message that there is no correct solution. Attention is focused on improvement, both of the organizational culture and environment and of the nature of the persons involved. The virtues perspective conceives of human action in the workplace as continuous, rather than in terms of one-off acts or special cases (Koehn 1995: 536). Past actions, by moulding character, become the cause of future actions. The virtuous manager and organization are concerned with building an environment that will encourage the practice of virtue, in part by relieving the pressures that push one to vicious acts. However, true excellence of virtue leads to supererogatory behaviour as well. The virtuous person's acts are not totally determined by the current environment or the cumulative effect of past pressures. Furthermore, the truly admired manager overcomes pressures to compromise, at times even changing his values and habitual behaviours.

What Virtues are to be Taught?

Teaching virtues requires an understanding of what virtue is and what qualities or virtues a manager needs to excel. Although virtue ethicists tend to presume the answer, often adopting a list and the underlying definitions of essential virtues from tradition, this can be too abstract and even misleading for contemporary business people actually trying to practise ethical behaviour in the tumultuous workplace. Indeed, MacIntyre (1985) observes that since the Enlightenment there has been an inability even to agree upon a catalogue of the virtues, and even more fundamentally, an inability to agree upon the relative importance of the virtue concepts within a moral scheme in which notions of rights and of utility also have a key place. Moreover, there has been no consensus as to the content and character of particular virtues. This suggests some qualifications to the imposition of an ethic of virtues.

First, presuming too much too soon about the nature of virtue and the meaning of individual virtues and vices involves risk. For example, Rohatyn (1987) and Levin (1989) represent those who argue that business ethicists should produce students who conform to traditional industry norms—i.e., inculcate conventional morality and virtues. But this view can lead to compromise of the legitimacy of business ethics as an academic field and a lack of respect towards individuals as responsible actors. The virtues perspective should involve wise evaluation of values, norms, and rules. Business ethicists can strive to promote growth in morality according to some standards (see Marsden 1994) by encouraging the development of prudence, or *phronesis*, and those other personal qualities that enable and dispose people to live and work ethically. But this must be done carefully.

Second, it would be a mistake today to study virtues as philosophical ideals outside the context of a modern society or organization. Ancient Greeks were active members of the culture of their city, possessing a world and life view that served as a practical contextual base, a common language for their studies and debates. Modern academics have no such advantage. Modern society is disjoint, with a great diversity of philosophical perspectives, a situation that often leads to irreconcilable differences, according to MacIntyre (1985). Moreover, many academics are not 'men of the world' to the same extent that the ancient Greeks were men of theirs. In particular, relatively few contemporary academics are in daily touch with a representative sample of the men and women working in the modern corporation, small business, or government agency. This raises the methodological question of whether contemporary ethicists can fully understand the moral character required for business today merely by deductive theorizing based upon the writings of great thinkers of the past (see SORELL). The point is that by its nature, a virtue or vice cannot be understood outside of its social and cultural context in space and time.

The most appropriate list, relative importance, and even meaning of the virtues for a manager filling a role in a business organization vary. Ethical theory, including virtue ethics, needs to be verified as it is understood and applied by people working at their daily occupations. This is an area where research is very much needed. Social science methods can be used to identify the qualities of virtue that a manager requires to excel in his or her role within an organization (Whetstone 1995). Then the ethicist can concentrate on practical implementation—how can virtue be taught?

2. HOW CAN VIRTUE BE TAUGHT? A TRADITIONAL SOLUTION

The Aristotelian Perspective

How can virtues be taught to adults preparing for or practising business? Aristotle said that moral virtues result from habitual exercise—by doing acts virtuously. But how can one do a just (or brave) act if this requires a just (or brave) character that can only be acquired by doing just (or brave) acts? The answer is that one must start by attempting to do virtuous acts, although these acts at first, if ever, are not completely virtuous. A person becomes more just by doing just things and becomes more courageous by doing brave things.

Virtues are not simply habits, but they involve judgement and flexibility in application. Intellectual virtues (wisdom, understanding, and prudence) owe their inception and growth chiefly to instruction—and thus need time and experience. According to Aristotle, both skills and virtues are produced by trial and error, practice, and feedback, being honed with practical experience. Developing virtues is thus a learning process, facilitated by interactive teaching by someone with moral and intellectual virtues. This suggests the value of the leader–follower dyadic relationship as a method for character development.

Other Perspectives

But there are many perspectives in the contemporary multicultural world (see Darling-Smith 1993: 13). Several are mentioned below to show that in spite of their many presuppositional and methodological differences, there is at least one widely accepted method of character cultivation—personal mentoring.

A faithful Christian believes in the process of moral character renewal called sanctification in which she or he is spiritually enabled to grow in the virtues exemplified by Christ. The person, other people, and environmental factors are instrumental factors in this character development process. The Buddhist's understanding of ethics is that the good is subjective, the test is in experience, not in principles or laws. Righteousness is attained through self-cultivation (Smart 1993). Explicit mechanisms for acquiring virtue in the Islamic Kerkennah culture of North Africa include self-conscious child-raising practices, religious training, formal education, and different kinds of mentoring and apprenticeships (Platt 1993). The secular humanistic view is that virtue is a cultural ideal, a cultural product that is learned.

Character Development through Mentoring

But in spite of such pluralism, support is widespread for the practical use of personal mentors and mentoring relationships for building character. It is the one means universally practised by adherents to various forms of Christianity, as well as to other great religions, by Greek philosophers and secular social scientists. Socrates and Gandhi both approved of teachers whom they believed could not so much teach virtue as help people get to the place where they could learn it for themselves (Rouner 1993).

In this century moral development has remained a controversial issue within developmental psychology. Although Hartshorne and

May's research appeared to deny that virtue can be taught, it actually only demonstrated that top-down instructional methods such as lecturing are ineffective (Sprinthall and Sprinthall 1988). More recently, James Rest et al. (1986; 1988), following Kohlberg (1981), demonstrated through psychological research that moral development continues throughout formal education, particularly among young adults. Moreover, deliberate educational attempts (through formal curricula) to influence awareness of moral problems and to influence the reasoning/judgement process can be effective. Not only can a person's moral character be neutralized and repressed by socialization (Bellah et al. 1985), but a person's ethic can be influenced positively as well. The formation, refinement, and modification of a person's operational value system—the attitudes and beliefs that motivate conduct—are ongoing processes throughout one's life; it is never too late (Josephson 1988: 28).

It is generally believed that character is best taught not through lecturing or sermonizing, but through some combination of experiential learning and role modelling. There can be many sources of positive and negative influence, including environmental and cultural factors and relationships with parents, children, friends, co-workers, people at church, neighbours, and others. The cultivation of character dispositions, requires multiple experiences within oneself and among people (Streng 1993), best approached as if set within a family relationship rather than in a top-down manner. The implication for teaching is that a practical approach cannot be limited by the physical and time constraints of the classroom—virtues and vices are exemplified or modelled at all times and places, at school, at home, on the job, at recreation.

But is there a place for promoting character development of students as part of an academic curriculum? If so, how can such an effort be organized? Although their goals do not include the development of virtues, McDonald and Donleavy (1995) do helpfully list specific organizational questions that a business ethics programme needs to consider. They are paraphrased as follows:

(1) Who should teach ethics courses — philosophers or those with considerable business experience?
(2) Should business ethics be taught as a separate course or integrated into other courses throughout the currciulum?
(3) Is there a need for training the teachers?

(4) Should ethics be taught early or late in the degree programme?
(5) What are the goals of the course?
(6) Should alternative teaching models, such as role playing, be used?
(7) What innovative means of teaching could be used?
(8) How is the course to be assessed?

McDonald and Donleavy's discussion of these questions is helpful, although the answers might vary if character development were an explicit epistemological objective. There is a need to teach ethical sensitivity and moral reasoning skills in the classroom, possibly in a separate course. However, the importance of context and tradition and the belief that virtue is best taught by example and personal experience, favour the employment of teachers with personal experience. Such seasoned teachers can coach and mentor students rather than merely lecture to them. Moreover, since character is generally developed slowly as well as experientially, there would seem to be an advantage to spreading ethics education throughout the curriculum. However, each teacher must not only be convinced of the need for ethics education, but also be able to devote scarce time to it. Staff training is needed, especially if non-traditional methods are used. The gradual nature of character development suggests the value of a continuing effort, rather than limiting ethics training to either an early or a late course.

Alternative teaching models such as dyadic mentoring and experiential learning should be encouraged. Innovative means might include assigning classics of literature as suggested by those proposing to consider business as a humanity, discussing biographies of moral heroes of business, using faculty and business leaders as mentors and as guest speakers, and requiring internships. Opportunities given to the students to participate in social, athletic, and service projects could be perceived as laboratory exercises for character development. Assessment and transferability of course content is unusually difficult for a programme of character development. Longitudinal studies are necessary, pointing to a continuing need for research.

Faculty and other staff, and the more mature students, could adopt the role of moral mentor for younger students. Mentoring programmes could be encouraged by the institution, although the moral code and telos of such programmes need to be carefully developed and thoroughly communicated to all those involved — an heroic task in a multicultural, post–modern community. Indeed, even the most heroic cannot and should not be imitated blindly, since his formative experiences and role may differ. The importance of tradition and role for defining what is meant by excellence in a particular community undermines the validity of a universalist approach. Moreover, such corporate modelling requires not only full institutional support, but exemplary moral behaviour in financial and all other respects by the institution's agents.

On the contemporary campus, it would be far simpler for a single teacher, or a group of faculty members within a single department, to implement a mentoring programme. In particular, a group of business faculty members could undertake such a programme, not only as a way to incorporate the moral character development within business education, but also as a way to conduct longitudinal assessments and further research if they are able to follow the business careers of their students after graduation.

Because of the gradual and continuing nature of the process, mentoring and monitoring of its impacts might best be done in the workplace. Indeed, as discussed below, a traditional method of character development is workplace mentoring. It is to the workplace that academic researchers need to turn, perhaps learning from the world of practice how better to teach virtue ethics in the academy.

Mentoring in the Workplace

The remainder of this discussion will focus on why and how mentoring can be used in business organizations for moulding the character of adults engaged in business. Mentorship is not the only or necessarily the best method, but it is a well-recognized practice in many businesses and professions, long associated with master–apprentice, physician–intern, and teacher–student dyadic relationships. An organization can benefit from successful mentor–protégé relationships. Those employees who have been mentored are generally better educated, better paid, less mobile, and more satisfied with their work and career progress (Kram 1980). Mentorship is the most important element in the psychological development of men (Levinson et al. 1978) and is an important device for influencing commitment and self-image (White 1979). It is also important for the career success of women (Henning and Jardim 1977; Roche 1979), although women can have difficulty in finding suitable mentors (Stewart 1976). Dyadic mentoring relationships at work influence the development of personal character qualities, including loyalty, honesty, and a work ethic (Whetstone 1995). The right mentors help their subordinates to mature by equipping them with technical competency and offering them a worthy vision, a virtuous purpose. This finding is consistent with the observations of Parks (1986; 1993) that ethical consciousness and commitment continue to undergo transformation at least throughout formal education. Parks noticed dramatic changes in young adults attending business school, concluding that maturation can depend upon worthy mentors and mentoring environments.

The use of mentors in the business organization, as well as on the school campus, is consistent with at least two of the major streams in the development of Western education described by Kohlberg (1981): traditional cultural transmission and progressive pragmatism. Consistent with more traditional education, a mentor strives to teach the values, knowledge, and skills needed for advancement in the organization or community. He meanwhile holds the subordinate to performance standards expected by the various stakeholders— the management acting as agents for the owners, customers, suppliers, other employees, and the broader society. In terms of progressive education, the mentor also encourages and guides, allowing the student to practise and even to fail in actual or simulated experiences. As a coach, teacher, and counsellor, the mentor learns through their personal interrelationship as well. The more mature partner challenges, provides feedback, and exhorts the subordinate to reach towards successively higher stages of technical and moral development.

But what is the specific objective of character development? That is, what character standard should mentors establish? A traditional answer is to refer to heroes.

Heroes and Heroines as Mentors

The traditional approach for 'making good' lies with finding moral examples to emulate. The hero narrative is an ancient model used for moral education in many cultures. Confucius said that the superior person seeks to perfect the admirable qualities of others and does not seek to perfect their bad qualities. Anderson, reviewing Bennett's *Book of Virtues* (1993: 59), comments that the 'early building of character depends heavily on examples, both in this world and in literature. Children—and adults to some degree—emulate people, not ideas.' People today still achieve excellence in a field such as baseball or rock music by identifying with the finest practitioners (Martin 1991).

Heroes and heroines play a critical role in developing the values of an organization:

> Values are the bedrock of any corporate culture. As the essence of a company's philosophy for achieving success, values provide a sense of common direction for all employees and guidelines for their day-to-day behavior. These formulae for success determine (and occasionally arise from) the types of corporate heroes, and the myths, rituals and ceremonies of the culture. In fact we think that often companies succeed because their employees can identify, embrace, and act on the values of the organization. . . . How do values come to be shared in a company? Through the reinforcement provided by all the other elements of the company's culture, but primarily by the culture's lead players—its heroes. (Deal and Kennedy 1982: 21)

Identification of the heroes in an organization and their apparent character qualities offer a key to finding and developing excellent managers in the contemporary workplace. Heroes as exemplars are especially important for an ethic of virtues (Williams and Murphy 1992).

What makes someone a hero? Must he or she risk life or limb for another? Workplace heroes possibly fit the first, and most formal, definition in *The Concise Oxford Dictionary* (1990): 'a man noted or admired for nobility, courage, outstanding achievements, etc.'—although this is perhaps too grand. The so-called *Great Man* theories, long out of fashion, reinforce the concept of the leader as a person who is endowed with unique qualities, ones that capture the imagination of the masses. But modern society deprecates the role of the hero, often seeking social order in rules, paper processes, written controls, and other impersonal, bureaucratic mechanisms. Modern Western man does not want to admit that any specific person is admirable or steadfast or generous.

Heroes as the Most Admired Exemplars in the Workplace

Investigation within an American corporation found that its managers almost without exception can readily identify individuals whom they greatly admire as role models, even as heroes (Whetstone

1995). While no one was perceived as being the personification of the ideal manager, those interviewed believe that their personal workplace exemplars have been instrumental in their moral as well as their technical development as managers. In particular, it is the supervisor–subordinate relationship that offers constructive feedback through an interactive personal relationship, allowing and even promoting a dynamic process of trial, error, and correction not possible from reading the 'great books' or even from emulating distant hero figures. This is especially significant in an era when many no longer read the classics and when historic figures and many contemporary leaders are besmirched in the cynical media.

The Nature of Workplace Exemplars

The consensus description of the most admired and least admired managers is summarized in Table 11.1, based on interviews with thirty-seven managers in a US food retailer. The most admired manager or heroic exemplar manifests both the technical capacity to be productive and a sincere concern for other people, a combination of effectiveness and relational values. Subsequent analysis, including the administration of a survey questionnaire to a larger sample, developed a prioritized list of the specific virtues of an excellent manager in the particular organization, with honesty the most important. Workplace heroes are understood as being basically morally decent persons (Sorell and Hendry 1994), rather than magnificent heroes or saints. The following is a representative comment by a manager in the US food retailer:

A lot of store managers helped mould me. I saw some do really terrible jobs. I worked for an older guy who was a highly ethical and moral guy, a great store manager, a people person. He helped us a lot. He took me under his wing. . . . I don't know if store managers now have the time or temperament to take kids under their wings. If under pressure, you aren't just sitting there worried about whether everybody else is happy.

Three-quarters of store managers testified that they were most influenced in their personal and career development by an immediate supervisor, particularly in the areas of morals, technical skills, people skills, and the work ethic. Such influence was not always positive,

TABLE 11.1 Characteristics of Heroes and Antiheroes in a US Retail
Corporation

The most admired manager (work hero)		The least admired manager	
Rank	Percentage of Respondents Specifying	Rank	Percentage of Respondents Specifying
1. Moral, virtuous	70	1. Immoral, weak in character	73
2. Competent in job	68	2. Uncaring; NOT concerned for employees	59
3. Caring; concerned for employees	54	3. A poor motivator	54
4. A teacher; a coach	43	4. A poor communicator	35
5. A good communicator	43	5. A boss—NOT a teacher or coach	30
6. A hard worker	41	6. NOT firm, NOT well-balanced	30
7. Firm, well-balanced	32	7. NOT a hard worker	22
8. A good motivator	30	8. NOT competent	14
9. Enthusiastic	16	9. NOT enthusiastic	8
10. A family man/woman	14		
11. A community servant	3		

however. They were most critical of managers who exhibited vices
such as dishonesty and sexual immorality.

What makes one admirable and thus a workplace hero? In the
organization studied, they are not described as being like Pym's
(1985) almost invisible, suffering servant exemplars, but neither are
they superhuman heroes in the classical sense. They are human
beings who are exceptional as leaders. Specifically, these people are
coaches who have established a personal rapport and a relationship
of loyalty with their subordinates. As a result, people are empowered
to achieve company goals and feel a personal obligation to them to
do so. To be admired, a manager must be competent in his or her job;
relational skills and other personal qualities are insufficient. In general, admired managers know the business, even the details, while
remaining learners and creative innovators. They exhibit leadership
skills and qualities as planners and visionaries who are also able to
analyse and make decisions in a timely manner. They behave in a
well-organized manner, being aware of goals and how to allocate

resources to achieve them. They know their people and have the self-confidence to delegate, although they continue to observe and follow up as needed to ensure that a job is done.

The exemplary manager represents a composite of the objective (Homeric), subjective (Aristotelian), and instrumental or utilitarian (Enlightenment) types of hero (see Francis 1990). In the workplace, he or she is admired for a combination of virtues, being well suited to their role in the organization (objective), being a person who by nature behaves virtuously (subjective), and being skilled in getting the most out of available resources—i.e., maximizing his or her contribution to company profits (instrumental and utilitarian).

The function of the mentor is not static, however, but dynamic in the sense of helping others to grow technically and morally. The comments of one manager offer insight into the moral development process, placing particular emphasis on the mentoring relationship between supervisor and junior employee:

I was just divorced and had a bad attitude. I stayed out late by habit. One morning this supervisor came into my department, took me out of the store, and gave me 'down the country'. He said I was wasting my life, letting alcohol rule my life. I reformed. I may have done this on my own later, somewhere down the line, but he excited me to do some things earlier. Some of my feelings about the business came from him. The business changes, but it remains a people business.

Establishing an Environment for Teaching Virtues in the Organization

However, workplace heroes as exemplars and a cadre of excellent managers are not enough. As Plato suggested in his narrative of Gyges' ring, people practise justice when they are unable to do wrong. Structures are therefore needed to constrain the unethical behaviour of the just and the unjust. The virtuous can be tempted, while the vicious can act correctly if there are proper restraints. Rules and codes, physical and psychological and social constraints, and a system of rewards and penalties are needed to implement an ethical system. While virtue can oft prevail against environmental opposition, a consistently good management outcome requires both developing the character of managers and a supportive and con-straining social environment.

However, this balanced approach is not always made explicit in extant business ethics theory. For example, Weber (1993) proposes a multi-component model for institutionalizing an ethic that considers managers primarily as decision-makers who address one problem after another in a logical, even mechanical, fashion. The four components influencing organizational ethical behaviour (the model output) are organizational ethical culture, code of ethics, employee ethics training, and organizational enforcement mechanisms (ibid.). The problem with this model is that it reflects the same deficiencies associated with much business ethics research and teaching. Indeed, by focusing upon the cognitive decision-making process, it is deficient because it is incomplete, omitting any explicit reference to the personal character perspective. However, if such a model were applied using practical judgement and other virtues, with consideration of the values, needs, and potential contributions of the people in the organization, it could prove more beneficial for establishing an ethical culture.

One approach for addressing this neglect of the personal character of the actors is to adopt a deliberate programme for mentoring. To do this a business could provide the physical environment and organizational culture for encouraging mentors, allowing the time and opportunities for relationship-building. Management could also establish a deliberate incentive programme, even tying a portion of a supervisor's performance rating and bonus potential to peer and subordinate-rated improvements in the performance of subordinates and to the number of subordinates promoted. But this approach may raise objections. A strong corporate culture can be viewed as an imposition of social conformity—in apparent conflict with the full expression of an employee's individuality, treating the employee as a means rather than an end. Is such socialization itself morally acceptable? This is a particularly sensitive issue for a management that is undertaking to influence the future development of people's values and thus impact their character. To do so seems utopian and certainly manipulative.

But a human organization cannot expect to avoid imposing values, although there is a need to apply care while doing so. Indeed, if an organization does not rely on informal social controls (conformance to a culture), it tends to turn to formal financial controls and bureaucratic procedures to achieve its aims. The more important concern thus is not whether an ethic should be institutionalized, but how. The rather 'low-tech' method of dyadic supervisor–subordinate mentoring relationships remains a reasonable response.

If understood in its proper role as a complement to cognitive perspectives, supervisor–subordinate mentoring can address the problem of fragmentation in business ethics by offering a practical means for on-the-job teaching of virtues. This traditional approach not only provides experienced guidance for the up-and-coming manager but also helps the mentor to grow as a responsible leader.

Is the Age of Mentoring Over?

The traditional manner of on-the-job mentoring may be growing obsolete in the changing international business environment. Companies of all sorts are making do with fewer and fewer middle managers, and those they do retain often require different skills (Bleakley 1995). The basis for such rationalization is economic. A significant portion of the 'fat' that many companies cut in their rationalizations is made up of the middle managers. However, the companies' computations may not include the cost of losing experienced managers who are needed to serve as moral and technical mentors. As a result, younger employees may not develop as well as they would under the personal guidance of an experienced mentor. This increases risk over the long run in terms of the number and intensity of ethical 'incidents', possibly even endangering the long-term integrity and viability of the organization.

Traditional mentoring relationships are growing more difficult to maintain as organizations 'flatten' and decentralize. However, the people remaining are assigned greater responsibility for meeting performance expectations appropriately. These people thus have even greater need to be excellent in terms of technical competence and moral virtue than in the past. There is a continuing need to stress the importance of moral mentors and the responsibility of business organizations to encourage mentoring relationships at a time when this seems less and less practical.

Nevertheless, all is not dark. Telecommunications advances can be applied towards establishing new ways for supporting mentoring relationships if people properly appreciate the need. Then the Age of Mentoring can continue in new ways with the traditional positive effect.

3. SUMMARY

A lack of consensus as to what business ethics is and should be has produced an increasing fragmentation between and among business ethics researchers and business practitioners. Business ethics—and, thus, business ethics teaching, research, and practice—need to focus on the common aim of helping people to understand and improve their workplace behaviour. This is not always the clear aim. More specifically, business ethics teaching is deficient because of an over-emphasis on cognitive analysis of individual acts, a preoccupation with the most difficult dilemmas, and the message that there often is no correct solution. The most comprehensive of several proposed solutions is to promote the development of personal moral character of ethical actors as well as their cognitive decision-making skills. This would serve to focus business ethics research, teaching, and practice on the improvement of workplace behaviour over time. It would require teaching virtues to those people, primarily adults, preparing for and already engaged in business practice. This chapter argues that not only is this needed, but it can be done.

After briefly discussing several recent proposals for improving business ethics teaching in the university setting, this chapter suggests the critical importance of a traditional method for teaching character virtues in the workplace itself—superior–subordinate mentoring. Historically this has been accomplished through personal face-to-face interactions between mature and younger employees. Research indicates that virtues as standards of excellence can be exemplified by more experienced managers, most particularly by those admired as workplace heroes.

But recent trends in corporate restructuring, including decentralization and downsizing, are making personal mentoring relationships more difficult to establish and maintain. While intended by some to respect and empower people, elimination of middle manager supervisory roles can involve an unrecognized cost. Indeed, this side-effect of the trend towards 'flatter' organizations may be undermining an important mechanism responsible for workplace character development. Nevertheless, if the risks are recognized and addressed with the help of new technologies, mentoring in some form can still be a good way for teaching virtues.

REFERENCES

Anderson, D. (1993), 'Lost and Found', *National Review*, 15 November: 58–60.

Aristotle (1976), *Nicomachean Ethics*, trans. with intro. J. Barnes (London: Penguin).

Barker, R. (1993), 'An Evaluation of the Ethics Program at General Dynamics', *Journal of Business Ethics*, 12: 165–77.

Bellah, R., Madsen, R., Sullivan, M., Swindler, A., and Tipton, S. (1985), *Habits of the Heart* (Berkeley, CA: University of California Press).

Bennett, A. (1989), 'Going Global: The Chief Executives in the Year 2000 will be Experienced Abroad', *Wall Street Journal*, 27 February, A1.

Bennett, W. (1993) (ed.), *The Book of Virtues: A Treasury of Great Moral Stories* (New York: Simon and Schuster).

Bleakley, F. (1995), 'Job Searches Still Last Months, or Years, for Many Middle-Aged Middle Managers', *Wall Street Journal*, 18 September, B1.

Brenkert, G. (1994), 'Business Ethics and Modes of Ethical Reasoning', in Donaldson and Freeman (1994): 196–213.

Ciulla, J. (1994), 'Casuistry and the Case for Business Ethics', in Donaldson and Freeman (1994): 167–83.

Confucius (1955), *The Four Books*, xii, trans. J. Legge (Taipei: Wen Yu Shu Tien).

Cowton, C. J. and Dunfee, T. W. (1995), 'Internationalizing the Business Ethics Curriculum: A Survey', *Journal of Business Ethics*, 14: 331–8.

Crabb, L. (1987), *Understanding People: Deep Longings for Relationship* (Grand Rapids, MI: Zondervan).

Darling-Smith, B. (1993) (ed.), *Can Virtue Be Taught?* (Notre Dame, IN: University of Notre Dame Press).

De George, R. (1991), 'Will Success Spoil Business Ethics?', in Freeman (1991): 42–56.

—— (1994), 'Business as a Humanity: A Contradiction in Terms?', in Donaldson and Freeman (1994): 11–26.

Deal, T. and Kennedy, A. (1982), *Corporate Culture: The Rites and Rituals of Corporate Life* (Reading, MA: Addison-Wesley).

Derry, R. and Green, R. (1989), 'Ethical Theory in Business Ethics: A Critical Assessment', *Journal of Business Ethics*, 8: 521–33.

Donaldson, T. and Freeman, R. E. (1994) (eds), *Business as a Humanity* (New York: Oxford University Press).

Dunfee, T. (1994), 'A Response to Richard T. De George's "Business as a Humanity: A Contradiction in Terms?"', in Donaldson and Freeman (1994): 33–41.

—— and Cowton, C. (1993), *Bringing a Global Perspective to Teaching Business Ethics* (Philadelphia: The Wharton School of the University of Pennsylvania).

—— and Donaldson, T. (1995), 'Contractarian Business Ethics', *Business Ethics Quarterly*, 5: 173–86.

Duska, R. (1991), 'What's the Point of a Business Ethics Course?', *Business Ethics Quarterly*, 1: 335–54.

—— (1993), 'Letter to the Editor', *Harvard Business Review*, November–December: 188–96.

Foglia, W. (1993), 'Overview of Ethics Project', in Robertson (1993*a*): 1–6.

Francis, J. (1990), 'After Virtue? Accounting as a Moral and Discursive Practice', *Accounting, Auditing and Accountability Journal*, 3.3: 5–17.

Freeman, R. E. (1991) (ed.), *Business Ethics: The State of the Art* (New York: Oxford University Press).

French, P. (1994), 'Responsibility and the Moral Role of Corporate Entities', in Donaldson and Freeman (1994): 88–97.

General Dynamics Corporation (1988), *Ethics Program Update* (St Louis, MO: Barker).

Green, R. (1994), 'A Response to Richard T. De George's "Business as a Humanity: A Contradiction in Terms?"', in Donaldson and Freeman (1994): 27–32.

Henning, M. and Jardim, A. (1977), *The Managerial Woman* (New York: Doubleday).

Hoffman, W. M. and Fedo, D. (1994), 'Liberal Arts and Professional Education: A Response to Clarence C. Walton', in Donaldson and Freeman (1994): 142–51.

Holmes, F. A. (1991), *Shaping Character: Moral Education in the Christian College* (Grand Rapids, MI: William B. Eerdmans).

Josephson, M. (1988), 'Teaching Ethical Decision Making and Principled Reasoning', *Ethics: Easier Said Than Done*, 1: 27–33.

Kennedy, E., and Lawton, L. (1992), 'Business Ethics in Fiction', *Journal of Business Ethics*, 11: 187–95.

Koehn, D. (1995), 'A Role for Virtue Ethics in the Analysis of Business', *Business Ethics Quarterly*, 5: 533–9.

Kohlberg, L. (1981), *The Philosophy of Moral Development: Moral Stages and the Idea of Justice* (San Francisco: Harper and Row).

Kram, K. (1980), 'Mentoring Process at Work: Developmental Relationships in Managerial Careers', Ph.D. diss., Yale University.

Kristol, I. (1987), 'Ethics Anyone? Or Morals?', *Wall Street Journal*, 15 September.

Larmore, C. (1987), *Patterns of Moral Complexity* (Cambridge: Cambridge University Press).

Levin, M. (1989), 'Ethics Courses: Useless', *New York Times*, 27 November: 23.

Levinson, D., Darrow, C., Klein, E., Levinson, M., and McGee, B. (1978), *The Seasons of a Man's Life* (New York: A. A. Knopf).

Lewis, P. (1985), 'Defining "Business Ethics": Like Nailing Jello to a Wall', *Journal of Business Ethics*, 4: 377–83.

MacIntyre, A. (1985), *After Virtue: A Study in Moral Theory* (London: Duckworth).

Mahoney, J. (1990), *Teaching Business Ethics in the UK, Europe and the USA: A Comparative Study* (London: Athlone Press).

Marsden, G. (1994), *The Soul of the American University: From Protestant Establishment to Established Nonbelief* (New York: Oxford University Press).

Martin, D. (1991), 'What Makes People Good?', *National Review*, 9 September: 25–9.

Mehta, V. (1965), *Fly and the Fly-Bottle* (Baltimore: Pelican).

Monast, J. (1994), 'What Is (and Isn't) the Matter with "What's the Matter . . . "', *Business Ethics Quarterly*, 4: 499–512.

Olson, S. (1995), 'Old Guards, Young Turks, and the $64,000 Question: What Is Business Ethics?', *Business Ethics Quarterly*, 5: 371–9.

Parks, S. (1986), *The Critical Years: Young Adults and the Search for Meaning, Faith, and Commitment* (San Francisco: Harper Collins).

—— (1993), 'Professional Ethics, Moral Courage, and the Limits of Personal Virtue', in Darling-Smith (1993): 175–93.

Piper, T., Gentile, M., and Parks, S. (1993), *Can Ethics Be Taught? Perspectives, Challenges, and Approaches at Harvard Business School* (Boston, MA: Harvard Business School).

Plato (1974), *The Republic*, trans. D. Lee (London: Penguin).

Platt, K. (1993), 'Vicarious Virtue: Gender and Moral Education in Muslim North Africa', in Darling-Smith (1993): 105–23.

Pym, D. (1985), 'Heroes and Antiheroes—the "Bricoleur" in Community Reconstruction', *Futures*, 17: 68–76.

Randall, D. and Gibson, A. (1990), 'Methodology in Business Ethics Research: A Critical Review and Assessment', *Journal of Business Ethics*, 9: 457–71.

Rest, J. (1988), 'Can Ethics Be Taught in Professional Schools? The Psychological Research', *Ethics: Easier Said Than Done*, 1: 22–6.

—— Barnett, R., Bebeau, M., Deemer, D., Getz, I., Moon, Y., Spickelmier, J., Thomas, S., and Volker, J. (1986), *Moral Development: Advances in Research and Theory* (New York: Praeger).

Robertson, D. (1993a), *Integrating Ethics into the Wharton Undergraduate Curriculum* (Philadelphia: University of Pennsylvania).

—— (1993b), 'Empiricism in Business Ethics: Suggested Research Directions', *Journal of Business Ethics*, 12: 585–99.

Roche, G. (1979), 'Much Ado About Mentors', *Harvard Business Review*, January–February: 17–28.

Rohatyn, F. (1987), 'The Blight of Wall Street', *New York Review of Books*, 12 March: 21.

Rouner, L. (1993), 'Can Virtue Be Taught in a School? Ivan Illich and Mohandas Ghandi on Deschooling Society', in Darling-Smith (1993): 139–53.

Shane, S. (1993), 'Introduction to Management: Overview of Course and Relevance of Ethics', in Robertson (1993a): 89–97.

Smart, N. (1993), 'Clarity and Imagination as Buddhist Means to Virtue', in Darling-Smith (1993): 125–36.

Solberg, J., Strong, K., and McGuire, C. (1995), 'Living (Not Learning) Ethics', *Journal of Business Ethics*, 14: 71–81.

Solomon, R. (1991), 'Business Ethics, Literacy, and the Education of the Emotions', in Freeman (1991): 188–211.

—— (1994), 'Business and the Humanities: An Aristotelian Approach to Business Ethics', in Donaldson and Freeman (1994): 45–75.

Sommers, C. (1991), 'Teaching the Virtues', *Imprimis*, 20, November.

Sorell, T., and Hendry, J. (1994), *Business Ethics* (Oxford: Butterworth-Heinemann).

Sprinthall, N. and Sprinthall, R. (1988), 'Value and Moral Development', *Ethics: Easier Said Than Done*, 1: 16–22.

Stark, A. (1993), 'What's the Matter with Business Ethics?', *Harvard Business Review*, May–June: 38–48.

Stewart, W. (1976), 'A Psychosocial Study of the Formation of the Early Adult Life Structure in Women', Ph.D. diss., Columbia University.

Streng, F. (1993), 'Cultivating Virtue in a Religiously Plural World: Possibilities and Problems', in Darling-Smith (1993): 89–103.

Van Luijk, H. (1993), 'Coming of Age in Business Ethics', *Business Ethics Quarterly*, 3: 205–13.

Velasquez, M. (1994), 'Some Lessons and Nonlessons of Casuist History', in Donaldson and Freeman (1994): 184–95.

Walton, C. (1994), 'Management Education: Seeing the Round Earth Squarely', in Donaldson and Freeman (1994): 109–41.

Weber, C. E. (1995), *Stories of Virtue in Business* (Lanham, MD: University Press of America).

Weber, J. (1993), 'Institutionalizing Ethics into Business Organizations: A Model and Research Agenda', *Business Ethics Quarterly*, 3: 419–36.

Werhane, P. (1993), 'Letter to the Editor', *Harvard Business Review*, November–December: 198.

Whetstone, J. T. (1995), 'The Manager as a Moral Person: Exploring Paths to Excellence', D.Phil. thesis, Oxford University.

White, M. (1979), 'Psychological and Social Barriers to Women in Science', *Science*, 170: 413–17.

Williams, O. and Murphy, P. (1992), 'The Ethics of Virtue: A Moral Theory for Business', in Williams and Houck (1992): 9–27.

—— and Houck, J. (1992) (eds), *A Virtuous Life in Business: Stories of Courage and Integrity in the Business World* (Lanham, MD: Rowman and Littlefield).

INDEX